Peden: Prophet of the Covenant

Peden: Prophet of the Covenant

Robert Watson

Shoving Leopard

Published by
Shoving Leopard
8 Edina Street (2f3)
Edinburgh,
EH2 5PN,
Scotland

http://www.shovingleopard.com

First published as *Prophet of the Covenant* in 1983

Copyright © Robert Watson 1983, 2006

Robert Watson asserts the moral right to be identified as the author of this book.

Every effort has been made to trace possible copyright holders and to obtain their permission for the use of any copyright material.
The publishers will gladly receive information enabling them to rectify any error or omission for subsequent editions.

ISBN 1-905565-04-6 Paperback

All rights reserved. No part of this publication may be reproduced, stored in a retrieval system, or transmitted in any form or by any means, electronic, mechanical, photocopying, recording or otherwise, without the prior permission of the publishers.

This book is sold subject to the condition that it shall not, by way of trade or otherwise, be lent, hired out or otherwise circulated without the publisher's prior consent in any form of binding or cover other than that in which it is published and without a similar condition including this condition being imposed on the subsequent purchaser.

Preface

A nation's life is a continuous growth, and has its roots in the past that it may have its fruits in the future. The most heroic story of Scotland's Covenanters cannot be blotted out. Of these heroes, there is something weird about the history of the Rev. Alexander Peden, "Peden the Prophet." He was the John the Baptist of the Scottish Covenant. His lonely life for years, his wild hiding places, his marvellous escapes, the timely descent of the mist, or "the lap of the Lord's cloak" as he called it, the keen insight of his exact prophecies, and his final burial beneath the gallows at Cumnock which then became consecrated ground (as God's acre), have thrown an air of deep mystery round his memory, which time can not erase. His name lives on in Peden's Pulpit near Harthill, Peden's Stone by Colmonell, Peden's Cave on the Lugar, and even Peden's Hill, over the Border at Otterburn, a will o' the wisp to the end. This exciting novel attempts to capture something of that mystery.

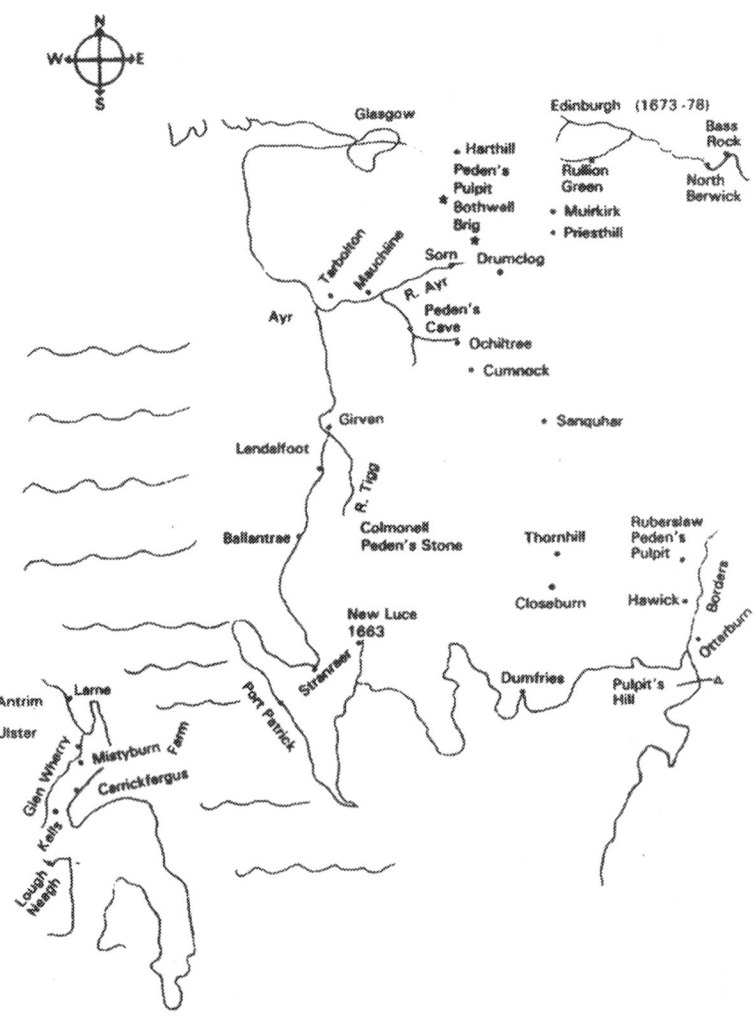

Peden's Movement's (1663-86)

Contents

	Page
1. The Signing of the Covenant	1
2. Deliverance by a Thread	9
3. Where the Carcass is, there the Vultures will Gather	21
4. A Fond Farewell	30
5. The Gathering Storm	38
6. A Moorland Conventicle	58
7. In the Mearns	75
8. Betrayed	98
9. Prisoner of the Bass	106
10. To be Transported	120
11. Return to Redesdale	142
12. A Judas Come to Judgement	150
13. A Glasgow Baillie	158
14. Dark Disaster	175
15. The Devil's Pride	186
16. An Unexpected Help	197

17. Strange Soliloquys............................204
18. Muckle John Gibb............................219
19. Faithful unto Death...........................229
20. The Glens of Antrim.........................245
21. Death not the End............................260

1
The Signing of the Covenant

It was the year of Grace, 1638, and the 28th of February and it was a very February day in Auld Reekie with the greyness of the skies matching the greyness of the tombstones in the famous Greyfriars Kirkyard. But there was little deadness about the scene. It might have been Resurrection Day for life was evident with a mass of excited humanity thronging the Churchyard. An observant byestander would be able to separate the merchant class, rich enough to endow private merchants schools, those who sold at the Luckenbooths, soberly dressed shopkeepers, earnest looking countryfolk, gracious looking nobility, and grim looking mercenaries, but all gathered in a motley noisy multitude as if unaware of their differences. Indeed the cause of their assembling was one of great national moment, enough to dissolve the barriers of class distinction. A voice could be heard above the din.

"A silence for David Leslie, a silence for General Leslie. We are about important business this day." Gradually there is a subsidence of the clamour with occasional ejaculations. "Woe to the tyrant! Down with the usurper!"

A small gnarled man with piercing blue eyes mounted one of the largest flat tombstones with not the slightest embarrassment at his unconventional stance for he was a man of military fame far beyond the confines of Scotland but newly returned from the German wars under Gustavus Adolphus, the Protestant champion and Lion of the North. His thin lips tightened with determination as with command his voice carried over the quietened throng.

"Fellow countrymen, fellow Christian believers, and friends of mine and Scotland's welfare, I ken weel that you are come from afar to be gathered here at Greyfriars Kirkyard in our capital city, from the land of the Lollards in Kyle, Carrick and Ayr, frae the hills of Galloway, the Border Burghs, the gentle Lothians and the wild rolling Howe o' the Mearns, not to forget those from our worthy Kingdom of Fife, that couthy corner of the land. Also equally weel ken I you come merchants, and burgesses, weavers and cobblers, noblemen and farmers, aye and even meenisters." Here a nervous ripple of laughter ran over the crowd in response to his wry humour. "Our purpose here is plainfold, the extirpation of Erastian doctrine and usurped Church government from our beloved and fair land of Scotland. An alien spirit has seized our Lords temporal and spiritual, it seems. Our purpose then is not only that we cleanse the throneroom of our land of all that is not of God but I say, that we stand by public sworn oath that we will abide faithful to Presbytery. As I read the Holy Scriptures I can think of no less did Amos, Isaiah, Elijah, Elisha, and a host of others against the blasphemous invocations of Baal worship and all that was perpetrated in the high places. What say ye, brethren?"

His brother in the flesh, Alexander Leslie, answered with a shout. "A Covenant, a National Covenant, brother David! The age old Covenant of God with Abraham became that prophesied by Ezekiel and Jeremiah, those prophets of old, to be fulfilled in the new by our gracious Lord and Master Jesus Christ. Our Covenant will be equally binding between all that stand firm in the nation and their God, aye and that by blood. We be no serfs nor feudal vassals but it is as constitutional subjects we aspire to be. The person of King Charles and his authority we jealously guard on the one condition that he preserve the true Reformed religion and the common weal. We crave no Republic here in Scotland. But this King I say has squandered our devotion and obedience." The neat moustache and goatee beard of Alexander Leslie, Earl of Leven, bristled with indignation like the energetic fervour of a bulldog waiting to be unleased.

David Leslie was quick to answer his brother with the aptest response possible. He was always the calmer of the two Generals. "But, my good brother, wit ye not that a Covenant has been prepared already by our young advocate of the Edinburgh courts and the Rev. Alexander Henderson of Leuchars who has proved to be the most worthy and statesman-like of our Presbyterian clergy. Let them be brought forward! Archibald Johnstone of Warriston and the Rev. Alexander Henderson of Leuchars!"

Two robed figures, both young, are eagerly handled forward by helping hands to a stand on a flat stone tomb. The one with clerical attire raises his arms in fervent prayer, "Beloved Lord, we are gathered here in your sight, and before men and angels in full cognizance of the Government of Scotland on this afternoon of the 28th of February in the year of Grace 1638 in the Kirkyard of Greyfriars, itself built where the monastery of the Franciscans stood in times past. We, 50,000, I am told, of the congregation of the just, are assembled here also to build upon the old and to witness a new Covenant. Deign, O Lord, to look upon your people who take their stand by your Word. Lord, as I cast my een out over the broad vista of the Grassmarket to the crags of our Castle of Edinburgh, so do You see the scope of our future restoration of true religion and we pray that in Thy predetermined will let the flame be lit which will set all Scotland on fire for the Lord!"

As his strident voice had risen to a crescendo, faces charged with passionate emotion encompassed the figure of Archibald Johnstone of Warriston. He cried, "See, I append my signature beside that of His Grace, the Marquis of Montrose, Lord Rothes, Alexander and David Leslie, the Earl of Loudon and our most worthy pastor, Rev. Alexander Henderson. Who shall stand by the Covenant? Who shall sign next? Who shall say that this is not a Book of Life other to that written of in the Holy Scriptures?"

The clamour was overwhelming as the concourse pressed forward eagerly to sign the ramskin which had now been laid out on a great flat stone. Tears of deepest emotion could be observed amongst the shouts of enthusiasm.

Turning to Warriston, Rev. Henderson exclaimed almost with a reverent awe, "Lo, Archibald, how many are subscribing it with their very own blood as they draw it and use it in place of ink. Truly they are pouring their own souls into this. See, some write after their signature, 'Until Death!' They offer their gear, their bodies and their lives as a living sacrifice, and regard it as their reasonable service. It will be many hours till this great work is done. But how great is our oneness, as we are told how pleasant it is for brethren to dwell together in unity. Even my Lords the Marquis of Montrose and Archibald Campbell, First Marquis of Argyll, those two men of noble eminence, hitherto so inveterately opposed for reasons personal and beyond our understanding, are now united in a common loyalty. United we stand, divided we fall. But they say that these two are like Caesar and Pompey, as the one would brook no superior and the other would have no equal. James Graham of Montrose, some say is the finest gallant in the realm but he has never loved Archibald Campbell. I do honestly think that he cannot brook that any should have greater respect among the Protestant people than he. And he presents a brave figure while our Marquis of Argyll, to those of observant mind, presents a nature so complex and involved, that it is difficult for even his closest friends to read. And indeed his dark and sasturnine complexion, furrowed forehead and downcast outlook, give the impression of a person frequently engaged in the consideration of important affairs and who has acquired an air of gravity and secrecy by long habit which he cannot shake off even when there is nothing to be concealed. He has a cast in his een which makes his west coast men of Kintyre call him Gillespie Grumack or Archibald the Grim. It is said he walks with that downward gait of his to hide his disfigurement. But his tall and thin personage is not without a dignity that becomes his rank in his deportment. Some see in his distant aloofness a coldness that seems sinister and compare it most unkindly with the gay demeanour of Montrose but somewhere the Spirit of the Almighty does whisper in my ear a dependency for the Covenanting Cause with Argyll but that some ill omen does surround our Marquis of Montrose."

Johnstone of Warriston turned on his clerical associate in the compilation of the momentous document and with almost a reproachful vigour, exclaimed, "What talk is this, good Minister, in the midst of the high tide of our movement? Would you have us sink under the stone of unbelief, yea and mistrust? There is a moment in the tides of history which must be ridden ere it ebbs. Let there be no mistake. For us it is this moment. Let us not have the doubt of St. Thomas quench our spiritual fire. There yonder is Captain John Paton of Meadowhead in the parish of Fenwick, a born soldier and man of action, though in his youth he was thirled to husbandry. But, volunteering for military service, he has served in Germany where he fought already under the great Lion of the North, King Gustavus Adolphus of Sweden, and was advanced to the post of Captain. The time for talking has come to an end and now is the time to take the Kingdom by violence if necessary. Surely even the Scriptures do admonish us to take the Kingdom by force?"

Henderson's abrupt look was full of authority. "Your interpetration of the Holy Scriptures leaves a lot to be desired, Mr Johnstone. God's Word commends entering into the Kingdom of God by a joyful faith. But it is now two hours into the afternoon. It will be dark before this great throng have all signed the Covenant and there are thousands of adherents still to win throughout Scotland!"

Here the statesman-cleric turned to the crowd, "This historic document must be carried throughout the length and breadth of Scotland, from town to town, and from village to village. Noblemen and gentlemen will carry copies from district to district."

"The Covenant! The Covenant! The National Covenant! Long live the National Covenant!" A deafening roar arose from the crowd.

The slender but impressive figure of the Marquis of Montrose turned to my Lord Rothes and the Earl of Loudon, "Aye, and I shall attend to St. Andrews, that centre of Episcopacy, and Aberdeen, that intractable and unnatural city, and persuade them by sense or force of the necessity of signing our National Covenant. This is our answer in which patriotism and religion are blended. Scotland will heartily acknowledge Charles, fight his battles and give him her unstinted allegiance but the King must not filch from her either her civic liberty or her spiritual birthright. This is the protest of a Church which loves its own simple creed and worship in which a man, be he of high or low degree, can approach the Almighty without the mediatorship of any priesthood and Christ only is the Head of the Church without any royal prerogatives. The stage on which we are enacting this historic scene is the most suitable, the graveyard in which our ancestors have been laid from time immemorial. It stirs our hearts. These ancestors are mute witnesses to our declaration of religious freedom." Montrose ceased from his declaraction of loyalty to the Covenant as he turned to listen to Rev. Alexander Henderson who was now reading from the document aloud to the assembled concourse. "We, noblemen, baronets, gentlemen, burgesses, ministers, and commons, and every one of us underwritten, protest, that, after long and due examination of our own consciences in matters of true and false religion, we are now thoroughly resolved in the truth by the Spirit and Word of God; and we believe with our hearts and confess before God and the whole world, that this is the true Christian religion, pleasing God, and bringing Salvation to man by the mercy of God, revealed to the world by the preaching of the blessed Evangel. This Evangel is believed by the Kirk of Scotland, the King's Majesty, and three estates of this realm, as God's eternal truth, and only ground of our Salvation. We abhor and detest all contrary religion and doctrine; but chiefly all kind of Papistry, now condemned by God's Word and the Kirk of Scotland. We detest and refuse the usurped authority of the Roman Antichrist upon the Scriptures, upon the Kirk, the civil magistrates, and consciences of men; all his tyrannous laws made against our Christian liberty his corrupted doctrine concerning original sin, our natural inability and rebellion to God's law, our justification by faith only, our imperfect sanctification and obedience to the law; the nature, number and use of the holy sacraments; his five bastard sacraments, with all its rites, ceremonies, and false doctrines, added to the ministration of the true sacraments without the Word of God; his absolute necessity of baptism; his blasphemous opinion of transubstantiation, or real presence of Christ's body in the elements, and receiving of the same by the wicked, or bodies of men; his dispensations with solemn oaths, perjuries and degrees of marriage forbidden in the Word; his cruelty against the innocent divorced; his devilish mass; his blasphemous priesthood; his profane sacrifice for sins or the dead and the quick; his canonization of men; his calling upon angels or saints departed, worshiping of imagery, relics, and crosses; dedicating of kirks, altars, days; his purgatory, prayers for the dead; praying or speaking in a strange language with his processions, and blasphemous litany, and multitude of advocates, or mediators, his manifold orders, auricular confesion; his desperate and uncertain repentance; his general and doubtsome faith; his satisfactions of men for their sins; his justification by works, merits, pardons, peregrinations and stations; his holy water, baptizing of bells, conjuring of spirits, crossing, anointing, hallowing of God's good creatures with superstitious beliefs, his worldly monarchy, and wicked hierarchy; his three solemn vows; his erroneous and bloody decrees made at Trent against the Kirk of God, and finally we detest all his vain allegories, rites, signs, and traditions brought in the Kirk, without the Word of God, and doctrine of the true reformed Kirk: to the which we join ourselves willingly, in doctrine, faith, discipline, religion, and use of the holy sacraments, with Christ our Head." Alexander Henderson continued on enumerating the various laws, statutes, and constitutions of the Confession of Faith of 1580 passed under James VI. The people to whom their religion meant so much more than in an age of materialism waited patiently and attentively. Not least they cheered the oath of loyalty to the Crown which came latterly from the Ministers lips. "With the same heart, we declare before God and men, that we have no intention or desire to attempt anything that may turn to the dishonour of God, or to the diminution of the King's greatness and authority; but, on the contrary, we promise and swear, that we shall, to the uttermost of our power, stand to the defence of our dread Sovereign and King's Majesty, his person, and authority, in the defence and preservation of the true religion, liberties and laws of the kingdom."

The four large skins of parchment on which the copy of the Covenant was written were subscribed by all ranks, high and low, until every person within the crowded walls of Greyfriars had first signed, and then they were taken out of doors and laid flat upon a gravestone for the signatures of those in the Churchyard. Many were crying but others were full of a triumphant pride. No longer were they the dictated to but the dictators. The subscriptions came so thick and fast that there had been at one time plenty of space on the roll, now many could only find room for their initials. Many hours passed and the appending of names still was not ended when the darkness came down. This twenty-eighth day of February, 1638, was a significant day for the nation of Scotland, the return of a nation to its first love. It was a day on which the Princes of the people came together to swear allegiance only to the great King whose name is the Lord of Hosts.

From the capital this enthusiasm went to the towns, the villages, and remote parishes. it was a spreading fire, being passed on as surely as if there ws a beacon flame on the hilltops of every hamlet. Copies of the Covenant were sent for subscribing and a nation not noted for emotion revealed a lasting and productive feeling. Copies were sent to the London Scots, and to the Scots congregations abroad and the Scots regiments serving on the Continent. It had hardly been known since the days of Israel of old for one whole small nation, men, women and children, to stand up as one living soul to call upon their God. The Bishops heard of the National Covenant and trembled. Archbishop Spottiswoode, when he heard of the events in Greyfriars Churchyard, exclaimed in raging despair, "They have destroyed in a day what we have been thirty years building."

Some bishops fled to London but others wanted to raise an army in the north to defeat the Covenanters. For an excited wildness now took possession of the Scots character, normally sedate, and strange things were done. In Edinburgh, Fife and some parts of the west country, the Covenant superseded all other public and private interests. Gentlemen and noblemen carried copies about in their portmanteaus and pockets, asking for subscriptions to it and doing their utmost to influence friends. It was subscribed publicly in churches with the minister exhorting the people. It was also subscribed privately in secretive meetings under the cover of darkness.

It was a great day for the people of Scotland who saw themselves bound to God in a holy cause, but Charles I, a doomed and infatuated Stuart King, sent up a message to Scotland, that he had ordered the use of the Liturgy, and so made the quarrel personal. Five years before, when the Dean of Edinburgh had begun to read the Liturgy, obnoxious to the packed High Kirk of St. Giles, his voice was drowned in noise, and Jenny Geddes, an old woman who kept a greengrocer shop in the High Street, in indignation cried out, "Villain, dae ye say Mass at my lug?" and hurled her stool — affectionately known as a "creepie" — at the head of the Dean who threw off his surplice and barely escaped with his life.

The next great step of the "Covenanting Party" was to summon a free General Assembly in Glasgow in November when Bishops and the Liturgy were abolished and Presbyterianism was restored. The Earl of Argyll, that influential figure of Highland and Lowland connection, here cast his lot in with the Covenanters. The Covenanters were really the true nation of Scotland, and 30,000 armed Scotsmen were raised to defend their liberty, with banners inscribed in gold letters, "Christ's Crown and Covenant".

Charles immediately raised an army in England and advanced to the Borders, ordering a fleet at the same time to blockade the Firth of Forth. When the blazing tar barrel announced that the 28 ships of war had appeared in the Firth, the population flocked in such great numbers to the shore that they could not land their 5,000 troops under the Marquis of Hamilton. His mother, a zealous Covenanter, came on horsebac to Leith with her retinue, and said she would kill her son if he ventured to land as an enemy of Scotland. She had loaded her pistol with balls of gold instead of lead to give him a right royal welcome.

Into this Scotland then of religious strife and almost unbearable family tensions, had been born an Alexander Peden, in the year of the National Covenant, a tall, straight twelve year old lad with the light of prophetic vision already beginning to dawn in his deep grey eyes. Born at the farm of Auchincloich, the Field of Stones, near Sorn, in Ayrshire, he was the eldest son of Hugh Peden, a small proprieter, and heir to the land. But, as yet, far from trouble, he was content to guddle speckled trout in the Lugar with the Boswell children from Auchinleck, and watch fascinated the spinning of the wool in the nearby weavers cottage, dreaming dreams of the future. Little did Alexander Peden think that the flame of the covenant, that was set alight that day in Greyfriars Kirkyard was to be a continuing fire in his heart to the end of his life.

2
Deliverance By A Thread

The National Covenant heralded a period of religious turmoil and tumult equal to the great Protestant Reformation a century before. Men still had not learnt to live together in tolerance and harmony with those of differing political and religious creeds. The controversy centred, as the Covenant said, on the all important role of the King, whether he was to be the spiritual head of the Church, even though it be Presbyterian, and then the rule of Bishops and imposition of a Liturgy and forms of worship with kneeling and prayers that were foreign to the spirit of the Presbyterian people of Scotland. The underlying cause was spiritual rather than political. A nation had queried the claim by a monarch to determine the form of government of a national Church. The first two Stewart Kings of England, James VI and Charles I, accepted whole heartedly the pattern of Episcopal Government as found in England, and Charles I in particular, urged on by Canterbury's infamous Archbishop Laud, determined to make Scotland bow willy-nilly to the Episcopal yoke. Then came the tremendous storm of protest of 1637, epitomised that July by the ominous stool throwing by Jenny Geddes, that Presbyterian virago to some but heroic woman of faith to others, when she cried out with holy boldness, "Will ye read that Book in ma lug?" Jenny Geddes was a kailwife who used to sell vegetables outside the Tron Kirk further down the High Street. That morning she had brought her own stool, known as a creepie, and just as Dean Hannay, was about to read the Collect for the day, she picked up her creepie and flung it at the head of the offending cleric. It was the signal for a general riot and the church had to be cleared by force. The English Prayer Book was the object of their

9

rejection and their belief in the freedom of the spirit refused to be bound by any of man-made religion, especially if it did not agree with the Word of God. Great was the power of sweetness of this Word to them. The Covenanting people of Scotland read every portion of it as if it had been spoken to them directly, by the mouth of God. It was the pasture on which they fed and it was pleasant to their taste. It was to be their constant companion wherever they reposed, in the caves, or among the brown heather, or on the green hillside, and in it they had recourse to the oracles of eternal truth for strength and comfort in their many perils.

Many years had passed since that historic event in the Greyfriars Kirkyard and the anomalies and contradictions of human nature, led first the Marquis of Montrose to fulfil the Rev. Alexander Henderson's prophecy, and, as a Royalist to the last, to espouse Charles' side and defeat the Covenanting army in a series of brilliant campaigns, and then secondly, for the Covenanting army under the Leslies to support the exiled Charles II against Oliver Cromwell and his invincible Ironsides. The army of Montrose himself, compsed of Highlanders and Irish mainly, defeated the Covenanting forces at Tippermuir, Bridge O' Dee, Kilsyth, and the forces of the Duke of Argyll at Inverlochy until in September 1645 he met his match when surprised by General David Leslie at Philiphaugh. But the Covenanting forces did not fare any better against Cromwell's Ironsides than the best armies and navies of Europe, including Holland, Spain and indeed half of the Continent but sadly for the Covenanters that high peak of English power and age of tolerance was to come to an end with the abolition of the Protectorate and the Commonwealth and the coming of the Restoration of Charles II in 1660.

Then the troubles of the Covenanters were only beginning, with persecution, victimisation, tyranny, exile, injustice, imprisonment and cruel death to thousands of Scots men, women and young people who were martyred or exiled as slaves to the West Indian islands of Jamaica and Barbados, or the sugar plantations of Virginia and South Carolina. This was only to be ended by the indeed Glorious Revolution of 1688 with the coming of William of Orange and Mary and the freedom of religion that accompanied a limited Parliamentary democracy.

But the scene goes back to some few years before the ill fated Restoration and the small village of Tarbolton in the Ayrshire parish of Mauchline and an Ecclesiastical Court, convened by the Presbytery of that bounds. In the judgement seat was a very gentle and demure looking youth of tall and straight bearing from what could be gleaned from a cursory glance even. His long limbs were cramped in the small box seat reserved for the sinners, repentant or otherwise. His eyes were downcast, but if observed closely, would be seen to be of a grey, penetrating nature. His hair was of a jet black hue. A group of men were arranged in benches opposite, men of an ecclesiastical demeanour, serious, venerable in their disposition, and authoritative in their air though not an authority foisted by themselves. The man who clearly presided was addressing the young man.

"Mr. Alexander Peden, you stand here before this Court of the church, accused of a most immoral act, to be judged in the sight both of men and Almighty God. As a teacher and precentor in the local congregation of Tarbolton the thought of such guilt is all the more heinous. In the witness stand is the innocent young lady who has had her virtue deflowered. We shall hear her sad story presently. But, first, Mr. Downie, Clerk to the Presbytery, is everybody in the Ecclesiastical Jury present?"

A small, neat, and obviously meticulous figure scuttled forward from where he had been unnoticed in the corner.

"Yes, your Reverence. The Revs. Morrison of Mauchline, Small of Ochiltree, Grey of Ayr's township, and McAdam of Alloway's Kirk as well as the Elders of Tarbolton parish. They are all present, Rev. Guthrie."

The Rev. John Guthrie, whose brother, the Rev. William Guthrie, well known Minister of the parish of Fenwick overshadowed his own ministry, continued his description of the accused and the charge against him. "Then, let us proceed. Let me recite what I know of the defendant. You can then correct me, Mr. Peden, if I have erred somewhat in any particular. You are a gentleman by descent and upbringing, born in 1626, in the House of Auchincloich, known to the locals as the House of the Field of the Stones, in the northern part of the parish of Sorn in the shire of Ayr. I ken myself these large flat stones with some strange inscriptions I know not what. I'm sure these stones could preach a sermon and tell some history if they could speak. They say they go back to Celtic times. Hem, hem, back to the matter in hand. Your father was a small proprietor and as the eldest son you became heir to the lairdship. Gentlemen have been your friends and prominent among them I hear, the weel kent Boswells of Auchinleck. You were well educated, a scholar of the University of Glasgow when James Dalrymple, now famous as a lawyer and statesman, was Professor of Philosophy. I believe apart from College escapades in which you were the prime mover in ruses to trip over Faculty members with, eer, ropes stretched across

Quadrangle doorways, sending firecrackers down the chimneys of other students and even on a disgraceful occasion that of a University lecturer, — you will appreciate, Mr. Peden that all these things have to be brought out into the open if we are to ascertain the truth of your character — so as I say, apart from these you performed your academic studies with great application, attentiveness and no little intelligence. Your Latin and Theological studies were particularly good. So it was that you graduated with honour and entered with an eager and sincere heart, for ought anyone could tell, into the work of schoolmaster and precentor in this parish of Tarbolton. You even became promoted to Session Clerk in which position I did give you my full support and trust in as much as the Session is the extra right hand man of the Minister. This is what makes it all the harder for me to be the executioner in this tragic case, Mr. Peden. Have you somewhat to say before we preceed further with the evidence?"

The young man slowly lifted his head as if weighed down by an unbearable burden. The youthful joy which it could be guessed usually suffused his face was overcome with the strain and spiritual pain evident in his eyes. In a voice tremulous with fearful emotion, he said, "All I can do, your Reverence, is to plead my total innocence of the charge. The woman in question I know only in a Christian neighbourly sense as a fellow member of Tarbolton parish. She has come to me for advice on the Banns the Church would announce on the occasion of her marriage. As Session Clerk, I gave her the arrangements on the times and occasions of announcement and also the pecuniary charge. She never did give away the name of the young man. I believe her enquiries were built on hope, your Reverence. I was led to believe that she works in the Inn of 'The Rising Sun' as a serving wench. I did not come across Margaret Laird often, as she did not come to the Church until she was intending marriage, and, without offence, sir, she is a little too old for my class at the Schoolhouse."

The lines of the grave leathery face of the Rev. John Guthrie grew even graver. "There is no need for a bitter spirit or sarcasm. You are in deep trouble, Mr. Peden, my dear young man. But I do agree that 'The Rising Sun' is of none too good a reputation, in fact downright disreputable for putting up all sorts of waifs and strays and gangrel bodies whom 'The Tarbolton Arms' would never entertain. I've heard some eldritch cries out of there during the hours of darkness. How long has Margaret Laird been there? Speak up, Mr. Downie!"

"Eer, sorry, sir, but I don't know exactly, though its no lang ago sin' she cam to Tarbolton. Naething much is known of her life previous tae this."

"All right, Downie, Bring forward the girl, Margaret Laird." A sheepish looking girl is brought into the courtroom form a small door in the corner. She is glancing nervously around as if in an air of unreality and her thoughts and very being were elsewhere. A coquettish air was still there, however scarcely hidden by her fears, and a quick fling of her shoulders cast her pale blond hair into a little more shapely form. An all encompassing lace shawl covered the upper half of her body.

"Now, girl, I wish you to give an account of your antecedents and how you came to make such accusations against Alexander Peden."

"Antecedents, sir? I don't know as I have any."

"Where ye come from, girl! Pray get on with it."

"Well, sir, a' come from the toon o' Ayr to find work as worthwhile work is hard to come by for girls like me with high hopes of advancement and the looks and smartness tae get it."

"Quite!" Rev. Guthrie answered testily.

"Aye, as I wis saying, your Lordship, sorry, your Reverence. They didnae appreciate me in Ayr. They're too high falutin' for their ain good!"

"Quite so!"

"So I moved wi' a my worldy possessions you might say, to this braw village of Tarbolton and the meenit my een caught sight of 'The Rising Sun' I knew that that was the place for me. Mr. Maitland is a rare, braw Innkeeper and treats me like a lady, no a slut."

"If you do not get on with it, I'll hold you in contempt of court though I doubt if you would ken what that means."

"Well, serving in the 'Rising Sun' I got to know the customers and the local Tarbolton folk very well. But as ye ken, no everybody comes into 'The Rising Sun' especially the Kirk folk. I cannae understand why no, as we serve the best ale. Anyway I was wanting to show myself a respectable buddie and gang to Kirk. I went along to the Parish Church regular like and its there that I met Mr. Peden. At first I never spoke to him, him being superior like, the toon Schoolmaster, far abune me. But then he came to me late one night when I was on my way home from the Inn tae my lodgings."

The countenance of Alexander Peden was suffused with indignation. "This is lies and hypocrisy!" There was no discernable malice in his voice and eyes.

"Silence! Mr. Peden! Or you too will be a wheen aff contempt of court. This is a Court of Justice!"

"So, as I was saying, he accosted me one night and said he wished to instruct me in the Faith. Being a trusting kind of girl, I took his word and he accompanied me home to my humble lodgings in the Nether Vennel. There I provided sic simple fare as my wages could allow. But after, though he did bring out his Catechism and begin tae question and answer, yet it did seem he was intent frae the stert and did force himself on me. Not wishing tae offend such an important person o' the Kirk, before I could stop him he was making love to me, and when I did protest and was near tears, your Reverence, Mr. Peden did threaten to report me to the Magistrate as being a woman o' ill repute. What could I do but surrender to his desires and he did know me, as I once heard it put in a preaching in Ayr."

"Why did you not cry out, woman? This is a respectable parish. We all need one another's help at some time or ither."

"Dae ye think they wid take my word, that of a serving wench of ill repute against that of a gentleman, a well respected man of the Kirk? Nae fear!"

"This is the Court of the Lord, a court of justice, woman. As the prophet Amos says, we ought to do justly and love mercy."

"Aye, that's what I mean tae get, your Reverence, justice. I'll make Mr. Peden a good wife. After he had had his way with me, he wanted to cast me aside like an auld rag that he wiped the pot with and had served its purpose."

"I think the evidence has been heard, gentlemen," said Rev. Guthrie, turning to the jury. "There is a distinct paucity of witnesses, unfortunately. Let us depend upon Divine guidance. Have you anything to say in your defence, Alexander Peden, or any other present indeed, before the jury pronounces sentence?"

Alexander Peden hung his head in silent submission to the will of God. The atmospere was pregnant with a tense anticipation that something was about to happen, something unexpected.

Suddenly an insignificant looking figure rose trembling to his feet from among the elders of the Tarbolton Parish on the jury bench, and a thin voice croaked out, "I am the father of the child, and the guilty one. The trial need continue no longer."

A gasp of shocked unbelief was audible through the Courtroom. Isaac Stevenson was a Kirk elder of untarnished repute for many years. Such a thing was impossible.

"Say your piece, Isaac Stevenson," said John Guthrie scarce believing the outcome.

Isaac Stevenson was a pathetic sight now, his thin face unnaturally pale. A man of middle age, he was at best a retiring person, and the guilt was out of character.

"As ye ken, I now and then frequent' The Tarbolton Arms' for company as my life is very lonely since my spouse Agnes died o' the cholera after twa years marriage." His reedy voice trembled as he continued, "Never did I dare glance at 'The Rising Sun' for less afford my custom but steered a wide berth, knowing its reputation. Nor was it for the drink that the Arms saw my presence and all I took rarely was a thin ale, as it does agree ill with my constitution, but it was for the company alone of honest hearted men. Never did I look at a woman with desire since my dear Agnes died till that evening when hurrying by the door of 'The Rising Sun' and the woman Margaret Laird called to me. Loath I was to wait but good manners do always belong to a Christian man, and I did engage in converse with her." Stevenson pointedly avoided the figure of the girl where she sat, now visibly spitting spite from her features.

"She told me in what seemed a sincere and confidential way that she saw the folly of her lawless and sinful life and asked to discuss her spiritual problems with me, knowing I was a man of God. In spite of my judgement, I succumbed to her wiles and attended the woman Laird to her lodgings in the Nether Vennel, which as ye well ken, reverend gentlemen," here Isaac Stevenson looked up obsequiously at the rest of the Jury, "'Tis a backstreet where even the loudest cries may not be heard. There it was that the woman did sexually entice me. I did continually turn her to the Bible to answer her spiritual problems. But she came ever closer to me, insisting that what she needed was love to solace her loneliness. The temptation of her womanhood was too great and I gave in to an hour of stolen pleasure in her recess bed. I am so sorry for young Mr. Peden for what he has suffered," he ended miserably to droop onto the bench before him.

With a face like thunder the Rev. Guthrie spoke, "Whether your naivete is greater than your guilt, let the jury decide. But the blatant fornication you have brought here, Margaret Laird, pronounces your sentence of guilt. You will appear before the whole assembled congregation in sackcloth and your half head shaved for several Sundays. Before that happens you will be doukit three times in the most foul deep pool in Tarbolton district; if that does not make you amend your ways, then you will be banished for good from the parish."

During all this time the girl had been reduced to a pale shadow of the once proud hussy, confident of the outcome. No longer did Margaret Laird hold up her head so that all could see her scorn of the religious body, whom she regarded as proud of their own righteousness. The Romany which existed deep within her, had caused a certain bitterness at the treatment of the gypsy people and the scorn poured upon their incantations, folk beliefs, and herbal remedies. She herself believed wholeheatedly that the blue of irises had the ability to heal bruises, as anyone could gather from their similarity in colour, that distilled water from the hawthorn flower drew thorns and blisters from the skin, and that the spotty cowslip was an obvious cure for spotty complaints. Ordinary people were ignorant. But now all her bitterness had deserted her as she realised that there was no escape from her moral sin. The denunciations that were hung up *In terrorem* for the crime of illicit love were both many and singular. The pillar of repentence or black stool was still the most conspicuous seat in the congregation and the number of culprits, both male and female, who occupied it in every parish of the Church, a public scandal. Generally the women predominated, as the other offending party was able to escape by running off to some remoted district. As the conspicuousness of such an exposure was so terrible to society then the female pentent often tried to mitigate it; but to prevent this no woman was allowed to ascend the pillar with a plaid, so that she was deprived of the power of muffling her head and face. A degree to this effect had been made by the kirk-session of Aberdeen. Sometimes when a male offender was to be exposed he endeavoured to bear down the shame by bravado or bufoonery, and the attempts to do this formed the standing joke of the parish, when no minister or elder was present to overhear it. It had been known for one to make a mockery of his public repentance by putting snuff in his eyes so that he cried tears, while he was privately winking and grinning to his companions below. But his hypocrisy was detected and he was punished with excommunication, the highest infliction of the Church, and only released from it by undergoing public penance for several Sundays. With poor Isaac Stevenson there was no such problem, as he was so broken in spirit that that would have been punishment enough. But for the women it was hard and for flagrant offences, additions were made to the common penalty. Two women who had accompanied the army of Montrose who had left the Covenant and rampaged over the Highlands defeating Covenanting armies, were compelled for a double crime to sit in the branks barefooted and in sackcloth at the Kirk-door between the two bells and afterwards to stand on the pillar during the time of sermon for several days, until the congregation had been satisfied of the sincerity of their repentance. Sometimes the worst parts might be avoided by a fine. The soldiers of Cromwell with their own ideas on religion, had thrown the stools of repentance out of doors but after they departed the pillar became more firmly rooted than ever.

Licentious conduct was from the first an object of severe observation to the reformed church and many sharp measures were taken and harsh punishments inflicted for its repression. A stool was raised in a conspicuous situation in each church, where penitents had to sit during service and afterwards hear the rebuke of the minister. They had often great difficulty in getting penitents to remain unmuffled and uncovered. The Aberdeen Session had ordained in 1608 that because in times past many women who came to the public stool or pillar to make public repentance, sat with their plaids about their head, coming down over their faces so that almost none of the congregation could see their faces or know who they were, the officer should take away from each penitent before her upgrading to the pillar. (In very gross cases, a paper crown was added to the external marks of infamy inflicted on delinquents.)

An Aberdeen Kirk session had ordained as its punishment, for the first offence, exposure before the congregation; for the second, carting and ducking; for the third, banishment from the town. Later a still severer punishment was imposed. For the first fault, the man as well as the woman shall pay the sum of forty pounds, or else he and she shall be imprisoned for eight days, their food to be bread and small drink, and afterwards presented to the Mercat Place of the town, bareheaded, and there stand fastened, so that he couldn't be removed for two hours. Additions for a second offence were cold water for food and a shaving of the head, while the third inferred ducking and banishment. When a marriage relationship existed, the man was ordained to be banished from the town but was first to be set up at the cross on three market-days, bound to the pillar by a pair of branks, and a paper-crown on his head inscribed with his crime; also to stand on three Sundays at the Kirk door, in haircloth, barelegged and barefooted, while the people are assembling; after to be exposed in like guise at the pillar of repentance during the whole time of worship. The Rev. Guthrie was speaking again.

"The life of the coming child is not to be endangered in your punishment. So, on taking thought, and showing the consideration of Christ and His Church, we will forego the punishment of douking. We are merciful and do not desire to cause undue suffering.

But as for you, Master Stevenson, I shall leave the Ecclesiastical Court to decide your fate though I strongly suspect that the cutty stool of repentance will figure largely in your fate." Here the Minister half turned to look at a high stool in a public and eminent spot at the lower end of the building. It had four spindly legs and no back, indicating how uncomfortable it would be for the culprit to sit on for long periods.

"God alone can judge the hearts but the Church has to be content with more outward signs of repentance. The cutty stool is the chief means by which the Church humbles its penitents. Be grateful that you are not in the time of Deuteronomy when stoning was commanded of the Lord for such moral sins. The culprit, as you no doubt ken, Mr. Stevenson, stands on our good stool but may be allowed to sit during sermon. Master Alexander Peden, I am glad to say you are completely exonerated and the Court begs your humble forgiveness for the slur cast on your character. I pray that no scar may remain. Continue your course as precentor and teacher as well as your studies to become licensed as a faithful Minister."

Sandy slipped self consciously from the congesting accused box, and, holding his head high, he advanced up the aisle. He held no antipathy towards the Court but experienced a vital sense of deliverance form on high. Though now coming on thirty years of age, there would have been an abortion of all his hopes for the Ministry. As he caught the glances of some of the ladies in the congregation, Sandy deeply appreciated the softness of their sympathy. The accusation was false; and his innocence was proved, as if by a miracle, on the very day when he was about to be excommunicated from the Church. But the anguish of the experience had been terrible and left its scar on a nature more trusting and friendly than most. By and by the wound was to be healed and he would remain unsoured. He was no ascetic and would continue to delight in God's gift to men. The bubbling fountain of his cheerfulness was not dried up, and, as he reached the door of the church and the Ayrshire fresh breezes enveloped him, he really rejoiced in life.

It was a day later, when passing the Kirk, that he felt a sore pang of pain. Standing attached to the gate post of the Kirk, by a chain with a hinged iron band, called the jougs, round his neck, was the broken figure of Isaac Stevenson. Hung round his breast was a large slate with bold characters placarding his offence. For three hours each day during the busy morning hours, he had to suffer this public indignity. Going over to the unfortunate man, Sandy Peden clasped him round the shoulders in a loving embrace. Man's outward judgements often belie their inward feelings.

"The weakness of human nature is common to us all and we are bound up in the bundle of life. It saddens me to have to see you besmeared with broken egg yolks in the jougs at the Kirk door where mischievous callants and ill-behaud in women think they are privileged to fling all sorts of rubbish in your face, Isaac. The strong refined look that was to remain etched clearly on Alexander Peden's face, despite the great suffering that lay ahead, was never more evidenced than at the moment. He felt no hint of a vulgarity that delighted in legitimate punishment. Sandy's trusting, friendly, nature was scarred more than Isaac Stevenson's reputation was ruined, if truth be told.

"The accusation was more heinous than what I did, Mr. Peden. But my young friend, I am receiving my due reward. The lass was clear with her intentions from the start, and, for a moment, I solaced my loneliness with an excitement of the flesh. I only ask that you do not cast a' thing in my direction but your forgiveness, and, when I've tholed my excise to depart Tarbolton Parish forever. The former elder's lugubrious look resembled a forlorn dog whose master had sent to the out house with a kick.

"Neither eggs, nor stones, nor any rubbish will I cast, Isaac, under the law of Christ. The jougs are already too heavy for you." The metal was cutting painfully into the man's thin neck. It had been adjusted too cruelly by the court executioner of punishments, and threatened to throttle him. "As for the future, I see it in the bonnie toon of Ayr wi' a quiet prosperity from polished stones and fancy trinkets. But she who came lately from Ayr will have a sad ending in a place close by where God was very precious tae me." Leaving the astonished man, he walked slowly down to his lodgings in a humble biggin off the Ayr road.

For the schoolmaster, session clerk, and precentor to the Rev. John Guthrie the next few years were full of study, church life, pastoral assistance to his superiors, fun playing with the bairns in the parish, and not least of all much frustration with his desire for ordination that he craved being continually blocked. Isaac Stevenson duly departed in disgrace from Tarbolton but his latter years saw Stevenson set up a thriving shop in Ayr making necklaces and brooches made from agate, jasper, and the like, much in demand by Glasgow merchants for their beloved spouses. Margaret Laird, form descending to the lowest gutter of the social ladder, was found dead in a rocky linn near Tarbolton, and was thought generally to have fallen by accident, though local rumour put it otherwise. Sandy meantime laboured studiously on his Latin, Hebrew, and theological studies, appearing before the ecclesiastical courts at Biggar and Lanark five times on trial for license. The court were severely critical in their examination, and Sandy despaired but finally on a sunny August day in the year of grace sixteen hundred and fifty nine, he delivered an exposition in dusty Latin on Divine Worship, which satisfied their tight restrictures, and late in the year came his preachers ordination.

With a light heart and fresh spring to his step, the Rev. Alexander Peden packed his books and few belongings, having abandoned his claim to the Farm of Auchincloich as heir to his younger brother Hugh, and set out on horseback for his very own parish of New Luce in the region of Galloway, a green pastoral land of glens and hills. Though to some it was a solitary and wild land, to Alexander Peden it was the land of promise, a green and pleasant land. A whole horizon in which to extend the Kingdom of God lay ahead of Sandy. Glen Luce, seemed to live up to its name, Valley of the Sun, as if beckoning him to the light.

3
Where The Carcass Is There The Vultures Will Gather

The year was 1660 and if an informed observer were present, they could have been excused if they had concluded that gathered there in a state room of Edinburgh Castle were the three most powerful men in Scotland, the arch-instruments of the Government in London for the central and general subjugation of that land under Charles II. Gathered in malicious conclave were John Mar, Earl of Middleton, the King's Commissioner; the Earl of Glencairn, William Cunningham, now the Kings Chancellor of Scotland and, not least of all, Sir Archibald Primrose, the Clerk Register. The Earl of Middleton, a big, coarse man whose habits, even in an age not over nice, were noticeably gross and boorish. He was addressing his companions in conclave with a fuming indignation, clearly inflamed with much alcohol. He had carved his way to office by his military ability. A poor soldier of fortune he had sought distinction in foreign service and from being a pikeman in Colonel Hepburn's mercenary regiment of Scots in the army of France, Middleton had become a peer of the realm and the representative of Charles II in Scotland when the Restoration took place. Certainly a fearless officer and skillful, audacious soldier, yet with a violent temper and an arbitary, revengeful nature, he could not be a wise civil governor. His vicious words bore this out.

"It is outrageous that these recalcitrant, stiff necked Covenanting hypocrites with their bold as brass faces should be allowed so free and by God, singularly imperative that they be seen and condemned as the traitors they are. Their double-tongued and double-minded equivocation will find no scope from now on. We have caught them like rats in a trap. It only needs the right bait. This Pied Piper will lure them tae their doom tae the right tune and it's the right tune I'll be playing. Primrose, read me that Oath of Allegiance, the bonnie document, that we may read the tune. We'll soon see where their loyalties lie, when their traitorous words condemn them. His Majesty, King Charles, may his name be reverenced and adored, will welcome our application of the Oath. Well may the day of his glorious return, the 29th of May, be remembered for ever a holy day unto the Lord, after the thrice cursed tyranny of these Puritans, Quakers, Covenanters and such spawn, under that blasphemous regicide, Cromwell!" Middleton's voice here became thick and blurred by alcohol and rose to a roar of rage. "Now, Primrose". Middleton, obviously the worse for liquor, slumped back into his chair.

Sir Archibald Primrose, almost living up to hisname by his prim and proper manner of speech and address, read from the Oath of Allegiance as if it was something of delicate substance instead of a harsh and proud claim. "His Majesty, King Charles II alone shall choose the Officers of State, his Privy Councillors, and his Lords of Session. He alone shall call, prorogue and dissolve all conventions and meetings and enter into treaties and leagues. He alone shall make war or peace. The day of his glorious return shall be for ever a holy day unto the Lord. His Majesty shall be granted an annual amount of £40,000 Sterling for the expense of the Royal Purse and Household. God save the King!" The third and hitherto silent member of the triumvirate, the Earl of Glencairn, a burly figure of sanguine countenance and least likely to run the country's finances, responded with great enthusiam and not a little boisterousness, "God save the King!"

"Sir William Cunningham, my good Lord Glencairn, you are a Royalist to the backbone!", Middleton cried, clearly pleased mightily at this spontaneous reflection of his mood by his underling. "O that we had more of your ilk instead of these Covenanting breed with their brooding natures and in their hearts are lurking traitorous desires. One would never think they enjoyed a good stoup of wine or the thrill of the pursuit o' the game deer. Mayhaps pure red blood doth not flow in their veins, but a turgid mixture of milk and water, think ye? But all could be forgiven, their canting religious talk and everything, if it were not for their downright disloyalty to their Sovereign King and Lord. Well do I remember our standing together at Worcester and Preston against that blasphemer and regicide Cromwell, how we kept the flame of loyal revolt blazing in the Highlands when all others had deserted His Majesty. And right royally has he rewarded us his servants. When the King was across the water in Holland he sent me over to command his forces, there was such disunity that His Majesty said in richt despair that the enemy depends more on the divisions and animosities among you than upon his own strength.

"These Highland Lords, Lorne, Kenmure and Glengarry, with their puff-brained chieftains whose only interest is how much baggage and gear they can loot, were a thorn on my side but even then with my faithful mosstroopers we led those Roundheads a merry dance through the Heilans. But then wart face sent north Monck and Morgan, curse their names, I would not honour them with the titles General and Colonel, and Mother Fortune dealt us a bitter blow at Dalnaspidal on the shores of bonnie Loch Garry! But I had rare luck with my friends, my good friends, the MacLeods of Skye. Forby I had a rare time, roistering and carousing, for they had plenty o' the usquebagh, bless them."

Sir Archibald Primrose spoke quietly with a sly look on his ferret face, "Did my Lord Commissioner fight under the Blue Banner and wear the Blue Bonnet at Preston and Worcester? As there has been a reversal of fortune at the hands of Cromwell, has there not also been a reversal of your views, my Lord?"

For a moment the face of Middleton blanched a deathly white with a barely suppressed anger until a sardonic smile pulled down his lower lip. "Thou wert ever the cleverest tongue in Parliament House and the shrewdest intellect forby but it is a dangerously impudent one full of a personal impertinence which will get you the Grassmarket Gallows one day mayhap. You have the art of speaking to all men according to their sense of things and so drawing out their secrets while concealing your own. Words go for nothing with you. But you are right. I did carry arms for General David Leslie at Preston and Worcester in the campaigns of '44 and '45. But dinna forget that I carved my way from being a simple pikeman in the regiment of Colonel Hepburn in France, a poor station indeed for one of my calling. Indeed, when I returned from France, I became so zealous about the Covenant that I took the very copy of the famous document in my right hand which I wished to be the death of me of ever I forgot my vow. But ere long I was undeceived as these Covenanting breed were revealed in all their perfidy. They are all traitors at heart waiting to be revealed when His Majesty calls for loyalty in his hour of need. Then their canting religion will not let a man live his life as he wishes. As His Majesty has said many a time and oft, "Presbyterianism is no religion for a gentleman". Not that I am religious." Here his roistering manner ceased and his voice sunk to almost a whisper and a faint tremor could be detected. "Yet there are things which cannot always be explained. I do well remember before the Battle of Preston I and my bosom friend, the Laird of Balbegne, neighbour to my family home in Kincardine, were speirin' wi one another if we would see the battle's end. When I asked him if there was a battle what would become of us if we died, he said, 'No matter! We shall be free from our vexations hereaway'. But as not being convinced that all is of lotus eating afterwards, I did ask him, 'What if there is a future life and world?' Balbegne opined it was an empty fable of the ministers which I would fain believe and yet do, My Lords, I assure you."

Middleton was blustering at this point. "Only some accursed germ in my brain did nag me to declare, 'But, suppose that some things turn out otherwise?' So what did Balbegne and I compact to do? I do declare that the veritable madness of a daft child must have seized me — for we entered into a compact that if one died, he should return, if that were possible, from the land of mystery, to inform the survivor of what he discovered there. At Preston, Balbegne fell and I forgot the bargain but I tell you, some time later while a captive in the Tower of London and sitting alone with two sentinels outside guarding the room, I was somewhat idly turning over the pages of a Bible which I found in the chamber, for what purpose I know not, it having been so little my custom. When I lifted my head and looked to the door I saw a man standing there in the shadows of the corner. 'Who is there?' I asked, and the answer came, 'Balbegne'. 'That cannot be for I saw you burried after you were slain in battle." But the ghostly figure glided forward, caught my arm, and reminded me of the agreement. Nay, laugh not. If you can account for it my my fevered brain caused by the incarceration under these cursed Puritans, I would be mightily pleased. Mayhap it was my fertile imagination regarding my old friend for his hand was hot and soft, as indeed it used to be, and was Balbegne in his ordinary likeness.

'I am permitted to stay one hour,' the apparition said, 'So let us sit down and put your watch before us.'

"He did not say how I should escape from my dungeon, how the King was to be restored, how favour and honour awaited at Court for me, and even how the sunshine would be covered over with clouds of calamity. Then when the hour was over, good Balbegne rose and took his leave, lingering for an instant at the door in its shadows before disappearing. Truly much to the relief of my distempered mind was his departure. Verily it must have been the lack of good wine that so affected me in my solitude! Methinks it is said that it has the opposite effect on others, my Lords. Let us have another stoup. I must take the good and leave the bad from such visions, my friends the same way as I do my wine. "Middleton returned to his roistering ways.

Glencairn broke into the awkward reverie that had fallen during the strange story, "Do you know what these humbugging Covenanters have called our lawfully elected Parliament? They say we are the Drunken Parliament, not knowing how good wine improves our spirit of understanding and agreement. I hear it said that when we issued the Act of Proclamation banishing from their manses and parishes all those Ministers who had not obtained a presentation from the lawful patron and collation from the Bishop of the Diocese before the 1st of November, 1662, we were all so drunk that day that we were not capable of considering anything laid before us. From that turncoat the Duke of Hamilton, this traitorous libel did come, I hear. It would seem that this contaminating evil spawned by these Covenanter boors is spreading to our classes, my Lord."

"I'll give them evil. Do you remember that night when we drank the Devil's health at the Cross of Ayr? That was a night to remember, at midnight too! You'd think auld herny had been at their tails the way these Whiggish Covenanters took to their heels. I sometimes think the De'il's in these fanatics. But that was a good tour of the West Country, aye the most rebellious we had after the rising of the second Parliament in 1662, when a quorum of our worthy Privy Council did accompany us and we did quell the Presbyterians and enforce the lawful rule of Episcopacy. What greater men than Fairfoul, Hamilton, and Leighton could they want as Bishops? And of course my Lord Archbishop of St. Andrews. These people plainly do not recognise the stamp of authority. When their Ministers do not take collation from the Bishop they are contemptuous of the royal authority, for the statutory states that forasmuch as the ordering and disposal of the external government and policy of the church does properly belong unto His Majesty, as an inherent right of the Crown, by virtue of his royal prerogative and supremacy in causes Ecclesiastical. The King is right. Presbyterianism is no religion for a gentleman."

"We have been accused of bringing in cowherds from the northern Highlands as Ministers and Curates, my Lord". Primrose showed by his expression that he may have believed the report. "But the matter of their snash will be swiftly eliminated by the system of fines which we will be introducing for each day's absence from the parish church. If the agricultural labour is not present, the farmer will be responsible for the fine and if the farmer fails then the landlord will be brought in. Truly we have perfected a system, my Lords, to end their rebelliousness when it hurts them most, in their pockets".

He rubbed his hands gleefully in prospect. "And it will not only improve church attendance but it will put down these unlawful Conventicles, especially when they find it's a double fine to that for non-attendance at Church. Our new Curates will help in the when they submit a list of all the offenders in the parish to the officer in charge of our dragoon troops, General Tam Dalziel, but lately returned from the land of the Muscovite. He knows how to deal with traitors. They say he has got hold of a new type of thumbscrews which he learnt in Russia under its Czar. Our official will be at the church door with lists of the parishioners to make sure absentees are noted and don't escape the net. If the guilty are unable to pay the money on the spot, the soldiery will be sent to quarter on him, his cattle seized, and his family beggared and then compelled to wander about like the wretches they are. We all know only too well that the Act of Fines was imposed for the relief of the Kings good and loyal subjects who have suffered in the late troubles. But equally we all know that the worthy Lords, Annandale, Airlie, Atholl and Drumlanrig are dependent wholly on fines to save their fortunes. The creditors of Annandale only stayed his bankruptcy by giving him time to exact fines from the rebels."

Middleton broke in with an indignant alcoholism, "Aye, the Duke of Hamilton is become our chief publican. And my informers tell me that the Marquis of Queensberry is building Drumlanrig Castle on his income from the fines."

"To quote the Scriptures, gentlemen, "Where the carcase is, there the vultures will gather." Luke's gospel, chapter 17 verse 37. That's a legacy from my religious upbringing, be assured, and one that I am trying to bequeath to others, since I find no use for it, except in the present case, of course.

"As I said before, Primrose, you were ever a subtle one, too much so for me. But this I know. These guilty curs claim to be moral and pious and chargeable with nothing but being Presbyterians. But for me that is quite enough. For it is the religion of a rebel and a traitor. Also you have no need of to tell me that Carmichael of Easter Thursten who is bankrupt gets the fines from these peasantry so long as the Commissioners take one half of the plunder of all estates and the other half goes to the Crown. But let me inform you of the latest good news, my friends. Our Lord Lauderdale is about to issue a royal proclamation."

While Middleton was hopelessly endeavouring to retrieve his erroe of imposing weak and false curates upon the Lowland Presbyterians his career was inexorably drawing to a close. The machinations of his rival Lauderdale prevailed and he was summoned to give an answer to the various charges brought against his administration in Scotland. These were neither light nor few. He was accused of having deceived both the King and the Parliament, of having passed Acts without consulting the King, of having ratified by the touch of a sceptre an Act by which those forfauted by the last Parliament wer exempted from pardon, even though the royal clemency should be brought to their support. He was accused of inflicting fines on the innocent, and allowing the guilty to escape for a bribe and misapplying public money. Middleton had usurped the right to appoint a receiver of the fines that belonged to the King. Lastly but not least he was accused of introducing a species of ostracism, like that of the Athenians of old, into his administration, by which ministers of the State were condemned by secret ballot without trial, and without the power of clearing themselves or appealing to His Majesty's clemency. The answers of Commissioner Middleton to thewe charges were so unsatisfactory that the royal confidence was shaken, and as Charles because of his unbounded prodigality was always in want of money, he was easily induced to believe that the fines which should have flowed into the Royal Treasury had been diverted into Middleton's own coffers. While his fate thus wavered in the balance one on the corrupt Commissioner's rash actions consummated his disgrace. Availing himself of his rival's greed and impetuous temper, Lauderdale moved the King to write to the Scottish Council, commanding them not to continue exacting the fines until his further pleasure, and to dismiss the collector whom Middleton had appointed. Middleton, alarmed at this arrest upon his power to reward and punish, wrote to the Council, countermanding the royal order. They then acted according to their Commissioner's dictate. Launderdale hurried with the tidings to his master. Although Middleton pleaded in his justification that the King had given him a verbal promise, through which he had been induced to countermand the royal order, Charles had either forgotten or was unwilling to remember any promise. Middleton was displaced from the management of Scottish affairs and Launderdale, his rival, exalted to his place.

Middleton's end was to be ignominious and fulfilled the dark vision. Charles II had married a Portuguese Princess, Catharine of Braganza, and as part of the dowry, England was given Tangier, one of the Barbary States. There had been almost continuous hostilities between England, France, Spain and the Italian States of Venice, Genoa and the Kingdom of Sicily, and the Barbary Corsairs who raided and pillaged the coasts of Italy, France and even Ireland. Once or twice Denmark had claimed only their unwelcome attentions. These pirates carried off not only plunder but slaves. One of England's finest sailors, Admiral Blake, had been sent by Cromwell with a fleet to bombard Tunis, another of the pirate states, and for a short time brought order to the Mediterranean where peaceful merchantmen had for many years gone in terror of these wild freebooters with their flashing scimitars, swarthy features, and exotic oriental turbans and earrings. The problem was that these North African ports had narrow shallow, bays in which the large men o' war — requiring a deep draught — could not enter. The Arab dhows slipped into port and frequently frustrated their pursuers. The North African coast was difficult and dangerous. Shallows extended far out, and there were few harbours. When the wind blew from the sea to the shore, as it did more often than not, a sailing ship was in grave danger of being forced aground. The danger was made greater still because there were no reliable charts and because the shore lay so low and was so featureless that it was hard to determine one's position. A north wind meant terrible danger, and a south wind was likely to blow the blockading ships away from their station. But before Columbus discovered America, Portugal achieved the conquest of Tangier and held the city for two hundred years. But danger was constant and fighting frequent, and the occupation was expensive in money and men, while the returns in terms of trade were poor. The Portuguese could not make the place pay any more than the Moors could without piracy. So in 1662 Portugal was glad to rid itself of the burden by giving Tangier to England as part of the dowry when Charles married Catharine of Braganza. England raised a regiment to take over the occupation. York Castle was built in honour of the Duke. To this far flung outpost Middleton was sent as Governor. Charles had felt a kind of pity for the discredited magnate. He lived for a few years until the old weakness of drink caused his end. Falling headlong down the stairs of his Governor's house, he broke his arm, the bone of which protruded through the flesh and penetrated his side and finally his heart. As he died in agony, Middleton recalled the words of the poor country woman at Coldstream by the Tweed in the land he once loved, that, since he had been so busy to destroy their Ministers, he should never more have power in Scotland. But even more clearly appeared the vision of his old comrade Balbegnic in the tower of London and his prophecy that the sunshine would be covered over with clouds of calamity. When the news finally reached Scotland an ejected minister of the Covenant wandering over the wilderness, tangled and cold, between the rivers Stinchar and Nith, brooded sadly over the unhappy end of this rough soldier who had once been for the Covenant. Alexander Peden did not triumph over the unnecessary fall of those who were once in the truth.

4
A Fond Farewell

The sun is glinting strongly in the late afternoon, glancing through the small narrow windows of New Luce Parish Kirk down near the Solway coast in the heart of Galloway. A figure stares from the pulpit, over a packed Kirk. His heavy hands grip the edge of the structure, his emotion showing in the whiteness of his knuckles and the gleam of his twinkling eyes. Rev. Alexander Peden, as he now was, had come a long way from the trial by fire in the courtroom of Tarbolton. For three years he had been the faithful pastor and preacher of this rural area and God had singularly blessed him. The upturned faces, eager and attentive, were witness to the respect and affection in which he had come to be regarded. For his happy face and couthy humour had endeared him to all. Shepherd, cowman, farmer, nobleman and doctor, all were the same to Sandy Peden. His strong frame carried him over his moorland parish with unceasing vigour to comfort the sick and bereaved, to teach the children, to administer the ordinances to remote shiellings and farms. Nature was always his friend as he was a friend of God he said and he had often sheltered in the nook of a linn of some wooded copse in the fold of a hill when the rains began to sweep remorselessly over the wine red, bracken clad, moors of Galloway. It was as if nature had equipped Peden for her rawness, for his frame was tireless. Those whom God calls He equips, he had preached himself. Prophecy was unerringly coming to focus on this prophet of a man.

"Beloved ones," His voice trembled like a leaf in the fresh spring air and tinkled like a silvery stream. "Ye will recall how this very morning we dwelt on the words of the blessed Apostle in the twentieth chapter, 'Therefore watch, and remember that, by the space of three years night and day I ceased not to warn you each one and how I wept over you.' Well, like St. Paul, who preached the unsearchable riches of Christ, I have never ceased for three years since I came to you in 1660, to give you the message of the faith once delivered unto the saints. I have declared unto you the whole counsel of God and kept nothing back. I am free from the blood of all souls. In this same chapter concerning the primitive church which took the faithe from golden Jerusalem to imperial Rome, I have expounded from verse seven in the aforesaid chapter. No man's fate can be laid at my door. I have taught you how you must have repentance before God and trust in our Lord Jesus Christ. Beware lest you be like the youth named Eutychus who when Paul on a Saturday night around midnight was celebrating the wonderful life giving Feast of the Last Supper, commemorating His death for us, grew more and more sleepy and so fell from the height of the third storey where he was seated, to his death it seemed until the grace of God brought back Eutychus to life when the apostle embraced him. The Lord is rich in mercy. May the breath of God's spirit continually infill you with His life giving power and I ask for you to pray for me as, like St. Paul, imprisonment as I an to now be expelled from this my parish of New Luce by King Charles II and his minions. As you know it is for nonconformity with their Episcopal yoke". Here Rev. Alexander Peden was distracted by an elder who was motioning in a half embarrassed way that everything was not all in harmony. Whereupon Peden signed with a most affectionately natural sweep of his begowned arm for the man to draw near the pulpit. "Whit's troublin' ye, Adam Gillespie?"

The red faced elder, trying to maintain his Presbyterian dignity, worked his way to the front through the packed benches, separated by only a couple of feet. Clearing his throat he kept his voice to a grave level. "Sir, there be many more outside on the hillside cannae get in and they are setting up an indignant clamour to hear your last sermon. But whit can we do? It's no the Temple at Jerusalem nor even the Ark that Noah built."

"Quite right, Elder Gillespie! The Lord is no respector of persons and He owns the cattle in a thousand hills forby the hills themselves. So let us depart this wooden and stone Tabernacle, albeit a holy one, for the even more holy one of God's cathedral of the sky. We shall be of necessity to partake of such surroundings in the forthcoming years. The hills, glens, linns, caves and lonely moorlands will be our friends from henceforth. Let us make their acquaintance this sunny evening." With a swing of his great spare limbs, Peden was out of the box pulpit with a large Bible in hand and, hands encouraging here and clutching eager handshakes there, he was out of the door and heading for the green sward in a smooth flow down from the heights of the wooded linn nearby. Already assembled were hundreds who acclaimed his appearance with a great shout of joy. Their disappointment was completely forgotten. The man of God whom they had trudged over weary miles of rugged countryside to hear, was returning their faithfulness.

A group of the congregation rushed off to the nearby wood to return shortly with great logs of dead wood off old trees that had been blown down by the merciless moorland wind. These logs they piled up into a rough structure of a triangular nature and had it situated on the brow of the hill. In the lea of this structure Alexander Peden took his place from where he could be protected from the breeze which though gentle on this golden evening was yet enough to catch his words and blow them to the airts. Also his view from the vantage point took in the assembled listeners as they gathered below in the hollow of the valley round the New Luce Kirk.

Peden had hesitated and glanced up to the skies as if listening to some unseen voice. Then as a loving smile crinkled his eyes, he continued his address,"As I was saying, brethren, Charles has determined to make us a scapegoat for his self centred tyranny. The Merry Monarch he is called down in London I hear but how sad the day for Scotland when the faithless Stewarts were restored to the throne this three years gone. I will not before God, take the Oath of Allegiance and engage in regularity to these petty puppets of "curates", bags of lifeless wind as they are, who move as their Bishops pull the strings and who are themselves controlled by a godless military who will in vain try to crush out the independent spirit of our Covenanting people. But in the sight of God He does own us all equal and has taken away the Veil of the Temple to end the division of all peoples. As for myself, I set no store by my life. So it is nothing for me to seek the moors where the wild winds blow, the sun shines, and the rains fly, where stand the hillsides of sheep and the howes of the vanished silent races. There the whaups and the pee-wees can be heard as they give their lonely cries over the wine red moors. There the air is austere and pure, God's very own country in truth.

"Great issues hang upon this our controversy with the King; not only the civil and religious liberties of Scotland but the Protestant cause itself is in danger. Notwithstanding all that they suffered at the hands of the Stewarts, our Covenanting people blindly and foolishly invited the Prince in exile to Scotland and crowned him at Scone in 1651. Ye recall an Act was passed, leastways the elder among ye, to say that Charles would consent and agree that all civil matters should be determined by the Parliament of the Kingdom and all ecclesiastical matters by the General Assembly of the Kirk. In the Coronation Sermon, Robert Douglas told the King that there must be no tyranny in the throne-room. It is good for our King to learn to be wise in time and know that he receives power to govern, but a power limited by contract and these conditions he is bound to stand by. Our worthy Samuel Rutherford has truly said in his work on our constitution that the power of creating a King is from the people. Power is not an inheritance from Heaven as the Stewarts do believe, but a birthright from the people. Little did our Protestant leaders know that they were dealing with a double dyed hypocrite.

"While Charles swore to uphold the Solemn League and Covenant, and thus repudiate Prelacy, he at the same time negotiated with Rome and Madrid for help against those Cromwellian rebels as he called them, against God, the Church, and Monarchy. He showed in his dealings with the Scottish nation an ingenious dissimulation and insinuating familiarity which won them and induced them to take up his defence, his cause and his establishment. But he has realised too late that the principles of the Covenanters are opposed by all that is true to the absolutism which he has inherited from his father and grandfather.

"The struggle has only begun!" His arm swung in a great challenging sweep to show his determination. "Charles does represent Prelacy which does mean Absolutism. It is for this stand against religious dictatorship that I am expelled from this my pulpit and parish with other faithful Ministers throughout our land. Murder shall stalk red-shod in every valley and household in the south-west. We shall be hunted like beasts of the field from place to place. You shall never see my face again in this pulpit." Crying and weeping broke out with great feeling among the multitude which had now reached well over a thousand. Many a male eye was moist and a brow pale with deep spiritual emotion.

"Bide wi' us, Mr. Peden! Bide wi' us! Dinna lea us. We hae need o' ye!" The anguish was equally evident among the men and women. Peden raised his hands for silence and a hush gathered in the hills again.

"I have already prolonged my Ministry here in New Luce for some months since Middleton's Ejection Act. It is for your sake, I have to sustain you for the trials ahead. When the Privy Council in Glasgow did declare that all Ministers who failed to obtain the authorisation of patron and bishop must leave their parishes, they laid down a time of the first of November. It is now February. The time has come now to bow to the inevitable will of God, a God who determines all things. The Privy Council thought that there would not be ten of such incorruptible faith and constancy that they would be unwilling to retain their salaries and comforts by compliance. How they were deceived in the blindness of their minds. In the depth of winter between three and four hundred of our Scottish national clergy, rather than wound their consciences by accepting their holy office from any but Christ Jesus, have abandoned stipend and parish and home. So it is that I maun be true to my other brethren as well as my God. I must leave you to the mercy of that same God and true Sheperd. He has given the gift of foreknowledge to puir auld Sandy. Yea, some ca'it second sight but I ca' it just God's first sight, and He has given me a vision like to that of the prophet Ezekiel. The land shall be filled with horror before it is sated with the violence of all who stay there. Inhabited cities shall be deserted and the land shall become a waste. The time with all that the vision points to, is near. There will be no more false visions, no specious divinations saying there will be peace when there is no peace. Ye will be scattered o'er the hills and moors of Galloway, Ayrshire and, aye, a' the Lowlands. Frae the Highlands, where they are a barbarous people, a host of caterans and thieves will be sent down to pillage, murder, rob and in effect, cow us into a submissive fear if it were possible. But, in the words of the Psalmist, God will be our strong tower."

The strong winter sun was beginning to set on this bright and brisk winter's day when the Rev. Alexander Peden emerged from the rough shelter to look upwards at the transparent sky with its wintry clearness and wisp of yellowish cloud, as if waiting for a sign from heaven.

"And now, my friends, I am gaun to warn you anent the future, as well as to admonish you of the past. Ye'll see and hear nae mair o' puir Sandy Peden in New Luce Kirk after this days wark is o'er. As the Patriarichs, a wandering Aramean shall I be over the face of Scotland for the rest of my days. See ye that puir bird". At that moment a hawk had darted down in view of the whole congregation in pursuit of its prey, a fluttering terrified lark. It headed for the wooded gulley. "See ye that puir panting laverock which has now crossed into that dark and deep linn for safety and refuge from the claws and beak of its pursuers? I'll tell ye what, my friends, the

New Luce Parish Kirk in Galloway.

twasome didnae drift down this way frae that dark clud, and alang that bleak heathery brae-face for naething. They were sent. They were commissioned; and if ye had risen to your feet, ere they passed, and cried, "Shue!" ye couldnae hae frightened them oot o' their mission. They cam' to testify o' a persecuted remnant, and o' a cruel, pursuing foe, of a Kirk which will soon hae to be take herself, like a bird, to the mountains, and of an enemy which will allow her to rest by night nor by day, even in the dark recesses of caves or amidst the damp and cauld mosses in the hills. They came and they were welcome to gie us a' warning, and to bid me tak the bent as fast as possible, to flee even this very night, for the pursuer is even nigh at hand. But, hooly, sirs, we maun pairt till oor work be finished. As an auld writer once said — 'Till our work is finished we are immortal.' Look, see how the lark has escaped the claws of the fierce hawk." The wise bird had slipped into the thick bushes clothing the rocky face of the narrow linn and the frustated hawk swerved off, unable to penetrate the interlaced thorns. "I hae een done my best among ye. I hae this day the consolation to think that my puir exertions had been rewarded wi' some success. An' it had been His plan or His pleasure, to hae permitted me to lay down my auld bones, when I had nae mair been content. But since it's no, I hae a request to make before we separate this nicht. Ye maun a stand upon your feet and lift up your hands to swear before the great Head and Master o' the Presbyterian Kirk o' Scotland that till an independent Presbyterian Minister ascend this pulpit, you will never enter the door of that Kirk mair. Let this be the Solemn League and Covenant between you and me, and between my God and your God, in all time to come. Amen, so let it be."

With a concluding prayer and benediction, Peden led the great audience in a Psalm of David, which summed up their coming struggle, of which they held no illusions:

> For He in His pavilion shall,
> Me hide in evil days,
> In the secret of His tent me hide,
> And on a rock me raise.

The atmosphere was now almost overpowering in its emotion. The night cloud had come down the hill and the sun had set. In the twilight the united and full vent of the voices of praise from more than a thousand lips ascended. Peden descended from the tent to the door of the Kirk which faced east. He entered it and climbed to the pulpit. In the full view and hearing of the massed people certainly of those who crowded in by the door, he closed the Pulpit Door, and knocked upon it three times with the great Pulpit Bible, accompanying it with the words — "I arrest thee, in my Master's Name, that none ever enter by you, except those who enter by the door of Presbytery. "With these words on his lips and a courage born of grace in his heart, Alexander Peden ascended the wall at the Kirkstile, spread abroad his arms to their utmost stretch and in a solemn manner, dismissed the multitude. His warning was to be heeded and his prophecy fulfilled.

5
The Gathering Storm

Four horsemen, gaunt from hunger and the weariness of pursuit, were kneeing their short hill ponies from the Galloway hills towards the clachan of Dalry, not far from the beautiful sparkling waters of Loch Ken. As they made their way from the fastness of inland Galloway, vigilance characterised their every movement. A large military figure with an air of authority was clearly their leader. But it was another who broke the silence of these hillmen, accustomed to the quiet solitude.

"Captain Paton, it has been a hard time this, even you will admit. These last weeks in the hills, mosses and moors of our beloved Gallowa' would have made a husk of any man. Hunger is a thing that affects the spirit even of a man. I ken that the Lord said Man shall not live by bread alone but He did mean that we should live by bread, bannocks, kail broth and venison as well. To sleep abroad, lying on shepherds plaids with our hands almost continually on our swords, sniffing about the outskirts of a hamlet with a cocked ear, does take its toll of our resources of spirit, mind and body. Sometimes the moorland seems like a shoreless sea as it stretches to the horizon, a sea of mist with the firs as dim islets. The whistle of the whaup can fill me with fear and a flock of wheeling plovers send me skulking among the bushes of some mossy glade." Here the speaker, a young man of noble bearing, still unable to hide the depression of his spirit, sighed deeply and glanced at his stalwart companion. "This is no world to live in. It is not for this that I was born in my mother's womb, afraid of the rap at dawn on the shuttered window, and some panic stricken messenger of woe announcing that the enemy is upon us, only for those bloodthirsty dragoons and their even more bloodthirsty general, that 'mad beast of Muscovy' Tam Dalzell, to wreak their savagery on us and our loved ones."

Captain John Paton seemed to have difficulty in manoeuvring the moorland pony with his great thighs, more because the sorry beast was indeed weighed down by its cumbersome burden. Captain Paton was also accustomed to a magnificent Spanish steed comparable to his build, as he had possessed in the army of Gustavus Adolphus when fighting his Catholic foes. But now, his eyes, soft with compassion in their deep brown, he addressed the young Laird. "Do not be downhearted, my faithful Laird of Barscobe. It is not for us to see threat and fear on every hand. How often have we been in glens with no menace of conspiracy and no shape of fear. The river has chattered away in friendly fashion and a thousand birds have warbled in the rain. The cries of the whaup, pee wee, and curlew are magic to the ear and the wild flowers fill the atmosphere with the very breath of innocence. At such times, I think that mankind might never have been there before me and the world of passion seems remote. And you do know, my good friend, that I am a man of passion. There is an occasion when the tang of wet heather does no longer sooth my senses but they are stirred to action, most violent and fierce, as when you mention such a man as Tam Dalzell. When he enlisted under the forces of the Czar of all the Russias, he doubtless saw nothing but tyranny and slavery, and tyranny and slavery have filled the cup he is mixing for his fellow countrymen ever since. The mad beast of Muscovy right enough! How strange are the twists of life, for he fought beside me as a comrade in arms at Worcester and a more valiant one there could not be. After our disastrous defeat he was sent to the Tower from whence, I know not by what means, he made his escape and journeyed to Russia to be a mercenary, like so many of the flower of Scotland when life is cheap and living is dear; we make bonnie fechters for other lands than our ain Scotland, Barscobe. Leastaways, the Czar made Tam Dalzell his General, and there in that land of Oriental autocracy and vile servitude, where the Eastern Orthodox Church does but serve the whims of its Czarist Master, that man learnt his lust for slaughter. He was always bred up hardy from his youth, both in diet and clothing, never wore boots, nor above one coat, and that close to his body with closer sleeves, like what we call jockey-coats. Nor did he ever wear a peruke, as you can imagine, but a beaver hat to cover his balding head. But what he does lack on his head he does more than show the beard which he has sworn never to shave since the execution of Charles. Both white and bushy, it reaches almost to his girdle. Such is the strange figure who after the Restoration became constituted Commander in Chief of the Royalist force in Scotland. They say that unworthy King holds him in high esteem for his valour and virtue! Men can be perverse."

Barscobe, not to be outdone in his knowledge of their opponents, interrupted, "For eight months this our land of the south west has been confined by Sir James Turner who has commanded the King's troops, with his headquarters at Dumfries. He is a man who delights in the study of human letters and history and reads the controversies of religion between us and the Roman Catholics but I have also heard it said of Turner that he fought as an adventurer in the Thirty Years War, now on the one side, now on the other, in the battles between Adolphus and Wallenstein, and that he swallowed a dangerous maxim, that so long as we serve our master honestly, it is no matter what master we serve. Truly it is a hard taskmaster he serves, for he harries the Covenanters of the south-west something harshly. He protests his clemency, insisting that he has been far from going to these excesses in extortion which his instructions have sanctioned but the truth does cry forth in an agony of protest that hundreds of families are being beggared by the fines extracted. He is a proud and loud mouthed soldier of fortune. Is it not extraordinary that the farmers, cottars, and people of this countryside, have not been goaded into revolt? The nobility of Scotland are not worthy of its peasantry. Far from being an example to those of lower station, they act like the offscourings and ruffians of society."

"Turner was indeed a turncoat in the German Wars," the Captain observed, "but to his credit, he is not of the bloodthirsty mould of Tam Dalzell. However he is less of a man, I'm thinking, with the courage of the majority. I dinna hae to tell you, Barscobe, that sic a quality of watered down courage is common to these dragoons. After the defeat by Montrose and his rabble of Highlanders and Irish at Kilsyth back in '45 when our lack of a harmonious command was a continuing weakness, I escaped to find myself trapped in a bog with my companions, one of whom was sadly drowned, but I soon won free and rode off to join my comrades, Colonels Strachan and Haket. We encountered fifteen of the enemy, all of whom we killed but two. When we had gone a little further thirteen more attacked us and ten of these were sent to their eternal destiny, only for eleven more Highlanders to approach. I can see by your expression that you find this tale of mine hard to credit, my friend. This I do not take kindly to as my word is the word of a gentleman. So if I may continue, Colonel Strachan was by this time somewhat low in strength as well as faith and said that unless I did something we were all dead men. But fear was far from me. Neither was I going to yield nor flee. My Andrea Ferrara sword in all its forty inches did stand me in rare stead again as nine of these Highland caterans were put to their account and two lived to tell the tale that the men of the Covenant are worth ten times the enemies of God in the field of battle. We do mighty deeds for our God while these slaves of tyranny are governed by fear and a greedy desire for pillage. These who have visited the north assert that they live in these Highland regions like primitive cattle, slaughtering one another in clan feuds, raiding the sheep and kine from each other, and living in hovels of deplorable conditions. It is little wonder that their courage is threadbare in the face of men of stature.

"Like begets like, John. For none of these creatures has regard to the morals of a godly life. Dalzell of Binns leads a lewd and impious life, like his royal master. Marriage, which the whole of nature altogether, apart from divine revelation, does show is an ordinance of God, he shows a mighty contempt for. It is well known throughout London, a by-word in fact, that this sad representative of a once royal line does openly consort with any and every woman who takes his fancy. God will send His judgement on him and Dalzell of Binns for their wickedness. Not the least of their crimes is this cruel imposition of crushing fines upon an almost impoverished people."

The hills had opened out from their folds as if some invisible hand had led them through their labyrinthine maze and even the horses seemed surprised at the new terrain. Ahead smoke curled from distant cottages clustering in the far corner of the valley.

"Come, my friends, let us descend to Dalry village for victuals and the shelter of a kindly roof for one night at least. It's good to be in the comforting Holm of Dalry after the wildness of the lands of Lochinvar. The only place wilder I'm thinking be the Rhinns O' Kells. Now there's a place for ye, up by Corserine, Millfire and Meikle Millyea where the snows lie langer than elsewhere and the winds blaw colder. One could get lost withoot trying in the Rhinns. But here in the green valley they ca' the Glenkens, humanity breathes again." With an exclamation of disgust and anger John Paton breaks off. "What am I saying? This is too much! They are bullying an old man! In addition to the persecution of the able and the young, they have stooped to the cruelty of abusing the old and infirm. There are a number of peasants being herded like cattle, do you see? Among them is an old man. The prophet Amos described such persecutors as those who grind the noses of the poor in the dust. They are probably Turner's men. Are you going to stand by, John MacLellan, and watch while your fellow countrymen, Covenanters and Gallovidians, are used so?"

"Let us not be too hasty and cause undue trouble. Maybe they have done criminal acts." The group of horseman had reached the square where four soldiers were jabbing the group of local peasantry with their musket butts. "Ho there, good fellow! What gives rise to this commotion?" The officer in charge turned with an aggressive swing and in surly manner, "Who be you, sir, and what hath it to do with you? I am Corporal George Deanes and these three are the King's soldiers of Sir Alexander Thomson's company of the garrison at Dalry. We are here on a fund raising business and are proceeding to thresh the corn of a recalcitrant and obstinate farmer, named Grier, to obtain the fine for absence from Church which Grier did not pay before he sneaked off from his farm. He's skulking around somewhere here, I'm sure. We'll get him, but meanwhile we'll take the lawful fine for his omission. So pass on your way, strangers, and cause us no bother before a worse fate befall you."

Barscobe spoke with great haste at the same time as grasping the arm of Captain Paton who seemed to be controlling with difficulty an internal convulsion of emotion. "Come, let us go, comrades. 'Tis none of our business. There is an alehouse, John." They began to reluctantly move their steeds on up the rough earth street. "Let us breakfast there in the hope that no one recognise us. Ale and bannocks will suit us fine." Soon they had seated themselves in a little hostelry whose atmosphere was as stale as the food, in the opinion of the Captain.

"This meat seems like it has been hiding away for as long as ourselves! We should have kept to ale and bannocks. It verily stinks and as for salted, I think it has been in the Solway for years. Ho, what is this outcry outside?" A local man, obviously of the Covenanting persuasion, had come running in, distress on his face.

"Grier has been seized and bound hand and foot like a beast to be carried away. The soldiers are threatening to strip him naked and set him on a hot grid iron because he cannot pay. Aren't you going to do something?"

"We certainly are." growled Paton, and grasping his great Andrea Ferrara in both hands, he rushed out the doorway. Barscobe and his fellow Covenanters followed with reluctance, as if fearful not of the

Captain John Paton who was executed in the Grassmarket of Edinburgh in 1685.

soldiery but of the consequences of Paton's fiercesome temper.

An old man cowered on the earth, trying to be brave but obviously fully aware of the cruelty latent in the dragoons hearts. His thick woollen jerkin was torn almost from his shoulders and a trooper was preparing a branding iron in a fire. Even Barscobe was visibly agitated by the proceedings which threatened great and possibly fatal suffering. He anticipated any action by his fiery friend by accosting the corporal, "How dare you use the old man so? Why do you bind him?"

"And how dare you challenge us again, the soldiers of His Majesty?" Corporal Deanes was red with apoplexy in his anger.

"Free him! Loose the old man! He is our kith and kin. Have courage! Acquit yourselves like free men and Gallovidians! Loose his throngs." The Captain was at this point so incensed that a great herd of wild Hunnish tribesmen would not have hindered him. The quarrel was becoming fiercer every minute.

With sudden decision Corporal Deanes shouted to his men, "Draw your swords men! A sight of gleaming steel will soon change their minds!"

"Have a mind, my worthies! Meet the sword of the Lord and Gideon!" The Corporal took the full brunt of the attack of the Andrea Ferrara which may not have been that of the Biblical hero but carried the same force. Meanwhile Barscobe had drawn his pistol but to his chagrin discovered that he had no shot.

"But no matter, these great many pieces of my tobacco pipe will do the trick," he exclaimed with a new found gusto. Hurriedly loading it, he aimed at Corporal Deanes who was about to chop down one of the Covenanters. Paton had meanwhile engaged two of the dragoons and beaten them both defenceless. When Deanes swung his sword for a likely fatal blow, Barscobe fired his unlikely ammunition and, staggering back, Deanes was seen to have some real deep gashes inflicted in his face and neck from the flying piece of pipe stem.

"Surrender or there will be more blood!" Paton bellowed. The three others sheepishly hung their arms, more defeated in spirit than in body. "Disarm them and bind the prisoner. Out of this petty scuffle, I feel, will spring a Rising throughout our land in which will be crowded a world of heroism, and pathos and pain." Paton was almost quivering like a hunting dog waiting to be released. His great face was flushed and the large grey eyes under the heavy eyebrows were vibrant with eagerness for the fray.

A local worthy piped up, enthused by this new infusion of hope in the form of the incomers. "Now is the time to strike when the iron is hot. Send to Balmaclellan where there is a Coventicle being conducted by the Rev. Alexander Robertson. Let us band together and capture the garrison here at Dalry. It has only sixteen dragoons. They will be punished by their implication in the fracas here otherwise, these good people of Dalry. Justice is not in the vocabulary of His Majesty's dragoons."

"Your ideas are truly guided by God, my friend. But not only that, for our only safety lies in capturing Turner himself and holding him as hostage till our grievances are redressed. I hear his garrison at Dumfries has had half its infantry withdrawn also for the campaign against the Dutch. They always were friends of the Covenant, these Hollanders. In October most of his cavalry left also. So Sir James Turner has only seventy men at his command. Let us march on Dumfries. Let us be bold! We can muster a force of two hundred at a count with half of them mounted and armed with muskets, pikes, swords, scythes, and forks. John Neilson of Corsock, I see you there. I know you are one of the landlords but I also know you are one with us and will join us. Who are with us? Give us your yea!" Seizing the basket hilt in both hands, John Paton raised the warlike standard high. A roar of consent rose from the populace.

The following day was spent by sending word through the towns, hamlets, farms and even houses of the nobility of the south-west as the standard was raised in secret, soon to be open. Groups and lone figures often could be seen converging on the centre of the rebellion where the sixteen Government soldiers had put up a token struggle, firing a few musket rounds before succumbing to the inevitable in such an area, so committed to the Covenant. It increased the growing confidence of the Covenanters force and soon the required two hundred were heading for the town of Dumfries and their major quarry, Sir James Turner. They arrived in the night by plan, catching the guards asleep at their gates. Equally embarrassing to their commander, Sir James Turner was asleep and rather sick when rudely brought to his window. His dishevelled figure was led forward between a file of armed men to the Covenanting leaders, dressed in his night gear. Sir John Neilson of Corsock presented him triumphantly, "Here we have the Governor of Dumfries, Sir James Turner. Albeit we found him unwell and in bed, with no more than twelve or thirteen men in the town, yet he still, when called on to surrender and he would have fair quarter, replied that he needed no quarter and could not be a prisoner, for the country was not in a state of war. But he soon found out differently! Prisoner you must be or die."

Sir James Turner had a saturnine looking face with a high bridged nose and pencil moustache and heavy ringlets which cascaded down his shoulders. His embarrassment was obvious at the state of his dress or lack of it. His words echoed his indignation.

"I protest most strongly! I, King Charles's officer, have been treated like a thrall and mounted on a low beast, without my vestraiment and the horse bare backed except for a halter on its head. I was then carried through the town in a most despicable manner. Who is your leader? This is infamous and plain rebellion!"

A shadowy figure in the group spoke out in a voice indefinably different from the tone of the other Covenanter, John Neilson of Corsock. "I am Andrew Gray, and have a commission of authority to lead this righteous rebellion. We assert our unchanged regard for the King but has not the Solemn League and Covenant, establishing Presbyterianism throughout England, Scotland and Ireland, been burned by the Government? Has not Episcopacy and the rule of Bishops been established contrary to the free wishes of the people? Have there not been fines, imprisonments, the quarterings of soldiers, and the inquisitions of the High Commission Court? Unforeseen and impulsive this uprising may have been but it can surely justify itself." Roars of assent and the cry of "Shoot him! Give him no quarter!" rose on all sides. Andrew Grey as he said his name was, withdrew quietly to the side and if observed closely in the dark, smiled a triumphant smile which curled his lip but touched not his humourless eyes.

As things were getting out of hand and Turner's life and limb were at stake, Neilson of Corsock's voice cut sharply across the din "You shall as soon kill me, sir, for I have given him quarter. Hugh Henderson, the Minister whom he outed from Dumfries, would even have you set at liberty, Sir James, but you will continue with us in our marchings to Edinburgh. Here are men of God, our chaplains, John Welsh, Gabriel Semple and even young Robertson, the probationer, who can deal with you seriously on the salvation of your soul."

A black garbed minister stepped forward and fixed Turner with a piercing gaze. "Gabriel Semple does say that you are lifted up in pride with insolency and cruelty over the poor people. But I honour you with the title of God's servant now in bonds, and I most earnestly beseech you for your conversion."

Sir James's face grinned sardonically "You will find this soil is most sterile and all but impervious to your pleas of religion. It would be hard to turn a Turner!" His laugh was noticeably nervous however.

"You may joke, sir, but sooner or later our deeds come home to roost. We cannot avoid our deeds, whether they be ones we can be proud of or not. We shall leave you to meditate on your position before Him with Whom we all have to do. Meanwhile you will be unharmed. Never will a rough hand be laid on you. We march immediately for Lanark by way of Ayr and Doon, and then by Lesmahagow to the Pentlands and Edinburgh, where we shall present our position to the Government by force if necessary. Our ranks will have swollen by then as the unbroken spirits in our land join us. Let us march forth under the Banner of the Covenant! For God, Scotland, and the Covenant!" The Covenanting force went full of praise to the Lord in motion and song up the main street of Dumfries. So was set the scene for the drama which was to unfold throughout Lowland Scotland in which the unequal military contest was overshadowed by the heroism of the Covenanting people of Lanarkshire, Ayrshire, the Lothians, Borders and Galloway and which saw the remote moors of these areas inhabited by a form of Christian martyrs reminiscent of the wandering Arameans of the Bible times.

The first unequal military confrontation took place on the Pentland hills on Rullion Green after the rising tide had swept from Dumfries through Lanark and across towards Edinburgh. The initial surge had somewhat subsided in the rains, hunger and weariness. Many had drifted off, doubtful if their protest would have any effect on the Government, and coming to realise what the alternative was. The mysterious Andrew Gray had just as mysteriously disappeared as he had appeared. It was rumoured that he could have been the Irish adventurer and informer, Captain Blood, who was in every national conspiracy, always escaping, pardoned, and let it be said, rewarded, by the King, even for the theft of the Crown Jewels from the Tower as he attempted. Double agents were well known throughout the political and religious life. But his place was filled by Colonel Wallace of Auchans, a veteran of the Cromwellian wars who had joined them at Ayr where they also heard a fiery sermon by Rev. John Welsh, their chaplain and the son-in-law of the more fiery Reformer John Knox of Haddington, the pilot of the Protestant Reformation. Colonel Wallace had put some resemblence of discipline into their ragged ranks which had then reached seven hundred with sixty muskets, forty pairs of pistols, and twenty pounds of powder as well as scythes and clubs. Despite the relentless and torrential rain this rough army increased to a thousand by Lanark. There they had two preachings of power and renewed the Covenants. From there they courageously plodded their way across the sleety moors towards Bathgate until within sight of Edinburgh in the suburb of Colinton. As they camped in the churchyard there, Captain John Paton came to seek Sir James Wallace of Auchans.

"It pities my heart to see so many faint, half drowned, half starved creatures, aye, and with all our enemies behind us and before us. We have found no help in the Lothians. The city of Edinburgh has even armed to resist us and I hear that the Provost, Sir Andrew Ramsay, has devised a new oath binding the townsfolk to defend the King's authority. The canon from the Castle's ramparts have been removed to the gates of the town and the strictest watch put on, so that no one is allowed to pass in or out. The stars in their courses seem to fight against the saints, Colonel Wallace."

"Aye, Paton, the dirge seems to have deepened every hour. Nothing could have been wilder than the weather, pitiless on our exposure. Well I remember as we came across the pitiful broken moors to Bathgate in an extraordinary, dark and rainy night, with the daylight gone two hours. No accommodation did we find there for our men, now seven hundred in number, wet, weary and spent. But, closely pursued as we were by Drummond's horse, we were constrained at midnight to march to Newbridge. When our brave Covenanters arrived there, they looked more like dying men than soldiers going to war and to conquer."

"But, Colonel Wallace, despite the torrents of rain, the cold, the fatigue, the hostility of the city of Edinburgh, and the regiments of Dalzell and Drummond, you have kept these soldiers' courage unshaken! It is not for nothing that you come from the stout stock that gave us Scotland's greatest hero. You are a Christian soldier, Sir."

"I am still a soldier who is jealous of that magnificent Andrea Ferrara sword blade of yours. You are privileged indeed to own one of these. By your wolf mark you have proof of identification indeed."

"Yes, the running wolf is certainly the genuine insignia of its author and I have long counted it a privilege to have this blade. Scotland also was privileged by the presence of the Spanish master sword-maker who graced our shores, by a strange stroke of fortune. Andrea Ferrara was famous throughout his own land of Spain when it is said his very own apprentice espied on his master's art and in a fit of rage he slew the apprentice. For this he had to flee the country and chose Scotland as a refuge. Whatever the wrongs of his crime, and a crime it was, Spain's loss was Scotland's gain. The quality of this steel has been proven as after Kilsyth when I slew a great number of these Highland miscreants. It's notches are proof.

Compare that with the numerous claimants of the Thirty Years War to an Andrea Ferrara which make the master swordsmith's age and capacity for work attain to impossible proportions. But, not to think that I delight in the deaths of these our enemies but only as they are the enemies of God and in defence of the civil and religious liberties of all free born Scotsmen. But I am very pleased that you have taken over the leadership of the Covenanting army, Colonel Wallace. Our first leader, Andrew Gray, was scarcely of the stuff of which leaders are made. Nae seasoned campaigner he, though I sensed, a crafty devil. There was something mysterious about him and about his participation in our venture. To the best of my memory, he seems to have presented a commission or recommendation to those in authority but no one knew exactly who he was or if he had been appointed by a General, Council or Committee. But when Mr. Gray began to realise the dangers ahead, he took the pett, vanished unexpectedly, not to be seen again by any of his party. This took place after we had marched thirty-two long miles to Dalry and then through part of the night to the safer wilds of Carsphairn. But maybe it wasn't so strange, as Judas betrayed Christ for thirty pieces of silver, and at Dumfries Gray ransacked Sir James Turner's chest, securing his papers and over six thousand merks. Our movement was not very organised then and the distribution of the money was not clear. I have a feeling that the mysterious Mr. Gray departed with his pockets fuller than when he arrived. But when you joined us at the Brig o' Doon, we knew we had a good man and a true Captain and skilled soldier. And of course to encourage my heart there also joined us my good friends, Major Learmont and Captain Arnot who fought with me at Worcester, standing shoulder to shoulder with General Tam Dalzell, now our mortal enemy. From an undisciplined crowd of over eleven hundred horse and foot in our greatest strength at Lanark, you have lifted them into a company of capable soldiery. Even Sir James Turner said when we were at Lesmahagow that he was driven into admiration against his will and confessed to me that when he saw the agility of both horse and rider in a practice skirmish, that he could but wonder that they had come to that perfection in so short a time. Being a learned man, and of a classical disposition, he did say that even the ranks of Tuscany could scarce forbear to cheer."

"Company of capable soldiery or not, when coming to Newbridge, they were a wretched, bewildered rabble and rather than fall out of the ranks, they had to tie themselves together, though a few deserted. But our desertions have been considerable, reducing us to nine hundred from that glorious eleven hundred. Here in this miserable bivouack in Colinton churchyard, newly mantled with frosted snow, we do present a less than glorious picture, if I am to be honest. Captain Lieutenant-General Dalzell, with regulars and probably some Midlothian Fencibles, in all has two thousand five hundred feet and six troops of horse. They have followed us from Glasgow relentlessly through Kilmarnock, Mauchline, Strathaven and Lanark and now by way of Calder to Currie. A confrontation there must be. In the words of the Psalmist, I lift up my eyes unto the Pentland Hills which look so pure and glorious but for that aid and safety which we so desperately need, let us look unto God alone. Though our hearts are unafraid, our eyes have been opened. There is no hope of new negotiations because the Privy Council are in no way satisfied."

"We have chosen our path," said Paton grimly, "and must travel on over its stones and thorns to the inevitable close; we are ready to die for the cause of religion and liberty. We shall receive no quarter from that butcher Dalzell."

"So is it, that if retreat is possible, that retreat is the advisable course. Let us march on the morrow round the southern slopes of the Pentland Hills. There is a particular slope called Rullion Green. I've heard it called Rullim Green, Yerlings Green and even Gallow Hill. Let's pray the last is not prophetic and ominous for us. It is an ideal position and vantage point. Rullion Green is well known to southern herds and drovers as a tryst and in Ayrshire folk style rullions as unkempt characters, like ragged sheep, I dare say. Its broad green slope streches up to a small plateau. A deep ditch bounds the slope on the north-west, intersecting the old drove road. Above is Turnhouse Hill, standing high and to the south, Lawhead, a famous high boss. Between Turnhouse and Lawhead we will take our stand. It will be an unequal fight for we have only sixty muskets, forty pairs of pistols and twenty pounds of loose powder. May the great God of Jacob, the Lord of Hosts, fight for us, for we are indeed a motley crew."

As soon as the tidings of the revolt reached Edinburgh, the Government was thrown into a panic equal to their former confidence; they knew that the oppressive orders they had issued had been applied faithfully to the letter. A double portion of this terror fell on Archbishop Sharp of St. Andrews, who, in the absence of the Earl of Rothes, was president of the Privy Council, and therefore, head of the executive. His preparations to meet the difficulty showed the extremity of his fear. Edinburgh was placed in a state of siege. The ferries on the Forth were secured and the bridge of Stirling barricaded; expresses were sent out to all the noblemen of the south and west, commanding them to join the royal forces. The chief hope, however, of the prelatist party was now in Sir Thomas Dalzell of Binns, an abler and more truculent soldier than Sir James Turner, having been trained in the service of the Czar of Russia. He was as inaccessible to pity as to fear and so it was thought he would deal conclusively with the insurgents. He would stifle the insurrectionists in their own blood. Dalzell was commissioned to hold his headquarters in Glasgow and act against the rebels wherever required. The rebellion had originated entirely spontaneously and grown with a plan.

The Council at Edinburgh summoned the insurgents to lay down their arms within twenty four hours but, as no promise of indemnity was coupled with this command, they knew that it was only a summons to the gallows, and were convinced it was better to die on the field. When they marched to Lanark, they had numbered nearly three thousand foot and horse, but they were imperfectly armed and wholly indisciplined. Yet it was then that the best chance of victory against Dalzell was theirs, but the majority wished to push on to Edinburgh where, they thought, friends waited to welcome the Covenanting army. Instead, disappointment was to meet them and two hundred turned back, alleging as their excuse, that they disapproved of the course which had been adopted. When they reached Edinburgh they had been reduced to nine hundred men who looked rather like ones dying than going to war. The cannon from the Castle ramparts had been removed to the gates of the town. A large supply of lances and pole-axes had been hastily ordered from Culross and Dumfermline. The city was so well fortified and occupied that hopes of an entrance into the capital were impossible. So early on a fine, frosty morning, close on the end of November, Colonel Wallace led his forces round the eastern front of the Pentland Hills until they crossed a narrow defile which intersected the range. Here they came to Rullion Green, already decided on as a vantage point. Through the pass on the opposite side of the glen came Dalzell's forces, three thousand, with the horsemen leading.

There was an initial skirmish in which the two sides fired their muskets across the ravine of the Glencorse Burn but, discarding them they came together with swordplay. Captain Arnot was fighting with great zeal, a man of normally quiet demeanour, and, with his party of about fifty horse, he opposed the onslaught of

Dalzell's men who had thought it was going to a butcher's shop. They were driven back to the main body and again they were driven back. Yet it was a momentary success which gave dignity to their final defeat and so with the dusk descending on the short winters day, Dalzell decided to advance the whole left wing of his army upon Colonel Wallace's right which was very weak in horse by this time. When the whole weight of the Royalist army fell upon them, charging over the ravine with vicious blades swinging, their numbers, discipline and weapons had their usual effect upon a weary, exhausted and untrained handful who, after a gallant but useless resistance, were routed. Forty and more were killed, eighty taken but the most, favoured by the gathering twilight, made their escape into the friendly hills. The clemency of the Royalist horsemen, who, being chiefly Scots gentlemen, had compassion for their foe, favoured their escape.

Meanwhile Captain Paton, being in the thick of the action, came face to face with General Dalzell, his old comrade from the Civil War and the Battle of Worcester, where they had fought side by side. Dalzell hesitated as between the whirling arms and bucking steads, his baleful gaze caught sight of the fair complexioned face of Paton, crimson with his exertions. The Muscovy bear felt a momentary pang in his breast. However immediately that recognition came to Paton, the Captain's heavy eyebrows lowered and he presented his pistols. Dalzell discharged both his pistols and in the heat missed while Paton's one loaded weapon found the target, only for the ball to bounce off the proof armour on his chest from which it hopped onto his boots. Calmly the Captain felt for the piece of silver in his jerkin pouch. He was too much the practical man of war and man of God to believe, as some of the more superstitious Covenanters, that a man like Tam Dalzell, so obviously in league with the devil, could only be killed with a silver bullet. But it could do no harm to think it had additional effectiveness. It was not to be, as that wise veteran, Dalzell, saw his purpose and withdrew behind one of his unfortunate dragoons, and the silver bullet smashed into the latters chest, throwing him lifeless back upon his commander, who, enraged, screamed at his soldiers to make an end quickly of the fray. Paton and two Fenwick men, with a mad frenzy coursing through their blood, hacked their way through the surrounding hedge of men five deep.

Captain Paton saw the battle was a lost cause and held the honest belief that survival was vital for the future regrouping of the Covenanting forces. Swiping fiercely with his great Andrea Ferrara in a motion designed as a threat to any potential enemy in his path, and as a public gesture to those in the Covenanters army with him to break from the circle of steel and flesh. "Break, break" His cry was full of authority and anticipation.

Dalzell's voice blazed above the din. "Follow him I want him alive." Three dragoons galloped clear in hot pursuit. They knew Paton was likely to have a sturdy horse and arrest must be made soon. It was two miles before, slithering down an oval depression, the Covenanting captain saw ahead a green scum covered marshy pool of about fifteen feet breadth. Three Galloway men were dragging their steeds from the mire on the far side. There was some panic in their clutching movements as the mud sucked at the hind legs. Paton could see the sweat starting out on their brows as he hauled violently on his reins. "What will you do, Captain?" One of them was in his regiment. "I have only three antagonists to reckon with." With these words he urged his steed forward and soared over the mire. He growled at these comrades to get home to their biggins. As his Andrea Ferrara flashed out, the first dragoon had about navigated the bog but his doom was written. His skull was cleaven and his mount stumbled back into the morass carrying along with it the other two troopers cursing vehemently.

"Take my compliments to your master and tell him that I cannot sup with him tonight. But he will meet me again before the end."

When he caught up with the Galloway men one of them gasped, "They've captured Neilson of Corsock and the Rev. Hugh McKail as well as John Parker of Busby from your own troop. They had no chance." Paton groaned and muttered between gritted teeth, "There'll be a reckoning," and urged them on till they could see the Ayrshire hills.

Those among the prisoners from Rullion Green of any position of consequence were in need of revenge for their unjust fates. Dragged to the capital, they had short shrift after the mockery of a trial. Counsel was denied them. They were convicted of rising in arms and renewing the Covenant without the King's authority. In vain they pleaded that they had surrendered on the assurance of quarter. Many were condemned to public execution but the punishment of death was now to be refined upon by the addition of torture. The chief instrument used on this occasion was the boot, a devilish thing used in exteme cases in France, and not altogether unknown to the ancient Romans. It consisted of a framework of four wooden boards nailed together, into which the leg of the accused who refused to confess was placed, and into this, wedges of different sizes were successively inserted and driven down by a heavy mallet, until the flesh of the limb was burst, or the bones shattered, according to the amount of infliction that might be found necessary. By this horrid instrument Neilson of Corsock was interrogated. Like hawks his enemies gathered in the dungeon of Edinburgh Castle. The pale face of the turncoat Archbishop Sharp of St. Andrews, one time professed follower of the Covenant, gleamed yellowly in the dim light of the guttering candle as a gust from some hidden ventilation from the subterranean recesses of Edinburgh rock threatened to bring physical to the moral darkness pervading the scene.

"Is it true that you refused to attend the ministrations of your parish curate? Do you realise what that means?"

"I think I already ken what it means." Neilson answered gently. "I have already been fined and imprisoned, and afterwards driven with my wife and family from my home. All my substance has been sold and my crops ravaged by the soldiery quartered upon me. Yes, I ken what it means."

"Your insolence will only worsen your case, Corsock." Sharp was coldly delighting in his role as inquisitor. But James Turner, standing in the background, was wriggling with shame in his soul. His actions showed it clearly as he continually moved up and down the cell. Though his soldiers had been quartered on Corsock, he could not forget the incident in Dumfries when, at the mercy of the mob thirsting for his carcass, Neilson's entreaty had spared his life. His throat choking with the clash of fear and pity, Turner spoke appealingly to Sharp.

"Surely there's nothing more to be got out of this simple man, merely an unquestioning tool, of their fanatical leader. It's Wallace and Paton we are after."

Sharp snapped back like a cornered vixen. "Not at all, Sir James. He is privy to the plans of this rebellion which, thanks to God, has failed. I have already sent reports to His Majesty of its seriousness and a little more truth will not go amiss. Madame Brodequin has the answer to shy tongues." It was as if his tongue flickered like a snake. Turner turned his face to the wall as the guard carried forward the framework. Lord Rothes, now commissioner since the demise of Middleton and Lauderdale had delegated power to him, took up the inquisition.

"Confess, Corsock, that the whole rising has been contrived and planned with order these past months. You can yet save yourself." Neilson had not murmured as his bare shin, fairly spindly from hunger and unaccustomed exertion, was forced into the space.

"The rising was unconcerted and nothing but the general

oppression caused it." The mallet descended, gouging out the skin and flesh with the wedge. Blood spurted and Sharp recoiled with a hypocritical disgust. But not a sound as yet came from the pursed lips.

"Give him another touch." Rothes had a cruelty unsoftened by the drunken boisterousness of Middleton. Again and again a third time he gave the command. Agonized screams were now coming from the poor man whose spirit was stronger than his flesh. The limb was now nearly mangled. Turner intervened.

"Nothing can now be gathered from his words. Any further torture is futile and evil, my Lord."

"Be wary, my Lord, and tak tent that you give no room for suspicion yourself. Neilson of Corsock, you are sentenced to the gibbet as a rebel." Rothes addressed the senseless figure.

"Commissioner, there is another even more dear to me, who is requiring of the ministrations of the Boot, the false preacher and licenciate, McKail. This silver tongued demagogue has notions of himself as a Demosthenes but I think we can show him he has met his Philip of Macedonia." Sharp's bitter hate was rising. "His last sermon in Edinburgh was reported to me by my spies and he believes that the Church of Scotland has been persecuted by Pharaoh on the throne, a Haman in the state, and a Judas in the church. What need we further proof?"

"Cease your speaking in riddles, My Lord Bishop." Rothes snarled testily, "and bring him in." There was a shuffling and clanking of heavy chains as a youthful figure was hauled by the guard from a neighbouring cell and thrown forward sprawling to the floor. Hugh McKail, a comely young man of twenty six had but recently returned from the Continent, where we had spent four years in exile after Archbishop Sharp, enraged at his preaching in Edinburgh when he clearly called him a Judas in the Church, had sent a party of horse to arrest him. A fresh faced man, yet there was in his demeanour a steel like quality as he was to prove. With the frame forced over his shin bone, he retained his calm, encountering the ring of accusers menacing around.

"You have been privy to the whole design from the beginning, admit it," Archbishop Sharp's venom was in full thrust from his double minded spirit.

"Which are the several branches of this deep laid conspiracy and who are the chief agents?"

"There has been no conspiracy. How often must it be said before you believe?"

"Drive in the wedges. We'll change his mind," So it continued till ten strokes had driven in the wedges and the eleventh was poised. McKail, pale and fainting with agony, whispered.

"I know nothing more than I have told you. The insurrection I believe to have been a sudden rising occasioned by the discontent of the people with Sir James Turner. Although all the joints in my body are to be tortured as my poor leg has been, I can reveal nothing further." He then fainted away and the frustrated inquisitors had him hauled off but not before Rothes consigned him to glorify God in the Grassmarket with his fellows.

His few days stay in the Tolbooth were an encouragement to his comrades and a touch of humour even tinged his words. When asked how his shattered leg was, Hugh McKail said that the fear of his neck made him forget his leg. The Grassmarket was crowded with not a few having a ringside seat in the windows of the surrounding tenements. When the cart bearing McKail trundled across the square, even the mockers, with their appetite for bloodletting already whetted by the executions, were struck silent when the figure of Hugh McKail, neither dejected or sorrowful, stepped down from the cart and mounted to the scaffold. A groan went up and crying was clearly audible in the ensueing lull. Turning, he addressed the crowd with a shining face.

"Your work is not to weep but to pray that we may be borne through with honour. My blessed Lord supports me. Don't let me down in the last step of my journey." From out of his shirt, flapping in the breeze that made everyone shiver as it swept down from the Castle battlements, Hugh pulled out a small Bible and reading loudly to the now silent crowd the last chapter of the Apocalypse, turned happily to the hangman. The latter almost hangdog about his unwelcome task, slipped the rope quickly round his neck with an apology about his duty, but when he tried to put a napkin over McKail's eyes, the young minister raised the cloth from his face and uttered a protest.

"I want you to see the smile on my countenance. My reason is this. Here in the Grassmarket we have a great crowd, a scaffold, a gallows and many spectators at the windows. But in heaven there is a greater and much more solemn preparation of angels to carry my soul to Christ." Abruptly he broke off and turned his gaze to the cold Scotttish skies, caught as into another dimesion of the spirit. His arms were raised in triumph, a fact most irreconcilable with his condition. An old wifie in the forefront of the mob cried "he's fey, the young gentelan." McKail's last words were endowed with mystique.

"And now I will finish speaking any more to creatures and talk with you, my Lord; now I begin my intercourse with God which shall never be broken off. Farewell, father and mother, friends and relations; farewell, meat and drink; farewell, sun, moon and stars: Welcome, God and Father, welcome, sweet Lord Jesus, the mediator of the new covenant; welcome, blessed Spirit of grace and God of consolation, welcome glory, welcome eternal life, welcome death."

A great sigh swept over the concourse as the step slipped from under his foot with the last word. As he swung jerking into space, his cousin, a Dr. Matthew, flung his whole weight on the Rev. McKail's thin legs and shortened his agony. Ten others were hanged on one gibet, protesting that they were free, innocent, and peaceable subjects of their lawful Soverign, but none made a greater impression for his bravery and humility than Hugh McKail, a young man of twenty six, and preacher of the Gospel.

6
A Moorland Conventicle

The normally bleak moors of Auchengilloch, in the triangle formed by Muirkirk to the south, and Strathaven and Lesmahagow, its neighbours in Lanarkshire, to the north, were wearing a bright cloak of green, brown and purple colours. The weather had been scorching and the heather burned up to the extent that the two figures who made their watchful way across the undulating countryside, were not hindered by the clinging bracken. Captain Paton was fully taxed to equal the pace of the lean and alert companion who covered the heather with purposeful tread. Alexander Peden had become as natural a part of the hill scene as the birds which plaintively cried above them in mock alarm. New Luce was a picture of the past and a whole mode of life away. The life of the fugitive was now as familiar to him as preaching had been. Now the occasions of preaching were to be grasped like straws which could be torn from his grasp by a winter wind. It was for such a chance that they were picking their way through the gorse and bracken up the course of the Kype Burn from the direction of Strathaven, a town of known Covenanting sympathies. Strathaven, sheltered in the hollow of the Avon, houses clustered below the keep of Strathaven Castle, with the town burial ground standing out on the hill opposite, as if to remind everybody of the mortality of life. Peden and Paton had been fed and rested while word was disseminated to the local folk of the foregathering Conventicle. Curates had not lasted long in the Evandale Kirk, meeting, with, on a famous occasion, a volley of stones being delivered with gusto by the womenfolk. The man fled in great terror and ran straight out of town with his gown flapping, forgetting his horse and the long road ahead to Glasgow, the nearest place of a friendly reception.

As they strode up the bank of the Kype, Paton glanced with a side look at his strange but special friend. A dark, sanguine looking face, honed to fineness by the outdoor life of rigid discipline in eating, sleeping and continual movement, was crowned by a mane of long raven locks, lank on his shoulders. His eyes again dark but with a light grey tinge, gleamed with an inner light, as if the owner dwelled on something of great joy and also awe. Some said he communed with angels and saw visions indescribable by human lips. Paton had noticed on occasion that the Rev. Peden would stop for no apparent reason and breaking off his conversation listen as if to some unseen voice. But now he was solely intent on the path ahead and, even now slowed, with his arm like an explorer pointing out the discovery he had made with supreme pride.

"This looks as if the Lord had designed the place just for His people to foregather to worship Him in spirit and in truth. Here is a small hollow with natural surrounding heights to provide look-out posts for Daniel McMichael and Nathaniel Blackadder to be our sentinels if the dragoons of Claverhouse and Lag happed, by some unhappy chance, to come upon the place of our Coventicle. God grant it be not so! But Jerusalem did not have more sure and farsighted watchmen on her walls than these two doughty fechters for the Covenanted work of Reformation."

"Ye ken as weel as I, Rev. Peden, the suffering and death that has been inflicted on Presbyterian people. The supreme price has been paid by many in the Grassmarket on the gallows or at the gentle hands of the Iron Maiden. God glorify their memory! Some are heavily fined. A million pounds has been extorted from the south west, it has been estimated. Some are taken prisoner, never to attend such services again, as their consciences dictate. Some are imprisoned for refusing to give the names of officiating Ministers, while others still are sent out of the country into slavery in the islands of Barbados and Jamaica or to Virginia and South Carolina in the Americas. At the famous Hill O' Beath Coventicle John Vernor and Robert Orr were charged with the heinous crime of having their children baptised. Both were imprisoned and, when they refused to inform on the others, they were fed on bread and water, and John Vernor was so heavily ironed that, in the course of time, one of his limbs showed symptoms of gangrene. They were ultimately set at liberty upon the urgent representations of some people of rank, but only on condition that they found security to the extent of five hundred merks, each to appear when called upon. Ken ye the danger that you are in here wi' your conventicling, though even we be in a remote place?"

"Aye, I ken fine, my hinnie. Well do I recall when the sacrament of the Lord's Supper was also dispensed in God's open air under the dome of what some have called the great Cathedral of Immensity. Those present, like here, were those who could not receive it with a clear conscience from the hands of curates within the parish churches. It was held at East Nisbet in Berwickshire on the banks of the Whitadder. The preacher was Johm Blackadder, bless his name, him they nickname Guess Again. It was a green and pleasant haugh and most commodious, fast by the waterside. In both directions there was a spacious brae in form of a half round, covered with delightful pasture and rising with a gentle slope to a goodly height. Above us was the clear blue sky on a sweet and calm Sabbath morning, promising to be one of the days of the Son of Man. The Communion Tables were spread on the green and around them the people had arranged themselves on decent order. None ever were admitted without tokens, as is our wont. I hope Daniel McMichael and the elders distributed them to everybody yesterday. The flock are gey spread abroad o'er the southlands. Aye it was a rare sight that day, as the multitude were seated on the brae face, crowded from top to bottom. But I will agree with ye, my man, that the sword of danger is always hanging over us. My Lord, the Earl of Hume, had profanely sworn that he would make the horses of his troopers trample the Communion bread under their hooves and drink the sacramental wine. Rumours were spread abroad that the county militia intended violence. So it was deemed prudent to take the appropriate precautions.

Reconnoitring parties were formed and companies of armed and mounted yeomen drawn round the congregation in such places that they might still hear sermon."

"And were you attacked on that sacred occasion, brother Peden?" "No, the Lord was good to us and blinded their eyes from our hideaway leading them off to some trackless waste on the hills. It is not for nothing that they cry us the hill folk. Some ca' us Whigs of Whigamores, Covenanters of course, and even the Wanderers, but more especially, dissenters and traitors. But my heart claims the title of the Hill Folk since it is in these hills that my life has been these ten years and more. They have been my pulpit, my home, my bed, my refuge, yea and my friend." Peden's eyes were alight with another worldly look and Captain John Paton's heart warmed to him.

"I to the hills will lift mine eyes. From whence doth come mine aid, My safety comes from the Lord, Whom Heaven and Earth hath made."

"Yes. It is so. It is not the hills but the God Who made them and dwells in them. He owns the cattle on a thousand hills and the Hills as well. At the famous conventicle on the Hill O' Beath near Dumfermline, the Rev. John Blackadder did preach from that glorious injunction of 1st Corinthians, chapter nine and verse sixteen, 'For though I preach the Gospel, I have nothing to glory of; for necessity is laid upon me; yea, woe is me if I preach not the Gospel.' On the first Sabbath of January 1674, Blackadder did preach to a large gathering of Covenanters at Kinkell House a short distance from St. Andrews. There the word of God was on Psalm 2.'The Kings of the earth set themselves, and the rulers take counsel together against the Lord, and against His anointed'."

"You were in mortal danger so near to the lair of that evil and ambitious Prelate, Archbishop James Sharpe."

"It did indeed prove so. For before the service had proceeded far, the spouse of that turncoat prelate had become aware of our conventicling and, in the absence of her husband, did don his evil habit and sent out a mixed rabble of the militia, the town rascals, and some of the wilder students to disperse the worshipping congregation. To the honour of the students of St. Andrews, there were twelve or fourteen of the best affected of the scholars hearers at Kinkell.'

"Did you fight off these wretched people?"

"The arm of the Lord was revealed by His peculiar humour. When this motley company reached the scene the lecture was ended and Blackadder was beginning his sermon. The lady of Kinkell House did remonstrate with the lieutenant in charge for creating a disturbance on the Lord's Day, and having brought forth some ale for him and his men, succeeded in getting him to talk to the intruders. Thereafter the congregation gathered quietly together again to hear the Sermon. The Meeting did close in peace."

"Aye, ale and a woman's tongue can be effective weapons." Paton of Meadowside Farm smiled wryly, remembering his roistering days on the Continent and his cups in many a German hof as well as his loving but disciplined wife Janet at their steading near Waterside. He missed her sorely and then his heart repented as he thought of the loneliness of the single life of Alexander Peden, whose life style of persecution left little chance of the delight of wife and children. His own burden was light but the charismatic figure beside him bore the burden of all Scotland. "As for me, I have attended conventicles on

Cairntable, that mountain height, conspicuous to the inhabitants of the Muirkirk parish and Douglas in neighbouring Lanarkshire. Nature assists us in our purposes. It does make me sad that our enemies spread malignant rumours that we fear and dislike that beautiful bird, the green plover, in Scottish called the pease-weep, so that when their nests are found they are immediately destroyed. It is said that the pease-weep, by some instinct, are led to attend to and watch any human beings whom they see in their native wilds and thus by hovering overhead to guide the dragoons, those booted apostles of evil, in pursuit of the Hill Folk."

"Nature can be ravenous raw. But, like the Son of Man, I have not a place to rest my head, whereas the tods hae holes and the birds hae nests. I have in my moorland adventures visited these dens and nests and conversed in friendship and intimacy with these, God's simple creatures. They are my friends. But I have learnt their language, the language of the wind, the rain and the trees. One must listen." Here Peden cocked his head in an attitude of mute motionlessness. "But I will agree that some shepherds I have known have come on the nests of the pease-weeps and killed their young. I deplore their foolish cruelty. The whaups and pease-weeps can give alarm cries to the hill folk in their Field Meetings. It is for this reason that God can use Nature if we apply ourself to her power. I shall always be grateful to the Lord for that deliverance in Galloway, when, with Claverhouse's dragoons closing in rapidly, the Lord did cast the lap of His cloak around us and the thick mist cam doon over the moorland and hid us from the soldiers sight!"

"And yet your life is in danger! Yes, even in the midst of so called friends. Yon wig and mask ye wear are proof of this. The bairnies wid coorie doon if they saw yon, Sandy!"

"That they wid. It's a sad day come in auld Scotia when a free born Scotsman has to resort to lurking in the dark places and hide his face from God's sun and air to stay alive. It's a fine scary mask is it no, made out of chamois leather that our good friends in Christ, the French Huguenot Protestants have introduced with their leather making and weaving. It has come to my ears that trouble is also brewing in France for them and that soon we will be comrades in adversity. Scotland will offer her shores as a refuge to these heroes of the faith. God forbid that there should ever be a repeat of the Massacre of St. Bartholomew's Day near on a hundred years sin when 30,000 were murdered. Cardinal Richelieu is the most feared man in all Europe and the symbol of the might and cruelty of the Roman Church. I divine some malicious plot that he is hatching out

A Moorland Conventicle.

for the destruction of the Protestant Church in France. In very truth be afeared that the Frenchies are bent on destruction here and a judgement day be near when our shores will be set alight."

Paton paled under his deeply tanned, leathery skin, etched with the responsibility of countless campaigns and decisions to obliterate many a village of innocent German peasantry, whose crime was to be in the path of the warring princes in the Thirty Years War. "God is our refuge and our strength against such as he. For Cardinal Richelieu the Pope is his rock, but for us God is the Rock of our Salvation.'

"Talking of rocks, it is maybe time I was paying a visit again to my old familiar haunt, the cave above the River Lugar where its entrance to it is only possible for me by swinging on an overhanging branch covering its entrance! I feel it's like the life of some wild forest animal on occasion" He chuckled at his own life of wildness and discomfort.

By now about three hundred had gathered on the hillside, having filtered through the moors from all directions and looked like a people thirsty for spiritual water which only could come from the men of God. As he looked down from the preacher's position, Peden sensed tears gathering in the ducts of his eyes and was eager to meet these hungry searching eyes with his own as he dispensed the Word. Around he could see an elderly woman with grace in her features as she sat like a very emblem of royalty, the soft kindly folds of her fleshy face full of kindness and thanks to God. Her Bible was held tightly in her grasp as if in fear of some evil force to claw it from her hands. Some young men on the fringe of the congregation, roughly circular in its formation, grasped long barrelled muskets firmly in their hands, and had a distinctly furtive look in their eyes, as if uncertain whether to fix them on the preacher or the surrounding hills and potential danger, notwithstanding the grey shapes positioned on the distant ridge. These men were of stern stock and familiar with danger, and their minds alert and serious of demeanour. Some were bonneted in blue, others carried theirs as a mark of respect. All had a white cravat contrasting with their black tunic or cloak. Almost all had their hands folded across their breasts. Some even sat astride their hill garrions. These animals seemed aware of the whole situation, as if sympathetic with the whole Covenanting cause.

Of the dogs present, the two in the centre had their noses snuggled into their paws but the two near the fringe were busy making advances on each other, as if nature had her first part to play with them, before even their masters safety. A boy sat with his hands stroking his collie but his position was deferential, brought up in the fear and nurture of the Lord. An elderly couple sat slightly apart, he with his chin cupped pensively, and she with her shawl drawn protectively round her shoulders and even covering her mouth to the extent of resembling an oriental woman. The woman's face, like the others, was of serious expression and tinged with sadness. As he surveyed their hungry looks, Peden determined to start his sermon with a word of encouragement.

"Beloved brethren, here we be a fugitive preacher and a fugitive people out in the mossy wilderness where the raw winds blow cold and we have no company but the whaups, peewees and partridges and maybe some sheep or deer or other of God's creatures. We are a scattered flock and these many years now I have been hunted across and haunted these lonely hills and valleys since driven out by the hand of the persecutor and tyrant, Charles II, and his minions, Sharpe, Leighton and Paterson, who pretend to religion, and Grierson of Lag and Dalzell who pretend to none, and Clavers who claims to one and achieves the other. Every effort has been made to suppress our Coventicles but in vain. God has been our refuge and our strength. They have tried to apprehend us preachers. Militiamen and informers have scoured the countryside in search of us. Four hundred pounds sterling is being offered for Rev. Welsh and Semple and a thousand merks for Revs. Cargill, Blackadder, Veitch, Hag and Fraser and myself, alive or dead. There are always Judases ready to sell their souls for silver."

"But persecutions have made the field-missions prosper the more. I hear that eight or ten thousand persons assembled to hear Welsh, Blackadder and Welwood when they perambulated Fife and that the parish churches are empty. My Lord Rothes and his household were the only worshippers in Leslie Church one Sabbath. I feel sure it was a cold service and a cold Kirk and that the singing was throaty, thin and a veritable murmur that day, my friends." At this a ripple of rich laughter was welcomed by the silence of the moors. "Ah, but they have had it hard, these new curates in our Kirks, have they not?" His voice took on a gentle but amused irony. "The very Church doors have been locked in the incumbents' faces! And have not the tongues of the bells been removed to make the hour of worship uncertain? There wouldn't even have been a sounding bell or a tinkling symbol and I wid have given a lot to see the curate's face that day! These so gracious curates and pastors have even been terrified by rough tongued men or stone-throwing termagants who abjured them to stay away and not ruin amy more souls." The Prophet's voice took on the tone of the prophet.

"One ingenious herd laddie, God bless him, emptied a box of pismire insects into a curate's boots, so as to torment him during Service! And even more vulgar and vicious pranks have been played upon these unhappy gentlemen. They have described me as a highway man with my mask of disguise. But as the Scriptures say, one must be as cunning as a serpent."

"But let us not laugh at others. There is sin in our own camp. It has been said that awful sins are abounding in every congregation of drunkenness, adultery and superstition. My Lord, the Duke of Argyll, a noble for the Covenant, though not many noble are called, declared on the scaffold, 'I hear that swearing, whoring and drinking are never more common and never more countenanced than now.' Despite the earnest efforts of the clergy to uproot superstitions, old pagan faith and customs have remained in our land. There is a great show of religion in our land. If you crack a nut, there is a grace for that, but there is not order or decency in their divine or contumelious service. People cut dollops out of living beasts it has been said by visitors. People believe that spirits, good and evil, inhabit everywhere, especially haunting the scene of murders, certainly that of the dead person. Five men were executed and hung in chains to expiate and appease a dead man's ghost. Let us live by peace, for they who live by the sword shall die by the sword. But the list of superstitions is endless, for fairies dance round the 'Wirrikow' scarecrow, and little green men live inside knells and virile spirits lurk in wells and streams. The spittle spell is still in widespread use. I weel recall Margaret Lindsay being accused of spitting on a bairnie's face for the falling sickness. I have seen myself the Beltane fire lit with an unholy awe and each glowing hearth watched with vestal care on New Year morn, lest an expired fire should presage some calamity. The De'il is a very real personage to many o' oor folk in Scotland, but the frequency with which he turns himself into the shapes of animals, persons, and things, finds no warrant in Scripture. But worse is that he holds hilarious court with wizards, witches, warlocks, and 'cailleaich' crones so that the deluded sell themselves into the Satanic service in order to purchase the vaunted power to bless and curse their fellow creatures.

"Even the saintly Robert Leighton, one time Bishop of Dunblane, and now Archbishop of Glasgow, has sent us Covenanters to doom with the devil. The sin of reading auspices from birds and portents from sights unusual in the sky and earth, is insulting to our God.

The hapless Montrose believed in astrology and my Lord Rothes is said to have been bewitched by Lady Ann Gordon. Some uncanny persons are credited with the power of second sight, prophecy and even casting the evil eye. Now, my friends in persecution, I believe that the Godly exhibit their intimacy with the Most High by showing notions of the spirit which have lifted them to heights of ecstasy, and, in the spirit of humility in the presence of the Most High, I say He has seen fit to give His servant the prophetic gift to save and uplift the brethren in times of danger and trial. Lest an unhappy spirit of pride overtake me, I will not recount of the Lord's dealings with me in His revelations. How does one know of a prophet till after the happening of his prophecies? The Lord's prophecies are always fulfilled. But, as Paul would not recount the vision of thirteen years before, when he was taken up into Heaven, whether in the body or out he could not tell, and mayhap have been given the thorn in the flesh to keep him humble after such a glorious and transcendent experience, even so will I pass on to other themes. The spirit of the prophet is subject to the prophet.

We are gathered here, beloved, as a Protestation against the established Government and Church, inasmuch as they are hostile to the commands and ordinances of God. For this we are driven out of our homes, our churches, our towns, villages and all that is comfortable and familiar to us. If the two divine institutions of Church and State were considered, according to the Scriptural rule, as to the qualifications of its rulers, as to performance of the duties which God réquires in His Word both of rulers and ruled, compared with the present method of carrying on the two divine institutions of Church and State, it might be seen that the present methods in their whole taken both by rulers and ruled is nothing but a bonding against the advancement of Christ's Kingdom.

There is one sort of the present professors that are bending against Christ by immoral practices and blaspheming the name of God and are esteemed good members of Church and State. Where are to be found either in Church or State those who are executing the laws of Christ against those sins that God has pronounced against when in Isaiah He says,'Woe unto them that join house to house and field to field.'. . ? Truly Drumlanrig and such like so-called nobility are making themselves rich at the expense of the common people of this land. I have said it before and I will say it again. The nobility of this land are not worthy of its peasantry and common folk, nor so well educated. Some of them cannot write weel nor hae the learning o' the letters that you have, and I say that as the son of gentry. Woe unto them that decree unrighteous decrees to turn aside the needy from judgement and to take away the right from the poor of my people! Woe unto him that builds his house by unrighteousness.' Woe unto them that rise up early that in the morning they may follow strong drink! Woe unto him that gives his neighbour drink, that puts the bottle to him! Certain it is that the prophets Isaiah, Jeremiah, and Habbakuk have the word for today for our persecutors. Therefore all rulers and people who either are guilty themselves of these or other wickednesses which are condemned by God in His Word or justify or in any manner of way encourage or help those that are guilty in their wicked practices, are all banded against the advancement of Christ's Kingdom. Their proper names, character and work are recorded in Psalm 83. These consulters are called the Tabernacle of Edom and Ishmaelites, of Moab and the Hagarines, Gobul and Ammon and Amalek, the Philistines with the inhabitants of Tyre. Ashur is also joined with them; they have helped the children of Lot.

When God comes to call the roll of Scotland He shall find many blanks, dead ministers, dead professors, dead men and women though going about upon their feet. They are the living yet dead. There are many classes of pulseless, bloodless, soulless people. There are those who are plunging in the world and who excuse themselves by the plea that they must labour for their livelihood that they might trust God and give Him credit. If so, He will help you at all your work. I will tell you what He would do for you. He would plough your land, sow your corn, shear your corn, sell your corn, and bring home your money. He will even, as it were, rock the cradle, if it is necessary, for you. He will condescend as low as you desire Him. Then there are others who have a religious profession but no inward holiness. I fear Christ has quitted many of you and given you the farewell slap upon the heart, and He will reprove you no more. For you, the poor broken-hearted followers of Christ, to whom He has given grace to follow Him in the storm, I tell you, Grace is young glory. Where is the Church of God in Scotland at this day? It is not amongst the great clergy. I will tell you where it is! The Church is wherever a praying young man or young woman is at a dykeside in Scotland: that's where the Church is! O winna ye talk face to face with Christ? If there be one o' ye, He will be the Second. If there be two, He will be the Third. Ye shall never want company! There was a poor widow in Clydesdale, as I came through, that was worth many of you put together. She was asked how she did in this evil time. 'I do very well', says she. 'I will get more good of one verse of the Bible now than I did of it all lang syne. He will cast me the keys of the pantry door, and bid me take my fill.' Was not that a Christian indeed?

"The sands of life are running out in the hour-glass for me and the thunder clouds are massing themselves over our country. The time is coming for me no longer to expound the Lord's message but when Ministers and people must dedicate their strength solely to pleading and entreaty; they must take no rest and give God no rest. No, my friends, do not advise me. It is praying folk alone will get through the storm. Ah, John Clerk of Muirbrook in Carrick, I see you there. Dear John, there shall be dark days, such as the poor Church of Scotland never saw the like, nor ever shall see, if once they are over. If a poor thing should go from the East seabank to the West seabank, seeking one to whom they might communicate their case, or that would tell them the mind of the Lord, and he shall not find one. Many a conventicle has God had in thee, O Scotland! But er long God will hold a conventicle that will make Scotland tremble. He sent forth faithful messengers to preach to thee; but ere long He shall preach to thee by fire and sword. Yet I see a rose bud in the distant East. And John, the church shall arise from her grave; and at the crack of her winding sheet, as many as had a hand in her burial shall be distracted with fear. Then shall there be brave days for the Church, and she shall come forth with a bonnie bairn-time at her back. O John! I shall not see those days but you may."

The soft, wispy mists of early autumn were drifting over the north Ayrshire moors, now on the folding hills, now in the hollows, or clinging to the channel of the burns gently flowing towards the south. The air was still, increasingly so in the mist. The strident cry of a curlew echoed eerily across the loneliness, causing the watching eyes to alter their direction momentarily. The crowd had become silent after such a piercingly prophetic message. It was as if they were on tiptoe waiting for some unnamed event to take place which would decide their future. A bitter game was indeed being acted out on the moors of Scotland. Keen eyes searched the mist for the flash of a red coat or the glint of a musket. There was nothing. The wail of a psalm died in the wind and the droning words of the prayer of blessing came to an end. The white clothed table carried the simple elements of the Communion, a number of slices of plain rye bread, and three silver tassies full of wine. Peden reverently moved to the table and quietly distributed the bread to some leading elders who had come forward. One of them remained to offer the element to the minister as the rest mingled with the congregation, passing out the symbol of Christ's body. Not for these worshippers the belief of the mass, with it's unscriptural interpretation of the bread and wine as the actual body and blood with all its superstitious connotations and power vested in the priest, but a living trust in the very real presence of the Lord. With whispered blessings, this most ordinary of human diets was passed from hand to hand, a bond of faith with their God for Whom they suffered and one another with whom they suffered. Rough ugly hands of ploughmen and smooth tapering fingers belonging to those who kept accounts, both gently took a piece from the slice. Both had put their hands to the Covenant plough and kept short accounts with God. As they partook, a mystical unity with their God and even creation all around was experienced. So it was with the silver tassie's contents of blood red Burgundy, probably smuggled into such as Dysart by some Dutch brigantine. Rotterdam and Groningen in Holland were havens of refuge for many a Covenanting minister outed because he was not prepared to be patronised into his pulpit or thirled to the Book of Common Prayer. As the Service came to a quiet conclusion and Sandy Peden raised his hands for a benediction, the outlying guards breathed a sigh of relief and an extra silent prayer that Claverhouse or Lag and their wolves had not descended on God's people with musket and sword to slaughter indiscriminately or to hunt them like dogs over the wastelands, leaving them to hide exhausted in some bracken bush or wooded copse.

The congregation now began to disappear like wraiths from the forbidden Conventicle. All that soon remained was the table with Peden, Paton and a few elders who then carried it to a nearby biggin where a little food was laid on also for the Minister and those needful. Paton was overcome almost with a godly enthusiasm.

"My, that was a rare sermon, Sandy, if I may address your Reverence so."

"Aye, certainly, John. Anyone as famous for his bravery and greatheartedness as Captain John Paton, has the right to approach the King on first name terms though I doubt, John, as to whether you and His Highness, King Charles, would really be on speaking terms, eh?"

"Nae, Sandy, I doubt I would be too cultured for him, as I hear he is too busy carousing and generally putting the country's finances in debt to France by his draining them on his various favourites and ladies of fancy, to spend time on serious learning or thought. Indeed, I might forget myself so much as to run him through with my Andrea Ferrara blade. It already has many notches. One more will make its owner quite happy, honour it with royal blood, and rid the country of a tyrant."

Peden, with an amused gentleness, laid his great hand on the similarly massive shoulders of Paton. "Ah, John, you must hold back that warlike temperament of yours. Remember that those who live by the sword shall die by the sword. Methinks that you have spent too long with Gustavus Adolphus and the triumphs of that Protestant Lion of the North in Germany. That great sword of yours, full forty inches long, I'm but a true Scot not a lackey or indulged minister, looks as if twae men couldnae lift it above their heids. The sword of the Lord and Gideon indeed!"

"Tis an Andrea Ferrara and is my treasured possession. It was tempered in the workshops of Solingen in Germany. There and in Passau they produce metals of such superb temper that even the Gaelic bards in the north eulogise these Spanish blades as they name them, setting them higher than those produced by their clan armourers who work under primitive conditions. These German armourers hold us Scots in great regard who fight for all who stand for justice. They have inscribed on the blades a message suitable to a Christian knight. See, here are the words Sandy, 'God protect the honest Scots'. So assuredly it is the sword of the Lord to do the work of the Lord! And for me, the double handed whirling sword can do it much better than those pretty but puny single edged backswords. But apart, what can steel do against gunpowder when though our exiled brethren in Holland have sent us flintlocks from Groningen, the dragoon forces of bloody Clavers far outnumber us and outshoot us? Our forefathers would have been astonished by these weapons of death. Cannot your visionary gift tell us of what like war will be hereafter? Some terrible killing instruments methinks are the end of this invention. Truth be to tell, I be speirin' concerning these visions and prophecies of which you are famed among the Covenant folk. Would you open the secrets of God to an old friend in need of encouragement?"

The smoking fire in the centre of the biggin had by now given the room a mystical atmosphere in which anything was possible. In an age of superstition, belief in the supernatural was not hard for the godly, especially if it coincided with biblical belief. Life was so hard in its daily grind to eke out a living that desire for another world, where food, raiment and freedom were in abundance, was only too overwhelming. The age of rationality, with its deadening intellectualising of all thought, had not as yet overcome the spirituality of the people. Peden's sanguine features gleamed in the wreathed greyness and his head cocked to the side, listening.

"You are a close friend and, if it be of profit and spiritual comfort to you to give account of some of the ways in which the Almighty has seen fit to deliver His servant and vouchsafe him foreknowledge of future events, I will open my heart to you of His mysterious ways. Ever since my departure from the Auld Kirk in Glenluce, I have been a wanderer in these hills, like the wandering Arameans of ancient Israel. In the year of 1666 a proclamation was issued against me and others of the outed ministers for holding Coventicles, preaching and baptising children at Ralstoun in Kilmarnock Parish, and at Castlehill in Craigie Parish where twenty five children were baptised. When, as you will appreciate, I did not make an appearance at their citation, being shy of such noble company, I was declared a rebel and forfeited in both life and fortune. Then I joined the faithful party which, as you know only too sadly, was defeated at Pentland on the fateful Rullion Green. I had come the length of the Clyde where I had a melancholy view of their end, and so parted with them there. Here comes the bitter portion of my prophetic gift from the Lord. A friend did say to me that I did well that left them, seeing I was persuaded of their fall. I was heartily offended and said 'Glory to God, that He sent me not to hell immediately for I would have stayed with them, though I should have been cut to pieces.' "

"But no-one doubts your courage at all," bluff Paton was chagrined. "You are held in the highest regard by all!"

"Tis not so. There are those of the party who would assign me a coward's cloak. This is the price of the gift. To whom much is given, much is demanded. The psalmist tells us that the secret of the Lord is with them that fear Him and the prophet Daniel blessed the God of Heaven for wisdom and might are His, and He changes times and seasons; He removes Kings and sets up Kings. He gives wisdom unto the wise and knowledge to them that know understanding. He reveals the deep and secret things. He knows what is in the darkness. Nor, risking a cowardly accusation, I am more use to the scattered people while I can retain my breath. What good am I a corpse to my Covenanting brethren? Better a live dog than a dead lion. But my heart is sore tried when the brave lads are dying all around. My enemies cannot move a tongue against me, my time being not yet come.

There have been many occasions in my wanderings over hang and hill where the Lord has given me foreknowledge of His protection. When the bloodhounds were keen on the scent I have slipped away from Scotland to Ireland, from one bloody country to another bloody land. No-one has been attracted by the thousand merks on my head but one. There has been no other fause Montieth to sell this Scotsman, though Wallace was more worthy. The troopers dogs have sniffed at the entrance to the cave where I have hidden and passed on. The climb up the cliff face near Auchinliok to my cave is so fraught with danger of a slip that its refuge one of these days might no be needed. Forby every stoney edge in the cave floor has verily impressed itself upon my ageing frame that I could envy the animals their shape, as well as their straw beds in the byre.

But forgive me, Lord, then there were the beds of unthreshed straw where o' times I lay concealed myself and the soldiers would stab through the 'moo' and yet touch me not. They were beds o' finest comfort to me compared with a King's couch though often many o' God's tiniest creatures have kept me company' Sometimes I swam the Esk River where ford there was none. Sometimes where mist broods on Scottish moor and mount and I could run no more for very weariness, I did pray 'Lord, if Thou hast no more work for us in this world, allow us the lap of Thy cloak this day again. Twine them about the hill, Lord, and cast a lap of thy cloak over auld Sandy and these puir things and save us this one time.' And oft He who comes with the rainbow as his wreath and the storm as his robe, did bring down his mists and shield us in such a day. One deliverance for which I thank our great God for His Almighty Lordship of the elements and miracle of the mist, was when the enemy were coming upon me and my fellow Covenanters. They did pursue us a considerable way with both horse and foot. At last getting some little height between us and them, like the Israelites of old, I stood still to see the salvation of the Lord, encouraging my companions to pray here. For if the Lord hear not our prayers and save us, we are all dead men. Here it is the enemy's hour, day and power and they may not be idle. But, Lord, have you no work for them but to send them after us? Send them after them to whom Thou wilt give strength to flee, for our strength is gone. If Thou wilt but throw the lap of Thy cloak over this puir body and those friends we'll keep it in remembrance and tell it to the commendation of Thy goodness, pity, and compassion, what You did for us at such a time". And as the Lord is such a perfect gentleman, John, He did hear us and a cloud of mist intervened immediately between us, and, in the meantime, a post came to the enemy to go in quest of the Rev. James Renwick and a great company that were with him at another Conventicle. Hallelujah, Praise His Name!" His voice became serious again. "I tell you now and I will say it again before our time is come. The Stuarts will be pitten aff the throne and all the moyen in the world winna pit them back. As for you and I, John, our names shall be remembered by generations yet unborn when all Scotland shall be free."

Paton, then bluff soldier, sat in awed silence, as the power of the dictatorial Stuarts on the throne of Britain, seemed firmly established again and impossible to be shaken.

By this time Sandy was weary with the long day in the open and emotion of preaching, and begged leave to rest, retiring without ceremony to the straw lined cot in the corner, covered with a sheepskin quilt. Soon his quiet breathing contrasted with the deep snoring of the barrel chested Paton on the other side of the hearth. The elders had all reverently departed, apart from the cottar, and the sleep of the just was theirs.

7

In The Mearns

Lochgoin Farmhouse stood out in the very heart of a wild moorland waste in the Fenwick area of Ayrshire. It had become a favourite resort of the Covenanters during the period of persecution. It was like an oasis in its dreary surroundings. Near the house were a few patches of oats and potatoes, with a small garden for kitchen vegetables and the hardiest kind of flowers. Fruit trees were not to be seen, for the best of reasons, they could not exist in such a barren and exposed situation. There were a few of Scotland's hardiest trees but even these had a dwarfed and miserable appearance. The moorland can best be described by the fact that, as James Howie made hay in a nearby field, the ground oozed, two to three inches in depth.

    The farmsteading nestled in a shallow hollow, a long range of a house, part of recent erection, and part of great antiquity. The larger and most comfortable portion was devoted to accommodating the cattle. Captain Paton, squinting up at the lintel, shading his eyes in the watery sunshine, saw the date of 1178 distinctly inscribed there. He had known the story that the Howies were descended from a line of persecuted Albigensians or Waldensians. John was often confused by the multiplicity of religious sects in Scotland, England and the Continent, both before and after the Protestant Reformation. Political intrigue counted for more than religious conviction in the Thirty Years War. Paton was essentially a simple man. However he knew that the founder of the Howie family was one, Huie, who fled from the south of France to seek refuge in Scotland. But it seemed that he had just exchanged one bloody country for another. There had been three brothers, one of whom had settled in the parish of

Mearns, another in the parish of Craigie, and the third took up residence in the lonely farmhouse he built at Lochgoin between Glasgow and Kilmarnock, and was still occupied by his descendants after 500 years.

Captain Paton had been conducted across the intensely cold, limpid waters of the Lochgoin, two thirds of a mile in length, by two lads from a neighbouring farm who were going to help with the haymaking. Captain John was on his way to meet Peden the Prophet at the Devil's Plantain on the road from Eaglesham to the Mearns, and intended only to stop off for a little. He knew he was sure of a bite and a bed, as he had often received. Faithful James was labouring among the fields, a taciturn man of deep sincerity, while Isabel Howie was a buxom, ramsteegerous girth of a woman, who embraced everybody and everything in sight, including the great kitchen cauldron. But there was nothing ramstoorie about that spotless kitchen. John's knock was answered at once and thrown open and Isabel Howie stood there, arms apart, like a triumphant capercaillzie interrupted in the middle of its dance, feathers all on end. But her moon-shaped face, gleaming red from the peat fire wreathed itself in joy as she crushed even the ox-shouldered Captain in a crushing hug.

"It's yourself, Captain. Come away ben, for this is a house of bon accord with naebody turned back except those who hae turned their back on Scotland and truth and justice for her people. I'm rare glad to see you, for I'm just this moment stitching a Covenanting banner or twa, for who kens when they may be needed to lead the forces of the Covenant. Come and see the one I'm about finished. Give me your crack, and maybe suggest a banner design. The whole place is in a curfuffle and I'm ettling to get things redded up."

Shepherding the Captain in with a heavy fleshed arm, Isabel bustled over to the large hearth rocking chair. Spread before it was a sail like cloth of fine linen, pure white with the figures of a Bible and crown, supported by a thistle, rather rudely traced with a red pigment, and the motto, "Phinick for Country and Covenanted Work of Reformation." As Isabel Howie eased herself into the nine spoked seat, Paton wondered if it would hold.

John Paton let his attention wander from the bole hole with the family Breeches Bible, to the salt hole, also set in the wall, where that valuable commodity was kept dry, then to the round, iron brazier in the centre of the kitchen from which the rich smelling peat smoke wound up through the opening in the thatch.

"I would hesitate to take it upon myself to compose a title, but, as the living God has been our Salvation and Rock, let 'Jehovah Nissi', the Lord our Banner, and 'Jehovah Jireh', the Lord will provide, be our watchwords. Add the sting in the Scottish tail, 'Whaur daur meddle wi' me?'"

"Aye, our enemies will someday feel the thistle of the Covenant prick their pride. Rest yourself if'n you are a wheen wearied."

"I confess that I am though it's only from Meadowhead Farm across the hills I've daundered and up the Dunton Burn but life's a taut wire. My foes seem intent on seizing me even to laying a trap when I went to the burial of one of my younger daughters, Allison, at the Kirk of Fenwick but a friendly voice gave me forewarning." He sank wearily into the other high-backed seat.

"I was fair sore hearted to hear of the effects of the pneumonia on your bonnie wee one. God's ways are strange."

"Yes, fortunately the good Lord gave me a good wife Janet Lindsay though but for a little while before she died from consumption. But I'll not stop off for long as Prophet Peden has sent me word to meet him at the Devil's Plantain over between the Mearns and Eaglesham. I have an inkling that there's something important in the wind."

"The Devil's Plantain! That's an unco place! Eldritch screeches come from the midst of that hillock in the dead of night. Why on earth meet there? I ken it's called the Guid Man's Acre but that's just so as to no displease the Devil." When no answer was forthcoming, Mrs Howie looked up quickly from her banner-making, to see Captain Paton snoring gently, esconced by the fire. The soporific atmosphere and Isabel Howie's confident voice had relaxed his taut nerves.

For a while there was no sound but the click of the gudwoman's needles and the slow rhythmic emission of breath from the rise and fall of the soldier's powerful chest. There was a distinct wheezing as, despite the bull-like strength of the man, since a child the tendency to an asthmatical condition had afflicted him and the continuous soakings in his life of the hunted had taken its heavy toll. Yet for now danger was afar it seemed when suddenly the door crashed open and the menacing figure of Sergeant Rae of the Kilmarnock militia was framed in the dim light. It had been a stormy night and the chances of his hunters venturing abroad had not occurred to Paton. But a party had searched Meadowhead in vain and gone on to Croilburn, another rempte refuge, and so the alternatives had been cut down and the quarry brought to earth at Lochgoin. But, though fairly certain of success, the officer had guessed that the main body might be sighted, and so sent on Sergeant Rae ahead with five men to approach by a lesser known path over the hills. When they crept closer, James Howie and his son John were still out among the cattle in the byre.

"Dog, I have you now!" The startled Captain thrust himself towards the spence, the spare room beside the kitchen, used as a parlour and larder, containing the family loom. He would escape through the back but he had forgotten the courage and initiative of Isabel Howie.

"Take to the hills and don't be killed like a rat." Seeing only the Sergeant, she ran at him and with her needles caused him to retreat. Following her advantage, Isabel threw her full weight against his chest with outstretched arms and ran Sergeant Rae out to stumble headlong. The Captain, seizing the opportunity to put on his huge thigh boots, rushed out and vaulted onto his mare before the confused troopers could forestall him. Their Sergeant had sent them skittling. Paton was completely cool in his appraisal and headed for the bogs protecting the rear of Lochgoin. The mare knew the pathway without any touch whereas his pursuers would have to pick their way. They fired on but their guns had got wet coming through the storm. Paton turned in the saddle to fire a bullet — which passed so close to Sergeant Rae that it took off the knot of hair on the side of his head. The alarm had now been spread and the rest of the search party rushed up the path to Lochgoin but John Paton knew the gauntlet was not one without escape. Bounding like a deer from one tussock to another across the haggs which protected the rear, he in fact had begun to outdistance the heavy clad soldiers. For good measure, turning swiftly, he fired accurately from the knee and the Highland sergeant collapsed with a curse of anguish as the shot crushed his thigh. Further discouragement wasn't apparently needed. Paton had become aware that often these men were unwilling servants of the State, and on occasion, compassionate dragoons had given secret assistance where possible and the officer's attention was elsewhere. There had been the narrow deliverance when covered by a clump of gorse and heather, the main party of pursuers had passed his hiding place, but one soldier, a young recruit straggling behind the rest, spied his brogues peeping from the bush. To Paton's astonishment, a trembling youthful voice told him to pull in his foot and he would pile some heather bells over it.

By now he was ascending the heights of Ballygeich, which apart from Mistilaw and the Hill o' Staik, was the highest eminence in Renfrewshire, a thousand feet, commanding an extensive view, embracing many counties. It was directly on his route to Eaglesham and his appointment with Sandy Peden at the Devil's Plantain. The wispy haar cleared as if magically when the Captain reached the top. The sun shone with transforming power, and stretched out below were the Fenwick moors, the fertile woods and fields of Ayrshire, the giant rock of Ailsa, towering Goatfell in the distance, on the other side the great basin and vale of Clyde with Glasgow and Paisley, while a perfect wilderness of Bens arose proudly on the dim horizon of the Highlands. As a lad he had childlike imagined that the far clouds were fabled mountains with fabulously rich cities that he would someday reach. Though his childhood fantasies had long since disappeared, yet he still looked for a city whose maker and builder was God. Such was the desire of all Covenanted Scotland.

Putting aside his dreams, he descended from Ballygeich Hill, and passed by the Picketlaw, where many a sentinel had stood silent, hawkeyed for any signs of danger. The Norman village lay below, situated in a shallow valley on a gentle slope. The barony of Eaglesham had been for centuries the property of the Norman Montgomeries. Robert de Montgomery came to Scotland with Walter Fitzalan, created by David I the High Constable. He granted the Manor of Eaglesham to Montgomery. From the Picketlaw the battlements of Polnoon Castle could be seen, built from the enormous ransom gained by Sir John Montgomery of Eaglesham and Eglinton when he captured Henry Hotspur Percy, son and heir of the Earl of Northumberland at Otterburn in the county of Redesdale. As part of the continuous feuding which characterised the border country, the fighting had begun in the setting sun and continued by moonlight throughout the August night. Captain Paton himself had often sung the famous ballad of "Chevy Chase" in the Cross Keys Inn, celebrating a Scottish victory. He was in familiar territory as he wandered down the old green cut by the Linn Burn separating the rows of cottages. He rubbed his hand on the bark of Beckie's Tree, smiled a greeting at the womenfolk bleaching by the burn. But it was the village market that guided his steps. Alexander, eighth Earl of Eglinton, had a few years before been granted a Charter on petition from the King. Paton had known the patronage of Alexander, called Greysteel from the colour of his armour. The Earl of Eglinton had also been named the pious, after signing the Covenant in Greyfriars Kirkyard and fought alongside John in the army of General Leslie. His son, however, was of a different character and must be avoided at all costs.

The Market Fair was held in Cheapside Street, which was in fact so called after the cheapness of the articles. There had been an ancient Fair there before which only one venerable worthy remained alive to recall how cheap the wares were. Fairs had been held from medieval customs, being appointed in connection with Saints Days and religious festivals. The dedication of churches was also an occasion when tradesmen and merchants brought their wares to a convenient space in the vicinity of the church on its anniversary when large crowds collected. The Captain had heard that the famous Glasgow Fair ran for eight days in July and that folk from all over the West of Scotland gathered to buy and sell, meet old acquaintances, and see the shows provided by strolling players, acrobats, tumblers, singers and dancers. Although Eaglesham Fair was a much lesser event, yet, as with Glasgow, the laws of the Fair were now binding on local and foreign traders so long as they were within the jurisdiction of the marches. This John knew well and that it was often ordained by the town's Council that every booth-holder have in his booth a halbert, jack and steel bonnet, to quell any disturbances arising. He mentally resolved to firmly avoid any controversy. Words which bind were spoken with hand laid on a sacred stone or on the Market Cross. The breaking of that peace made the offender an outlaw. That peace was for those who came to the sports, wrestling, and mirth that preceeded the Fair.

As he left the Picketlaw he was passed by riders whipping their steeds, country men on country mares, neither built for speed. Then he understood, for it was a slur for your neighbours to pass you on your way to the Fair. All kinds of migrating persons were wending their way to the Cheapside — hawkers, perambulating showmen, all the tribe of the spoonmakers, and basketmakers, shepherds from the hill country, hill farmers, crofters, and ploughmen. A shuffling figure was making his way very deliberately down the path over the Common Green. His long coarse blue cloak flapping awkwardly as to emphasise his awkwardness in society, and John had no trouble in recognising the kenspeckle figure of the Gaberlunzie, the professional Scottish beggar or pedlar. He turned his head at the Covenanting Captain's footsteps and his long, bony features reddened by continuous tramping of the roads of Scotland, broke into a cracked grin.

"What wi' the skirling o' pipes, blowing of trumpets, ringing of bells, discharging of muskets, and the crying of these noisy booth-holders, the hum of the crowd, and the bleating of the sheep, one could think that the pealing of a thunderstorm would even perhaps pass unnoticed!" His high pitched chords chortled as his whapple bobbed. The Scottish mendicant was in a class which had some privileges. A lodging was usually granted to them in an outhouse and the alms of a gowpen, a handful of meal, was scarce denied by the poorest cottager. At the houses of gentry cheer was given him of pieces of meal and perhaps a "Twalpenny" which was expended on snuff and whiskey. It was in fact a sadly comic irony that some of these indolent peripatetics suffered much less real hardship and want of food than the poor peasants from whom they received alms. The Gaberlunzie man usually carried his food in various bags around his person. He was so named from one large leather wallet-purse slung over his shoulder. This particular Gaberlunzie man, shrouded by a long, light blue cloak and hood, rather ragged, to go with his broken brogues, but the big leather pouch was well filled by the looks of it, with bread and meal, spindles and whorls for sale to the spinners at the Fair. As a licensed beggar, he claimed the right to join a festival feast. A sturdy staff assisted him as he trudged along to the whistle of a merry tune.

"It's been a long time since I thrilled to the excitement of a village fair, Gaberlunzie."

"Aye, you'll be more used to the quietness of a country Conventicle, Captain!" He cocked his eye slyly down at the Covenanter, for he was very tall and thin. As the Captain looked with sharp alarm at this veiled threat, he couldn't but notice that the beggar's hair was of a singularly silvery grey.

"What's your meaning, man?"

"My meaning is that your secret is safe with a Gaberlunzie. He is an Aristocrat of the Order, who, though he is a King's Bedesman or Blue Gown, would never betray a brave Covenanter soldier to these dragoons. Many of them have the nature of beasts." So speaking, he threw off his hood, and revealed a blue Covenanting bonnet with a bright red, brown, and green pheasant's feather stuck jauntily in it.

"Travelling from one end of Scotland to the other, there's no a nook and cranny or the smoke haze of a hamlet I dinna ken. The affairs of King's men and Covenanters are equally my affairs, as are a' other things. As a King's Bedesman, I am expected to pray for the royal welfare and that of the state's in return for alms and on Royal Birthdays all Bedesmen have a new gown given to them and a pewter badge. He proudly pointed to the lead and tin badge which held the cloak clipped at his neck. "With our cloak we receive as many shillings Scots in our purse as the King is years old. These are supposed to stimulate an increasing zeal in our intercession for the Majesty's long life. But I answer to whoever pays the piper in public deference. I can also sing a good song, tell a good story and crack a severe jest with all the ability of a Shakespearean jester, though unlike him, without using the cloak of insanity. My guid Blue Gown is my guarantee of honesty and safety." His features at that moment were most intelligent, with a powerful expression of sarcasm. "But when a good deed is done for no return, I am eternally beholdin'. Though you Covenanters are a wee sicht too serious for the likes of me, yet I admire your heart's bravery. Forby, when I was confronted by an obstreperous innkeeper in Moniaive, who accused me of being a laxy ne'er do weel, and made to lay hands on me, I tapped his noggin with my little john." Here he swung his staff. "But he hollered for a band of soldiery in the aleroom, and these long legs had to be my answer. Some of the mendicant fraternity are less than popular for their perpitatetic indolent ways. On making a nearby wood, I was still in mortal danger when a dark cloaked figure with an unco frightsome mask grasped my arm from ahint a dyke so that I was almost hoisted across it by the force of his strength."

"Sandy!" John Paton breathed the name with affection and reverence.

"The Rev. Alexander Peden it was!"

"I never did acquire a name from him but he was a strange prophet man, and prophesied that I would encounter a Covenanting Captain soon in my travels. From his description I jalouse you are that man. Sandy's message to you is that this day you will meet the delight of your last years but nothing else is to delay your journey. Jings, I nearly forgot, your queer Minister friend hid me safely in a hollow cave beneath a waterfall, called the Creehope Linn near Closeburn. Its a natural refuge in a surprisingly secret glen as it's suddenly encountered coming across the flat fields."

"Prophet Peden is as good and trustworthy a friend as you will ever encounter in your wanderings, whatever your situation may be. His mask, wig, and cloak, are equally symbols of his office of suffering as your Blue Gown, badge, and wallet."

"Wat Atkinson, at your service, and I thank your Prophet Peden for the bonnie blue bonnet and the truths of God which he taught me that night. It'll no be the first time a man has donned a disguise for an unusual reason. The stories are told of the reign of James V, a kind King." The last remark he uttered significantly. "A Gaberlunzie had come to the Wedding Party of William Hume's daughter in the rented farmlands of Cairnkebbie near Duns. He entertained the company to the dirling of his pipe until they were intoxicated with the ranting tunes. He seemed extraordinar good.

Then a squadron of royal troops arrived and accused the Gaberlunzie man of stealing the Royal Mace from Duns where the Sovereign was residing. Although the precious symbol was seen to have slipped from under the blue cloak, Mr. Hume and the guests were so intoxicated by the music that they assisted the beggar to escape. The farmer's reward was the rent free grant of Cairnkebbie when it was revealed that the Gaberlunzie was the King disguised for a wager. In the same way, the King dressed as a Gaberlunzie when he found a poor carter whose produce of eggs and onions had been ruined by passing cavalry. The so called beggar took the carter to the Palace at Perth where he gained him recompense. Indeed it was a rare crack when King James said to the amazed man? "Tis this way, my friend, As I see it, one of the two of us must be the King, and if its not you, then it must be myself."

The Captain joined heartily in the laughter, so natural in the din of the crowd now thronging the Eaglesham Cross. The Burgh Officer was about to proclaim the peace of the Fair, and the two sensed the sounds die down. Clear and strong were the words. "Forasmuch as this is the Fair Day annually held in Eaglesham, I therefore forbid in our Sovereign Lord's name and on behalf of our Lord Alexander Montgomery, that none of our Sovereign Lord's lieges coming to the Fair do any hurt or trouble one to another for old debt or new debt, old feud or new feud, but live peaceably and use their merchandise and exchange under the highest pain and charge against them doing in the contrary. They will be held responsible for breaking the King's peace and troubling the Market."

"Come on, Blue Gown! Lets mingle among the stalls and sample the goods. Its not called Cheapside Street for nothing. You can get some bobbins and bangles and I some rich lettuce and soft juicy turnip."

The Captain smiled as he saw over by the Burn the Yapping Game with herds ranged on each side of the Burn who at the given signal, were beating the water with sticks, till one side gave way. The water was spraying in all directions as the loons roared with excitement and the watching lassies skirled. The vanquished would leave the Market and the victors had the exclusive right of treating the lassies to fruit and the enjoyment of their society at the dancing on the Green. This was the Orrie over which the Captain and his Gaberlunzie friend had approached the Fair. Paton was now munching happily on a large apple and wending his way through a flock of panic stricken sheep when his attention was arrested by the sight of a booth and ring, surrounded by a loudly baying audience.

In the middle of the ring was a figure of taurine frame, his torso matted to an animal degree, bald head shining, flowing moustache giving added strength to the fierce high cheekbones, and thick, protuberant ears. A crier was declaring to all and sundry that Gregorio the Magnificent was asking all comers to a challenge of the best of three falls. Gregorio, the bald giant from East European extraction intermingled with some gypsy blood, grinned sardonically, and John Paton felt his blood rise in his throat at the thought that he despised Scots courage even more than their wrestling skill.

But, suppressing his antagonism, he knew he must not draw attention to himself, and was turning away, to avoid a confrontation, when his eye was held by a brown twinkling pair belonging to a neat looking maiden in a frilled skirt and bodice bright with blue and yellow flowers. Part of a group of village girls enjoying the Fair who had gathered giggling round a stall of woollen garments from Glasgow to try them on, she suddenly separated herself from them to stare back at Captain John Paton, who by this time was smitten with love. The magic even held in the midst of the noisy crowd, and the Covenanter, imbued with a new power, turned back to the challenge of the arrogant foreigner.

With a bound he leapt through the circle of spectators and smashed the flimsy wooden barrier erected round the Green. Words were scarcely needed as John indicated his intention to the crier, who informed him in sarcastic tones that he would receive a hundred merks if he lasted one three minute round with Gregorio, and then added as an afterthought that he would gain one thousand merks if he overcame the champion. Gregorio was meantime grinning viciously beneath his thick moustache. A wolf could not have been more certain of its prey caught in the wilderness.

At first all the expected result seemed imminent as the hairy rippling body flung itself on the Captain and he went down under the massive onslaught. His own figure stripped to his breeches, felt crushed but the very grease on the champion's body was his help as he slipped from his grasp, kicking upward with his knee as he escaped. Mercenary fighting was no gentle art and money had been more important than chivalry or spurs. So it was by kicking and punching that he survived the round, though the huge Gregorio caught him twice with flailing blows from his windmill arms. The crowd were in an uproar and kept inciting John to continue after the round. The Captain already had the encouragement of two adoring brown eyes.

Wrestling, perhaps the oldest and most universal of sports known to man, had been practised in the camps of Gustavus Adolphus' army, and, unknown to the champion, Captain Paton had learnt some free style moves, more in a catch as catch can fashion. If he could keep out of the crushing embrace of Gregorio's grip, he could have a chance, as he depended on a hand blow on a vital nerve. Gradually as his waiting game paid off, and the war of attrition began to wear down the enraged champion, the latter became careless, exposing himself in his bull like lunges. At last when even the Captain's rock hard muscles were beginning to quiver, Gregorio's great neck was an open target as he slipped under the champion's guard. Drawing his knuckles down with crunching force he chopped the carrotid-sinus at the side of the neck. Gregorio went down poleaxed, and lay as if lifeless, while the Captain barely maintained his trembling legs upright. Almost unhearing, and unconscious of the roaring crowd, he collected the thousand merks from the champion's patron, sullen and unbelieving. His faculties now returned sufficient to recall the deep brown eyes he sought out.

Sure enough, the lass was slightly back from the admiring mob but admiring nonetheless, and quickly he cut through them to clasp her quietly outstretched hand. Modesty was yet in her demeanour.

"It is a day for handclasping, sir. Are you familiar with that custom?"

"As familiar as any here, for I am of good Ayrshire country stock many generations back, lass, and I ken all the traditions."

"So you'll ken that if a lad and lassie handfast at a Fair it means they can have a trial marriage maintained for a year and a day and end it after that, if they do not find it pleasing?"

"I think I would find it pleasing without even the trial, Madamoiselle — ah, I don't even know your name."

"Janet Millar of Eaglesham at your service, and I work in my father's weaving business in our cottage. My father is also a Burgess."

"My name is Captain John Paton, and I try to keep the farms of Meadowhead and Airtnock round Fenwick in tack, though I have to admit that I am somewhat on the move round the country, Janet. I so like that name. Janet Lindsay was my first wife, though she lived but a short time, poor girl."

The sparkling brown eyes were dulled and Janet said compassionately, "I'm sorry, Captain. Death comes unbidden. Are you maybe a Covenanter on the run? Dinna be concerned. My father is very sympathetic and would join their army tomorrow."

John Paton's hopes were fired and his hand slipped back to encompass her smaller. Words were hard in coming but any were stifled by the urgent face of Wat Atkinson thrusting through the mass, and his bony hand pulling at the Covenanter's shirt. "Word has been passed to the Earl of Eglinton by the rascal owner of that furrin beast you have just given his pakes to, that a Covenanter is loose at the Fair. The wicked creature can't abide losing his thousand merks and remember that the Earl of Eglinton is a King's man, no friend of the Covenanters."

Just then an alarm was sounded from the edge of the crowd and the clash of weapons made Paton turn quickly to Janet and "I will be back, Janet. Depend upon it." He touched her hair but before he could delay longer, the Gaberlunzie had almost to haul him away.

"Run, man. I owe you one for Prophet Peden."

Slipping quickly and as surreptitiously as possible through the market stalls, Captain Paton walked calmly up out of Eaglesham village, turning for a last glance and his heart almost stopped as he caught the glowing warmth still in the depth of Janet's brown eyes. His mighty chest constricted and his breath lost its timing. A vacuum had been left by his wife's death he never thought could be filled. But now he knew it could and felt a strange joy, and tramped Mearns way with a light heart. He needed it all for John Paton had never been too happy about the Devil's Plantain. He had never been in its vicinity but had hastened on with a shiver and sidelong glance at the weird hillock.

In the time before the blessed Protestant Reformation when superstition was rife in every parish, many parishes had an uncultivated plot of land called the Devil's Plantain or Acre. It was set aside for the Devil and his minions who were supposed to hold their revels there; oxen and sheep were never pastured there; few human feet trod it. Sometimes they stood in the middle of cultivated land, a dismal breadth of thorns and weeds. It was also known contrarily as the Good Man's Acre so as not to offend the horny one with whom they made a bargain to give him this plot on condition that he did not enter the hamlet. These gloomy crofts had been the dread of each hamlet and were usually isolated hillocks on otherwise gentle countryside. Paton understood that people used to be buried there. It did not make him feel easier. The Reformed Church had made strenuous efforts to prevail over the superstition hanging round the Plantains, and some had been ploughed down and brought under cultivation. But as yet the one on the Humbie road to the Mearns still remained unchanged.

The Captain had by now come off the pasturelands on to the path known locally as the Humbie, and saw again the strange hill with its clump of trees. It almost seemed that the skies had become overcast and the air colder. The tall bare trees soughed in the wind which had suddenly arisen and he consciously forced his powerful legs up the easy slope. Deadness was evident in the soil with little grass, but nettles, dockums, dandelions and deadly nightshade were in abundance. Why on earth had Prophet Peden brought him here? Why was he such an unco gangrel body? With a start he saw a dark cloak lying spread on the ground. The fact that it had no significance, vested it with a mystery which was increased by the atmosphere. Staring up at the tall, leafless trees, he saw them bend and shake as if by a giant invisible hand. All at once a figure detached itself from behind a tree trunk, dark and grotesque with sightless eye sockets.

"So it's yourself, John! I deemed it wise to hide in case it wasn't. I thought you'd never come!" Paton's frozen mind relaxed, as he secretly cursed Peden's ways.

"You'll be the end of me, Rev. Peden. That weird mask and wig are no dress fitting for a Minister of the Gospel. I can't think you delight in its appearance of horror. I have never known you to league yourself with the things of darkness."

Sandy laughed merrily so that the Captain's jangled nerves were completely relaxed and he loved again the quaintness of his old friend.

"Captain, you're still recovering from your fright. No, no, there is many an explanation for what seems of the devil though I never discount the horny one. No, take this hill for instance, though many see it as invested with evil significance, it is in fact an old tumulus or burial mound. If you were to dig down deeply into this hillock, no doubt there would be uncovered brooches, jewelry, weapons, pottery and tools. The pagans intended them to be useful to the departed as they had been useful in this life. So it is really quite innocent, but the superstition lies in the minds of an ignorant people."

"But you must admit that witchcraft is rife."

"True, there is still some folk thirled to a master who will pay them ill. Once I said so to an old body who had touched the black arts but she turned to the Lord. Yet so many are victims of malice. There were two women at Haddington that I knew, guid women, an old woman and her daughter, who, though miserably poor, had contrived to look fresh and fair, during a terrible famine in the

Lothian harvests, which reduced even the better classes to straits, and many even to starving. But all this while the two ladies, lived on without suffering and they neither begged nor complained. When brought before the jury and undergoing a wicked interrogation by Kincaid, a witchfinder, these poor women admitted to intercourse with the Devil, they were so terrified. Then Sir George MacKenzie, the King's Advocate and no friend of the Covenanters, visited them in private and urged them to tell the real truth."

"I can hardly believe it of MacKenzie! When he was elected Lord Advocate, he revealed himself as a thorough going Episcopalian and King's man."

"Don't forget that in the darkest heart a spark of light can exist. MacKenzie was once a counsellor of the Marquis of Argyll and defended the rights of prisoners after Rullion Green. Anyway the ladies told him that if they were set at liberty from the Bar, when they returned to their hut they would be met with violence and abuse from their neighbours, who would try to drown them. Sir George therefore said he would send them to his estate in the North where people did not know them, and, if they thought them witches, they would fear them rather than hate them. But the condition was that they would trust him with their secret. So the dear women told Sir George to remove an old empty trunk in the corner of the hut and dig the earth where it was stirred. He found concealed in the earth, two firkins of salted snails, one nearly empty."

"You mean the poor women had been nourished on this strange food during the famine?"

"Indeed, a very simple explanation, as there is for this mound. Now, let's make steps for the Castle of the Mearns which is in Covenanting hands now. We've been holding Conventicles in the castle with old Mr. Wodrow preaching in the great Hall. Mr. Robert Fleming is the Curate in the Mearns. The castle and Barony have just been sold by the Nether Pollok Maxwells to Sir Archibald Stewart of Blackhall. Sir Archie is a supporter of the Cause. It's a pity we can't use the Minstrel gallery for the singing of the Psalms. Rev. Wodrow thinks it smacks too much of an unpresbyterian ceremony to have a choir."

"Is it not in a dangerous position with Capelrig House and its grounds having been taken from the Muirs of Caldwell and given in a treacherous Charter to my old compatriot, General, Tam Dalzell? The King rewards his own slavish varlets. Capelrig is not very far away."

"It's about Capelrig that I have asked for you to meet me here. It's something that will excite you, money for our needs of material things. The money is in a secret place, a legendary treasure. There is time enough to talk when we reach the Castle of Mearns."

"Leading the way, having gathered his cloak, Peden led his soldier friend through the fields, rolling, pastoral, with patches of golden corn. Paton fleetingly glanced back over his shoulder at the dark Plantain and saw the trees still swaying. It was hard to eradicate irrational fears. Soon the rich farmlands of the Floors, Greenbank and Flinders, were reached. Fat cattle grazed and hordes of hens scurried round neat white cottage farms. The Mearns was a real cornucopia in comparison with the bleak Fenwick moorlands. Only as the road snaked out through Malletsheugh Farm and beyond to Langton and Floak, did the wildness creep in. Paton made a mental note to visit his close friends at Floak, known as Mid Floak, and felt it was long overdue.

At last the solid Castle Keep came into view on the hill which gave it a fine vantage. It was, Sandy observed with a twinkle, a real hill. It was most certainly a place of considerable strength. The spot had been chosen by Herbert, first Lord Maxwell of Caerlaverock and Mearns, for the panoramic view it commanded of the countryside, and for the natural defence provided on three sides by the landfall. On the east side, for greater protection, an artificial ditch was dug, and spanned by a drawbridge. The Keep itself stood forty five feet high, with the walls west, north and south eight feet thick, while the builders had precise instructions to make the east wall ten feet as it was considered more vulnerable. Its main entrance was often in time of danger, not the iron-studded door at ground level, but the arched doorway, eleven feet up the east wall. This was reached by the wonderful contrivance of a wooden staircase which could be removed or destroyed in the event of attack. The iron-studded door could be braced from within and was strong enough to withstand any onslaught. As they soon discovered, the castle had three floors.

A rough though joyous halloo for the Covenant and work of Reformation greeted the two from the battlements.

"That will be James Hamilton of Langton Farm. He's a real enthusiastic follower of the Blue Banner and has suffered for it with fining, as has James Pollok, Laird of Balgray. The Laird is very different in character, a religious, sedate, and sensible man, maybe a little too sensible." Peden had a touch of soft irony in his tone. Before the Captain could quiz him, he was momentarily struck dumb by the ingenious wooden staircase which had silently been lowered on chains from its four corners of the arched doorway about a dozen feet up the wall. The iron-studded door at ground level became meaningless. Planks had been nailed across the drawbridge as footholds and the ascent was easy, but, as he reached the first floor, the Captain's nostrils were assailed by a pungent smell, not altogether of a delicate fragrance.

"What have we here, Rev. Peden, human carcasses done to death by your friends of the Mearns after fiendish torture?"

"Nearer to the truth than you think, since below is the dungeon, and it is used as a freeze store for cattle which can't be kept during the winter and must be killed off and their salted carcasses are stored here. A hungry stomach has no sense of smell or even taste."

They had now come into an arched hall whose walls were of rough plaster hung with tapestries depicting hunting scenes in which the riders and hounds seemed to leap out with the flickering light of the log fire as they closed with the boar. Hung on the walls were the heraldic crests of the Stewarts of Blackhall, of laurel wreaths encircling a helmet, and the motto, "Avito viret honore", signifying the importance of ancestral honour for its flourishing state.

Robert Hamilton came forward cheerfully with outstretched arms. "Sir Archibald sends his apologies but he was called away on estate business urgently and leaves the castle to our devices. You didna' fall over that trip step on the staircase for surprising any who would be assassins in the dark. When they fall over the missing one it wakes up the sleeping guards too."

"I'm not likely to forget it with the tumble from the previous occasion. Anyway they're not likely to force an entrance silently without the drawbridge being lowered. The metal gateway is far too strong."

"One never knows with the occupation of Capelrig House by Dalzell. Our Conventicles in the Castle may reach his ears. Mearns Castle is within a whisper of the wind from Capelrig and rumour is soft as eiderdown. Make yourself at home, gentlemen. So you're the famous Captain Paton whose reputation for strength is not exaggerated I can see from your stature. John Hamilton of Langton here, and this is William Pollock, Laird of Balgray and Balgray Mains Farm in the Mearns, you ken."

Seated at the long trestle table by the log brazier fire, Paton removed his shoes from tired feet to rest them on the rush floor, while Peden closed his eyes for some minutes, and a meal of gruel, roast capon, and small ale was laid out. Then there was a polite restrained silence from their hosts whiles until they satisfied themselves. Sandy looked up as he finished, and observed, "There maun have been minstrels once in that gallery." The quaint structure, precariously projecting above looked out of place to Presbyterian thought.

"Aye, it's a real pity we didnae hae some o' the lilt of lutes, mandolin, and harps, like our medieval brothers. It would brighten up our days, and even our services."

"Such talk is sacrilegious, Hamilton," retorted the serious Pollock."

"If the natural voice was not good enough, God would have said so. The musical playthings were for the Old Testament. Paul and Silas did not have them in prison when singing Psalms, Hymns and spiritual songs."

"Blethers, Pollock!" God does not change from the Old to the New Testament. Psalm 150 gives ample scope for praising God with a full orchestra."

"Gentlemen, gentlemen! Peace be with you. I'm sure God will be pleased whatever you use for praise, even a penny whistle!"

Sandy forced his sleepy eyes wide, despite the thick, smokey atmosphere. The smoke would be allowed to escape only when they were about to depart, as watchful eyes were ready to observe tell-tale signs.

"Now to my tale, which may, if the Lord wills, bring help to the Covenanting cause. No doubt you will have heard of the Knights Templars?" The Laird of Balgray was quick to answer.

"Certainly, Minister. They were a military religious order in the Crusading times whose vow was to maintain free passage for the pilgrims who visited the Holy Land."

"Yes, they started with a vow of poverty and professed to have no means of substance but the alms of the faithful. They took the name of the Poor Soldiers, the Pauperes Commilitones, of the Holy City of Jerusalem and gave needed defence against the infidel Saracens. But like so many in the Papacy, they grew rich in estates, manors, castles and much gold and silver. Their army became so vast and powerful that the King of France determined to suppress it. The Pope, his instrument, summoned the Grand Master, and accused them of heresy, idolatry, unbelief and many foul practises."

"But what has all this got to do with we Covenanters?" Hamilton was signified and Paton himself a little irritated at his all too unusual friend.

"Ah, but did you not know during all your farming in the Mearns that Capelrig Estate was ecclesiastically founded by the Knight's

Templars, and it means Chapel on the ridge? Deaconsbank and Patterton can be seen for their Christian names, and association. So when the Knight's Templars were suppressed, many members were executed and their goods confiscated. The great wealth in coins and jewelry was not going to be surrendered easily. When studying the old parish records of the Kirk o' the Mearns, I came across a medieval document with a fascinating tale." The fire gleamed on his gaunt features and all eyes were fixed on him. "Well, as the story goes, the Templars of Capelrig buried their wealth on the estate within the boundary of three crosses. One is the famous Capelrig Cross which Muir of Caldwell showed when still in possession of Capelrig, as rightfully in Covenanting hands. It is a great broken stone cross of Celtic design, standing nine feet, many centuries old. The Ryat Cross is a small monument on Ryat Farm. The third is not described but whoever finds it will be able to discover a treasure equal to a King's ransom, for the three crosses form a triangle with two sides equal and exactly in the middle of this triangle the treasure is buried. There is a name for such a triangle."

Pollock burst in eagerly, "It is an isosceles triangle. I have read much of Napier of Merchiston who has composed a calculation called logarithms to facilitate the trigonometrical answers on navigational and astronomical work. He worked on multiplication and division by mechanical means."

"Yes," agreed Sandy, "he was a truly remarkable man, Napier, and a man of many parts, including advocating the use of manure and common salt for improving the soil. As a true Calvinist too, he was resolved to keep Catholicism out of Scotland with all his strength, and wrote a treatise on the whole Revelation of St. John. However, he cannot return from the dead for all his ingenuity! So if we are to find this wealth for the Covenanting cause, we must rely on our resources."

"It is indeed a strange tale." Paton spoke for almost the first time. "But is the danger not too great with Dalzell in possession of Capelrig after the wicked Charter of King Charles?"

"He does but rarely live there when he has the luxury of Deane Castle of Kilmarnock and his own Castle of the Binns near Edinburgh. There is usually only a token force. There is also much cover amongst the trees. You have many digging implements at your farms, gentlemen, have you not?" The two Mearns men were sitting intrigued, and now burst out together in assent, but Pollock added, "This will be a Godsend after the burdensome fines imposed on me for Conventicling. Robert Fleming, Curate in the Mearns, is a grasping rogue."

"So let us immediately meet back here tomorrow morning bright at sun up, and bring your mattocks, hoes and spades, and may the Lord bless our efforts for we seek this treasure not for ourselves, to satisfy our greed. It could buy food, clothing for some, and a passage abroad for others. When Hamilton and Pollock had departed, Sandy continued to talk on late with the Captain, who, strangely enough, was not happy with the thought of using gold and silver plates, chalices, and jewelry, gained by nefarious means, to help the Covenanting cause, this despite his freebooting and sacking of a number of German cities.

"But that was fighting as a private mercenary, and I only took for myself what would keep me comfortable. It's difficult to eke out a living at Meadowhead in the best of harvest times, far less a wet, cold summer. Would God be pleased to use such tainted wealth in a sacred cause?"

"The earth is the Lord's and the fullness of it," quoted Sandy. "All wealth is from Him, and if He is not in this, our labour will be in vain."

"How do you know it's not just a fable like Merlin and Arthur for the Britons and Ossian for the Picts?"

"I would not dismiss these as legends, Captain Paton. Around Drumelzier near Broughton in the Borders, the evidence is strong of a Merlin association and every borderer knows that King Arthur sleeps under the Eildons. Thomas the Rhymer prophesied four hundred years ago that there would be a Union of the Crowns of Scotland and England in his words,

'When Tweed and Powsayle meet at Merlin's grave,
Scotland and England shall one monarch have.'

"Vortigern, King of the Britons, summoned Merlin, who astounded him with his powers of insight and prophecy. Legend says that Merlin was conceived by the Devil but was saved for Christ by his mother's confessor, Blayse. Mist has clouded the story, but dinna say Ossian is a fable to a Highlander or he'll spit you on his dirk," Sandy laughed. "In Capelrig the facts are powerful chiels. As we know, the Order of the Templars became strong and wealthy with land on the Continent, as well as Scotland and England. The old document said that a Papal Bull in 1172 empowered the Knights Templars to erect oratories and these houses of prayer, being places of safety, were sometimes used for the concealment of treasures of

Kings and nobility. But what maun be maun be. In the end it will be more than silver or gold will bring us through. It will be a praying people." With that Peden turned away and rolled into his threadbare cloak on the rush floor.

Before the Prophet fell into a slumber, John Paton called over quietly, "Oh, I meant to tell you that I found that good thing in Eaglesham, that you prophesied to Wat Atkinson the Gaberlunzie man. She is cried Janet Miller, and has lovely deep brown eyes. I was lost from the start." Alexander Peden smiled happily to himself, and slipped off into a deep sleep.

The morning broke bright and early on the Lairds of Balgray and Langton returned to the Keep with John Faulds of Newton, John Rankin of Tofts, John Gilmour of Mearns, John Alison of Flinders, and not least James Greig of Castle Mearns estate, all equipped with mattocks, spades and hoes. They were all eager to delve for any wealth to be had. Their everyday life was threatened constantly with ruin from fines and taxes. Balgray especially was always bemoaning the high tax on Fingaltown mill and Balgray Mains Farm on his estate.

Silently, as the morning mist was still rising, they slipped across the fields towards Capelrig where the mansion stood on the Holm Farm of the Muirs of Caldwell, displaced by Charles II's dishonest character. The guard were still asleep and only a wisp of smoke arose from the fire of the night's revelries. Sandy headed for the pasture about 130 yards away just south of Barcapel Wood, and the Capelrig Cross standing there. He laughed when some cattle could be seen rubbing themselves against the stone Celtic Cross, seven to eight feet. The base of the sandstone shaft was about $1\frac{1}{2}$ feet in its length and breadth. There was strange interlaced work on the front, back and sides, in panels. The back had been weathered to a deep furrow where a huge flake had been broken off. There were figures of eight knots, and a clearly defined cruciform figure derived from a six cord plait. On the side were combinations of eight pairs of loops, four on the left and four on the right. An extremely high cross, Capelrig was nevertheless a usual Celtic type, with a ring meeting the head, shaft and arms at their respective intersections. When the community of the Knights Templars established itself in the Mearns district, Capelrig Cross had already been ancient. Its religious character could not be doubted, probably marking an ecclesiastical boundary.

"A remnant of popery!" remarked the Laird of Balgray caustically.

"Rather a beautiful and interesting monument, formed by an art born of much pious zeal," answered Peden. "It is well that, though many such were destroyed during the religious troubles of the Reformation century, this and the Barochan Cross near Houston have remained, memorials to our Celtic Christian forebearers."

"Good for the cows to scratch their midgie itches on," muttered Balgray under his breath, yet sufficiently loud for Captain Paton to chuckle to himself.

"Come, let's on to the other, the Ryat Linn. Where about is it?" asked the Captain.

"About a mile and a half south and west." Sandy led the way to a stone dyke belonging to Holm Farm. A whole line of moie skins hung out across it. One was conspicuously white.

"See, thee is a white mowdie amongst the skinned pelts. Is that no gey unusual?"

"I daur say," replied Paton, "but no matter their colour, these mowdiewarts are a real pest to a farmer. At Meadowhead they played havoc with a field so that I could hardly plough for the hillocks." John's chagrin was comical in the situation.

"Soon they reached the Ryat Cross, similar to the Capelrig, though much smaller, and the Laird of Balgray, who had some rudiments of geometry, having constructed his own mansion at Balgray, drew attention to the fact that he estimated it was the same distance back to a constucuous hill as from one Cross to the other. It could be the solution to their quest and the triangle formed. The situation was dangerous as the garrison would be awake now. Suddenly an answer dawned on his brow. "The place is Capelrig House itself which has been built upon some ancient Knight Templar house of prayer. The treasure is buried beneath Capelrig, aye and our hopes are buried there." The Laird expressed his deep disappointment, reflected in all their faces, and even Sandy Peden who never built on material hopes, felt for them.

"We can never be sure that hill is the site of the third point. Let us search further." In vain they sought through the woodlands and fields, continually avoiding observation from the House. Finally wearied they sat down in a hollow, and Alexander Peden saw now the vanity of their quest.

"What maun be maun be. You are right, Captain John, this treasure is like the spoil that Achan took from the city of Ai and we are not meant to find it. It may have a curse we can well do without. Gold there is and rubies in abundance, but lips that speak knowledge are a rare jewel. I'm sorry, my friends."

"What we never gained we never lost, Rev. Peden. We would have needed the wisdom of Proverbs to find it, certainly if it is somewhere below Capelrig House. Yet the cause of the Covenant will go on without worldly help. Blessed are those that trust in the arm of the Lord." Hamilton of Langton's enthusiasm was unaffected.

Sitting in the woodland hollow, a thought had come to Sandy and a mischievous grin puckered his acquiline features. Melancholy too often was a visitor there, an unwelcome one. "Lads, let's bring a little discomfort to our foes. Apply your mattocks, spades and tools so that this hollow becomes even deeper. Now let me change this document somewhat to entice the inhabitants of Capelrig to investigate further." Drawing the yellowed document from the fold of his cloak, he made some drawings with a charred piece of wood from an old fire once lit by some vagrant mendicants or gypsies in the hollow. Peden carefully surveyed from the rim of the dell the area surrounding, while the rest worked diligently at the soft earth. At last, he called a halt, and holding up the document, said cheerfully, "There is now a new resting place for the Capelrig treasure, and it's right here. If we light a fire here and leave the story and map to be of assistance, they will fly like bees to the pollen and busy themselves. Perhaps we can even watch their vain efforts." Soon a fire had been lit with the abundant dead leaves around to cause a smoke and they retired away from Capelrig as the smoke rose thickly.

"There is a round towered doocot nearby with pigeon holes which will make ideal viewing points as long as the doos don't come home to roost in too great numbers."

Sure enough, beyond the wood was a medieval, circular, stone doocot of solid masonry with eight pigeon holes set high on the fifteen foot wall, with a broad projecting ledge on which the birds could parade. Quickly they made for the Tower, thoroughly enjoying the anticipated hoax. The cotes set into the wall within were tenantless just then, though the soft cooing of the pigeons was distinct in the nearby trees. It was James Greig of Castle Mearns who spoke. "Some pigeons will be back as the sun rises, to parade themselves and enjoy the warmth of the sun on the ledge here, though it will be evening before they all come home to roost in numbers. That's when we like to shoot them at Castle Mearns."

Meanwhile Peden allowed the eight others to view from the holes and report on the scene. They had barely settled, standing precariously on the projection of the cotes to look out, when the red coats of the soldiers gleamed in the trees, making for the tell-tale fire. An animated discussion took place when the officer had examined the document, followed by feverish activity as they began to dig.

Clearly the ruse had worked, and they believed they had disturbed the treasure hunters in their task. All day they continued their labour, until the whole hollow had the appearance of a small quarry.

During it all, Sandy and his friends could only with difficulty contain their laughter. Meanwhile pigeons had begun to alight on the ledge just below the holes made facing south to get the full benefit of the sun. They had to be extremely careful that they did not give alarm to the proud pigeons, as they strutted arrogantly along the ledge beneath their noses, preening their feathers in fantail movements.

"These are the Jacobins, with the feathers on their necks and heads forming the fluffed hood and mane, but I love the Archangels with their beautiful, lustrous coats, and they make fine eating, which is more important. I'm not so keen on the Scandaroons with their long wicked curved beaks, and the Carriers with their developed beaks and eye wattles." James Greig was a wonderful source of information on the common cushat and its exotic cousins. "It's fortunate that the holes face south to get the sun and we can have a clear view of our friends frustrations."

By now the sun had reached its afternoon height and the anger of the exhausted diggers was obvious, and so the final result came when the officer kicked out at a soldier who landed in the hole. He then flung away his spade and marched off, after bellowing at the sullen men who trailed behind him. He had to try to explain their victory to Capelrig's authorities. General Dalzell must not hear of it. His temper was not to be tampered with.

Sandy Peden, John Paton, and their friends, all waited patiently, entertained by an amusement so rare in a persecuted land. The pigeons were beginning to come home to roost, and the flutter and soft sounds lulled them all to sleep, all except Sandy, who always sought times of prayer to His God. At last evening had fallen and safety secure, as they crept out from the old Doocot, watched by curious bird eyes, squinting and cooing their disapproval. The spades and tools were still there and taken back to the farmlands and the purposes for which they were designed. Sandy declined hospitality at Castle Mearns and also said farewell for the time being to Captain John, whose destination was Mid-Floak Farm out by the Black Loch where he had friends. Sandy did not reveal where his next lodgings would be, and everyone knew better than to ask. They knew that the path of Peden the Prophet was a solitary one, and no one else dare nor could tread it with him.

8
Betrayed

Sandy had been back to the scattered people of New Luce parish to encourage the congregation there who were suffering from depression at the continual persecution. There was a fine of twenty shillings Scots for every Sunday missing. But you cannot put soup in a basket and many could not pay, resulting in their pewter utensils being taken, or a pair of brogues, or velveteen jacket that a soldier hankered after. The spirit of hopelessness descended upon them and Sandy felt the great strain of lifting it. Some were for returning to the Kirk if a Curate were sent, but strangely, in accordance with his prophetic warning, not one false preacher ever came. Once one such had set out from Edinburgh and even reached Dumfries but on the last stage to New Luce his horse had stumbled unaccountably and the poor man broken his neck on what was very flat open road. A recollection of Peden's words caused a deep conviction and even the weaker brethren were confirmed. Sandy defied the world to steal one lamb out of his flock unmissed.

After a short stay he headed over the hills by the way which was trodden by few, ten hard miles as the corbie flew, straight to Colmonell in southern Ayrshire and the Water of Tigg where the stone known now as Peden's Pulpit stood in a nook of the Tigg as it meandered lazily. It was unnatural in its size and must have been the residual load carried down by some glacier in bygone aeons. But it was ideal for many occasions when Sandy had exhorted the faithful from its flat top as the waters swirled around and he was reminded of Jesus on the boat cast off into Galilee's Lake. The pulpit was hidden from immediate observation from afar unless at Glenover Farm above but there they were for the Cause. That very farm was his home for the night after the hillwalk and the next day the folk were to foregather after the word had been passed around. The morning saw him sauntering through the fields with the farmer and his boy labourer. The horses grazed there were of quality and though he had not ridden often since his days of refuge he turned to his host with a quaint smile.

"My Master is the rider and I am the horse. I never love to ride, but when I find the spurs. It is honourable to be a footman in Christ's company and run at Christ's foot from morning to evening."

"Aye, Aye, Master Peden." replied that worthy, a rather dour individual with a reputation for being apt witted, gleg as the country folk would say. "There are o'er monie horses that would go the wrang way if the spurs werenae used. One needs the guidance. Life is fu' o' unexpected events around Colmonell and Ballantrae"

His dour companion continued with a lighter voice. "Some Curates are a bit more understanding than most. The Minister of Kirkmichael announced last month that if those who objected to his ministrations were to enter by the west door and pass through the Kirk on a Sunday morning, he would consider that an attendance! I think if I sent my shadow, that would be sufficient. It's a bit of a farce really but, I daursay, kindly o' him. You might say he has a passing congregation though some are persuaded to attend by his gentility. It's a pity he believes in the State telling us how we should worship Almighty God, and all this Stewart Divine right stuff. There's no accounting for some folks' light."

With his words barely uttered, the farmboy wrenched at his smock, gasping out that a squadron of soldiers had mounted the hill behind and obviously sighted them.

"Whit dae we do? They're looking for you, I ween." The farmer tried hard to keep his voice steady and quell the fear flooding his stomach.

"Wisdom lights up a man's face. Boldness is the best policy and remember that they may not know my looks. This mask and wig have been my salvation often!" With a friendly grin he waved to the officer as the squadron slithered down the braeface. That young individual looked as if he was fresh to his post and assumed a stern countenance.

"Show us the ford across this river, my man. What call you this water? We are hard on the trail of a fellow Peden, pretending to be a proper minister to these outed hillfolk, and that without right ordination. Have you seen him? We have followed hard from New

Luce, so do not lie on your life."

Peden disarmingly replied, "I have surely heard of this man. They say he's a legend round here. But honestly I have not seen his face round here. However I ken the ford over this Water of Tigg. You maun cross down here gin you want to reach Ballantrae. I heard a rumour he was for Ballantrae." The right degree of courtesy and subservience was intended to impress the young dragoon with a sense of his own importance.

The waters of heavy rains had swollen the Tigg in spate and one by one the horsemen crossed up to their beasts girths. The captain turned on the other bank and waved back to Sandy his thanks. When they disappeared the Laird of Glenover came to the ford with astonishment in his manner. "Why did you go with them? You might have sent the lad."

"No, no, it was more safe for me for they might have discovered us by asking questions of the lad. For myself, I knew they would be like Egyptian dogs. They would not move a tongue against me, for my hour of falling into their hands and day of trial is not yet come. That abides me. Nor have I told him a speel since never have I regarded my own features since I arrived and I also intend to spend the night at Knockdow Farm on the Ballantrae road. Now, to business, since the dangers passed. Go gather the countryfolk and we shall rendezvous at the Pulpit"

Half an hour later the valley of the Tigg was alive with hurrying figures, sprouting from the emptiness. Sandy smiled affectionately and planted his buckled brogues firmly on the lichen covered rock. It would not do for the preacher to unbalance in the middle of his sermon! Let the rousing Twenty Third Psalm to the Covenanters tune be sung out. Soon the environs of Colmonell village were ringing to the forceful cadences. Somehow the words bore home to him that he would soon be in the presence of his foes. But shrugging off the fear with the confidence that the Lord would not desert him now after all his narrow escapes, he warmed to his message. The night before he had been preparing in the prophet Zechariah the vision of the ancient Israelite that one day Zion would be restored when old men and women would sit in the street, each leaning upon a stick because of their great age, and the ways would be full of boys and girls.

Young people would be free to come and go according to their conscience. His memory travelled back to when three hundred ministers had given up everything for their conscience's sake. Three hundred manse doors closed for the last time behind the manse families who had been happy there. Little people, not understanding, clutched their battered beloved dolls and animal toys carved from driftwood, and trailed after burdened parents, whose hearts were also sore burdened. "Pray you that your flight be not in winter" Jesus once said to his disciples. It was a bitter winter in 1662 when the outed ministers were cast out homeless. The Scots Mile Act came next forbidding any Minister who did not accept Episcopacy and appointment by patrons and bishops, to come within twenty miles of his own parish. Then came the dreaded Conventicle Act of 1670 by which Ministers must not preach or pray except within their own families. To hold a Conventicle on a hillside meant death and £30 was the price on the head of a Conventicle preacher. But what was still a wonder to himself, three years had passed since the conventicle Act and his preaching had been continuous, despite the fact that word had reached him that a reward of £600 was being dangled ever temptingly for his capture.

His mind returned to the sermon and he reminded his people that just as God promised Zechariah that Jerusalem would be a city of truth so Scotland would be a land of truth. "No longer will Sandy Peden have to wear this ugly and grotesque mask, and dank wig. He will be able to look upon his people face to face. It's enough to flecht the bairnies, I know. But again my own features may do worse." A ripple of laughter ran through the congregation, seated happily on the rivers banks, some in postures of repose with children nestling into their shoulders, other muzzling dogs and moorland garron ponies, and a few with muskets still shouldered in watchfulness.

He felt an embarrassment as he stared out from behind the anonymity of the clinging leather mask, imagining how his eyes must appear as sightless dark holes to these dear folk who loved him so. But life itself demanded it. As his view ranged over the grassy banks it came to rest on a lovely face and a deep feeling of hollow longing almost overwhelmed him, This beautiful country girl had corn coloured hair escaping from her spotless white mutch and a pinkness of face as of a rose in full summer bloom. There was a hint of a light brown freckle which to Sandy was always a healthy enhancement. The blue twinkle of her eye was a godly light, full of the joy of life and the Lord. Nostalgia flooded in and the courtroom of Tarbolton all seventeen years ago appeared in total outline. Yes, the scar was still there and he wondered about how life had turned out for the half gypsy Margaret and her poor pawn Elder Stevenson. He himself had never had a wife and children but there had been no vow of celibacy and he had always maintained his faith in his fellow creatures. This young woman was not aware of course that his attention was on her and so he was at an advantage. He could catch her expression and personality without any character mask, no less real than his. If he was to have been married this was the girl open and free like the hill country, with a welcome hearth and a well set table. But he felt sadly it was not to be as a life of uncertainty and almost continuous pursuit afforded no opportunity of domestic bliss. No woman's arms were to be his to comfort and be comforted by.

As he turned his face away, the tear starting but hidden thankfully he had his attention rivetted as by the fascination of an evil thing. This was a red topped face situated near the girl's. How different was the impression portrayed, though not outwardly. This man had a bland countenance of a very white skin surmounted by bushy red eyebrows and thick locks of the same colour. His expression was so expressionless as if to convey innocence but Sandy sensed an evil presence and hostility. Here was danger. Your enemies shall be those of your own house. The man, dressed respectably like a shopkeeper, seemed intent on his every word as if for very life. Sandy dragged his eyes away and finished the message on a note of triumph. Teh city of God would be restored and peace brought to troubled Scotland again. Descending from the rock he enquired from the farmer of Glenover about the red headed man who he found was indeed an elder in Colmonell background. Through the corner of the mask's eye flaps, he noticed the man had worked his way between the departing crowd nearer to Sandy and the elders but sadly the delighted lass was gracefully tripping over the fields to Colmonell village with her family.

"Major Ferguson, Laird of Knockdow, will not take no for an answer, Rev. Peden." The Glenover farmer was saying, "and wished the privilege of affording you his hospitality. Its just along the road by the Castle of the Kennedys of Cassilis and through the wood. I'll send the boy with you."

"No need, my friend. I know the house and I wish no company." His brethren were waving from the heights of the skylines in all directions and with love he returned the time honoured mode of comradeship, noting with satisfaction that the flaxen haired girl and her farming family were the last to swing their arms like comforting windmills. As he wandered along the track dappled in the spring sunshine a speckled mavis hopped out from the grass with a fresh gleaming worm it had just unearthed, but with its violent jerk it had swung the worm onto its back. For a moment it was nonplussed and then, disturbed by Sandy's presence, it flew off. The worm fell off its back and was promptly gobbled by a merlin which was careless of humans. He smiled gently at nature's way. Further along he came on a flutter of grey, green and blue, a wounded woodpigeon which was wandering among the birch trees. His heart was touched. The woodcrest fluttered in its helplessness and each staring eye registered fright. Her loose feathers came off in his caressing hand. Peden identified with its fears as if a presentiment was here. God was warning him also that his wings might be clipped. But laying the pigeon in a bosky hollow, he continued by the woodland path and the hoarse cough and chuckle of a startled pheasant cheered him up as it whirred across his tracks. Turning to the left he sighted Knockdow standing prominent on the hill, two largely built houses of roughcast stone. The Laird Hugh Ferguson was an old friend who had lodged him frequently not only when on his way to that other bloody land of Ireland, but right back in the time of his New Luce ministry, when all the world beckoned like a beautiful blue horizon even though his little country parish would never be numbered among the world's great sights. Hugh Ferguson would play his flageolet quaintly and soothingly to Sandy who had walked the ten miles from New Luce to have his mind challenged and spirit relaxed. Seated round the broad hearth before blazing peats' thick rushes on the cold floor, Hugh and he would sit back, accompanied by a cutty pipe, to discuss the eternal verities of predestination, justification and the sovereignty and limitations of God whose perfect Heaven was not this vale of suffering. Sandy groaned when the agony of the many who had died for the Covenant squeezed his heart till the blood cried.

Even as he trode the hill, if he had glanced back, Peden would not have failed to see a dark movement through the trees and a flash of red in the direction of Ballantrae. But Hugh's welcome for Sandy was so all embracing that all fears were forgotten for a time. A bearlike hug prefaced a vastly satisfying meal of peasebrose soup, soft baked bread made by his elderly housekeeper, succulent pork and rich venison steaks in thick gravy, rounded off by buttered bannocks and and a sweet home brewed ale, and the inevitable clay pipe of baccy from the Plantations. Sandy sometimes wondered if any of what he smoked was harvested by the sweat of Covenanting slaves but the Laird of Knockdow assured him that he traded with an honest merchant carrying for a humanitarian plantation who employed African slaves who were not troubled by sweating in the Virginian sun and were well fed and housed. Yet something still nagged at his mind.

"An instinct tells me it will be a dear night's quarters for us both, Hughie."

"Och, dinna blether, man, and relax! Only your own people know you are here and the soldiery are awa to Ballantrae, sent by yourself."

"Aye, my ain folk, but I smelt the taint of evil around and had an unco feeling about a red headed man there at the preaching."

The Laird paled and drew up sharply in his armchair carved from a great oak on the estate. "I knew that man was nae good! I hae seen his light on late at night in the back of the wee shop he keeps, and gathering some queer rare weeds down in the marshy areas. There's something unhealthy about him. But his outward credentials are fine coming to us about six months ago from the north somewhere, the islands I think, which is rather strange as they are not generally Covenanting country. Yet he is a fair turn at cooking exotic dishes, these herbal mixtures. So the eldership accepted him on his outward appearance and observance of religion as one of themselves. But I always thought there was an unnatural lack of feeling about his faith."

Shrugging his shoulders he grasped the flageolet and announced with pride "Suit this to your mood and life style, Sandy, for I've composed it for you. Its called 'The Cry of the Curlew.' " A haunting melody was emitted from the flute and transported Peden to the high moorlands again. Suddenly there was a whinny close by and Sandy startled to his feet with one hand feeling for the little poinard and the other his heavy walking stick. But with a crash the door was thrown back and by the dim light of the oil lamp red coats gleamed with drawn steel as they filled the room. There was no turning to escape, as there was none.

"You made a laughing stock of me once but not again." The young Captain he had duped at the Tigg strode forward, strident and proud. But a larger figure pushed him aside and bade silence.

"I am Major Cockburn, commander of the Dumfries garrison, and you are both arrested in His Majesty's name, you, Mr. Peden for being a continuous rebel to the State and the Church and flouting His Majesty's Indulgence to all outed Presbyterian Ministers, and you Ferguson, Laird of Knockdow, for harbouring and conversing with this rebel for which there is a thousand merks fine."

"Who are you to impose your unlawful authority on the free people of Scotland? Who gave you the right even to tresspass on my land?" The Laird of Knockdow was fairly spitting with anger. Many of the landowners were totally antagonised by the dragoons riding roughshod over everyone. "Where's your identification of my guest and what are his wrongs? Peden is merely a name to you, I trow."

"My authority is the only authority, Laird, the law of force, and I have it on good authority that he preached just this day at Colmonell wearing this heathen mask I've heard tell of, and which I jalous is under your doublet. Our informer is of unimpeachable character."

Peden spoke quietly, "It is a character that will send your red headed man to Hell, Major. As that man of God, the blessed Donald Cargill says, be not high minded but fear, while in the body. Even a Christian might go through nineteen trials and honestly carry through them, and fall in the twentieth." Turning to Ferguson he spoke with a laugh, "I told you it would be a dear night's quarters to us both but I don't complain of Christ. I let my expression of Christ be suitable to my experience of him."

"Cease your religious pratings, hill preacher. You've preached your last. I'm happy to prove you're no ghost." Cockburn suddenly roughly seized Peden's long locks and cruelly pulled him from the chair where Sandy had calmly remained. Four soldiers were needed to bind the arms of each of the two powerful men with leather horse thongs. "You will be conveyed prisoner backward on horseback to Dumfries and then Edinburgh where the Privy Council waits to give you a fair trial and me a handy £50 sterling reward, not to forget my good troopers." The mercenary was in his laugh as well as his demeanour, and they were hauled to Dumfries that very night. At last it seemed the will o' the wisp Covenanter had been trapped, that his days were numbered, and the gallows would be his share.

9
Prisoner Of The Bass

As Peden sat in the scuppers of the ferry boat pulling out from the shores of North Berwick, the ropes cutting into his skin frozen blue with the whipping wind and bitter salt spray that soaked his face and smarted his lips did not obliterate the memory of the courtroom in the Edinburgh Tolbooth and the sentence of the Town Council. It was etched with a cruel clarity. "The following has been passed by the Scottish Privy Council on this day of 25th June in the year of grace, 1673. His Majesty's Privy Council do recommend to the Lord's Register and Advocate, or any of them, to call for and examine Mr. Alexander Peden, prisoner in the Tolbooth, for being in the rebellion in the year of 1666, and who is to be transported, by five or six of the guard, from the Tolbooth of Edinburgh to the Isle of Bass and to be delivered there to the Governor, who is hereby ordered to keep him fast prisoner until further order."

He stared fixedly at the grey mass ahead as the waves thundered and reverberated round the rocky prison. On the south side he could see the Governor's house and above it the gaol and quarters for the garrison.

There was but one place to land for every other front was too high and too steep. Old Fraser of Brea had written about his island Patmos. Though he had never met Fraser, Sandy knew all and every piece of news that passed within the Covenanting community. He felt he knew Fraser already. His rheumatism had acted up in the cold rocky Bass but no persecution could break his strong heart. In his letter to his friends in the north east he had said that he read his Bible, encouraged others, and prayed with them as much as the Governor allowed and even studied Hebrew, Greek, and some smattering of Oriental languages. Sandy's dark eyes crinkled up as he thought that this man of the cloth could hardly have done more than if he had been at home in his northern manse.

The boat lurched as a giant North Sea wave broke over the lightweight ferry. Sandy yearned for the west and the quiet waters of Galloway and the Solway Firth with its silver sands. This North Sea was so cold as if it came straight from the Arctic in a unabated deluge with no alleviating warmth. Nostalgia misted his brain as he glanced over the side and twisted his neck to see the ruins of Black Agnes' Castle by Dunbar in the grey distance (Black Agnes was Agnes Randolphe, daughter of Sir Thomas Randolphe, Earl of Moray, and one of Robert the Bruce's chief lieutenants. She had married into the Dunbars. In 1337, Agnes heroically defended Dunbar Castle for months against the English forces under Salisbury) and the more full prospect of Tantallon where smuggling was he knew a way of life around the Castle's shadowy environs. Though he never participated he sympathised with any harmless embarrassments of the Government and of her cruel servants. A searing pain brought it home to him as the bearded half drunken ferry man lashed a knotted rope across Peden's shoulders.

"That's for you, you Whiggish dog! Just to stop you day dreaming. There'll be plenty of chance for day dreaming where you're going!" He laughed boorishly and made to draw it again but a more kindly disposed dragoon seized his wrist with a sharp command to desist. With a muttered curse he applied himself to the tiller as the boat keeled over in the gusting wind that had arisen. "Damned wind! She's going to bring us late into the Bass. The tide is ebbing and we keep veering away nae matter how I turn! You maun climb the stairs".

"Keep her right, you scurvy dog, or you'll see the whip end of that rope yourself." The troopers' Captain was angry with exasperation, knowing the added trouble of ascending the slippery rock steps without a full sea when one landed on the Bass. The only landing place on its three quarter of a mile circumference, if the tide is at ebb, then they would have to climb the artificial steps on hands and knees. Each step was so far above the other that often one had to receive help from someone above, and meant increased annoyance to the Governor, irascible at the best of times.

As the boat continued to drift, bobbing like a plaything at the mercy of the elements, and the sailor savagely wrenched at the sails to match the wind, a mad thing, Sandy saw clearly now the great white birds as they soared in their hundreds round the cliff and plummeted in exciting dives to the sea. His spirit was enraptured by their grace.

"They're cried solan geese but they're gannets for a' that." It was the kindly dragoon who had noticed his absorption.

"Aye, I kent there was a collection of God's feathered creatures here, but no' their names. Yet one thing is true. They're more in command of their flying than our friend the sailor is of this cockleshell. I think we'll end up in France or perhaps the Lord will deliver me to my friends in Holland. They are a real succour to the Covenanters in Rotterdam and Groningen, my guid soldier laddie."

The young dragoon smiled sadly, "We'll mak' the shore all right, Mr Peden. Sadly for you, your reverence, for its a gey queer place. But you're right about the solans. I have observed them for long on my lonely guard vigil and they are a joy to behold as they dive with a magnificence into the breakers; their long pointed wings, so white, and straight sharp beaks make fishing easy. All their four toes are webbed and so they grip the steep cliffs; they breed in large colonies and their nest may be a mere hollow or a mass of seaweed and mud. A single chalk white egg is laid and the chick fed when its mother brings up its food from its stomach. The chick is then abandoned."

"Does it then not love its young?" asked Sandy in a quizzical astonishment.

The young soldier smiled. "Not at all, Mr. Peden. Starvation at last forces it to leave the nest and take to the sea. Nature knows what it is about. Here they remain for three years, longer I hope than your stay." He had lowered his voice, and then he smiled wryly. "Sometimes the young gannets don't last that long either. They are killed for food and oil and often have I seen that look in their great staring blue eyes as if they were human."

Before Sandy could answer, the Bass had loomed up and they were watching the waves lapping as they ebbed from the shingle and the roughly cut steps which stretched up the slope to the prison and garrison quarters. The boorish ferryman leapt into the shallows and snarled that they disembark quickly because these tides couldn't be trusted. The dragoons, four in number, crunched ashore with the prisoner. Sandy's much travelled shoon were sodden. The soldier, whom he had spoken with, scrambled ahead, clearly experienced in the holds in the rock face. For all that, even he had to climb on hands and knees up the artificial steps, each so distant from its neighbour. The benefit was that now and then he might give help to some one below. So they worked their way up to the prison house. The governor did not even give him the privilege of a welcome, Peden thought grimly.

A thumping push from the dragoon captain sent him sprawling through the narrow gate and along the flagged corridor to a tiny cell. Here the Captain laughed grimly, as he ordered the vacant faced turnkey, who had met them, to open the heavy wooden door, forbidding with its iron hinges, a massive lock and many studs. "We'll be good to you and grant you the company of your other traitor preacher so that he can delight you with tales of the wonderful life here!" The clang of the hinges was as hollow as his laugh.

Sandy was thrust into a dark and diminutive cell in which the damp and cold hit him immediately. Light and air were minimal and that only through one small window that was placed at a height above the floor almost beyond reach. All this was grasped in a moment. But then he was aware of a shuffling figure in the corner who nevertheless came towards Peden with an obvious eagerness for all his pain. A small dark man with ragged beard and flowing locks, his swarthy looks were almost european. Despite the threadbare greatcoat which he huddled to himself as if in danger of being robbed, there was a dignity about this man.

"It is my pleasure to meet you, Mr. Peden, or is it Peathine? I've heard so much about you. I winna ca' you Reverend as I am a Minister of the Kirk. My name is James Fraser of Brea."

So this was the famous hill preacher from the land of the Frasers of Lovat. His small frame and saturnine features bespoke of a Celtic race existent in Alba long before the Caledonia of the Romans or the Kingdom of the Scots. In his minds eye Peden saw Fraser of Brea as a Pictish chief or even a courtier welcoming St. Columba to the throneroom of King Brude in far north Inverness.

"Either will do, Mr. Fraser. It matters not. In Heaven we shall have a new name, already written on a white stone. Anyways with my heathen like mask and black wig, I could hae been the De'il in disguise for a' my friends knew. If I wanted an attire to scare off friends and foes alike, I couldnae hae chosen better. I appear like one of the black bogles or Brownies that you scare the bairnies wi' stories of at night. But it aye comes in handy when the country folks lay out provender at night in the fields for the 'Broonie' as they say. In return for this I harvest their grain and such like. But also one had to be careful of informers, my friend, the chance o' sillar has always been present to tempt those wi' an Achilles heel."

The little dark man responded, "Aye, you're right. I clearly remember when that accursed Grierson was rampaging from his den of Lag like a voracious lion, to rout out God's people round Closeburn and Minnihive, we did find we had employed an informer, Watson by name, to find out the cave of refuge of a Minister Rev. Lawson, close to Minnihive. Lag himself was not above being disguised to inveigle himself into the secret counsels of the Covenanters. But the Lord gave us knowledge of Watson and before Lag arrived, we had spirited Lawson away and Watson the informer who had gone before to reconnoitre the cave, was dinged unconscious by our lads for his treachery and left in the cave. So it turned out terrible for him, as that Grierson of Lag built a fire round the entrance and did by error suffocate by a horrible death his own tool."

"They who sow to the wind shall reap a whirlwind. Be sure our sins will find us out. The Lord's eyes are upon his own. Nae doot but that the Lord has created a few queer buddies but also nae doot they have created their own bed and earned their own title. There was that traitor and turncoat Davie Mason, a noisy religious pretender. One day he came when I was preaching at Girvan, pushing forward and trampling over the people to get near. So I shouted, 'Here comes the Devils rattle-bag: We don't want him here.' In due season David Mason became, as I expected, an informer, and the name of the Devil's rattle-bag stuck to him like a burr. Even his family got affected. Well he deserves it too. But what brings you away down from the Black Isle of the Northeast and the Fraser of Lovat country to suffer with those faithful to the Covenant? I've heard that Aberdeen has always been inclined to bishops and their dictatorial ways."

"I'm a friend of the Independents and of the Quakers also. Therefore I am wholly pacifist. I have been against the rising tide of rebellion brought on by the long and bitter persecution. So I was an easy target for the dragoon forces after being ordained by a 'Field Presbytery' when thirty three years, and my preaching, which some called direct, made me popular but also someone to receive Archbishop Sharpe's special treatment. Some hotheads were for taking the sword and redeeming themselves from the hands of the oppressors but I opposed that rising in arms all I could. I exhorted them to patience and to courageously use the sword of the Spirit."

"Blessed are the peacemakers for they shall be called the children of God. I believe in the Lord's judgement on Graham of Claverhouse, 'Bloody Clavers', Sir Robert Grierson of Lag, Captains Douglas and Winram, the Laird of Lee, not to forget Johnston of Westerhall, but not in armed risings. Though I am imprisoned here for taking part in the rising in sixty six, yet I did not go to Rullion Green and did know that death and destruction

The Isle of Bass where Peden was imprisoned in 1673.

awaited them. At no time have I supported fighting the Lord's battles with sword and gun. My short rapier in its leather sheath is my only bit sword and that never did meikle mischief. But I hope my friends have stowed it away safely somewhere for when I get out of this unco hell's midden. My wee walking stick has a whistle on its end by which I have imitated the peewit cry and warned my fellow Covenanters. And without contradiction, be sure Mr. Fraser, we are going to be freed from this rocky Bass, as free as these geese that wheel and cry round its desolate cliffs. Its an unco place, this!"

"My heart's with ye. The way of peace is the hard way but the way of God. Amongst our numbers there are those who would take the path of violence to obtain freedom, amongst them, the Rev. Donald Cargill, that fiery impetuous James McMichael, Balfour of Kinloch, cried Burleigh, and a Richard Cameron, straining at the lease, exiled over there in Rotterdam. It comes to my ears that a young field preacher, James Renwick by name, is similarly a militant. But tell me, how were ye taken, whom I know the enemies of the Covenant thocht more a will o' the wisp than a man?"

"Well, James, it was only last June at Knockdow in the parish of Colmonell by Girvan that this genie was put in his bottle. I had been holding a conventicle near by on the river Tig. A large flat topped rock in a fold of the riverbank affords an ideal preaching and praying spot. Afterwards Hugh Ferguson invited me for some sustenance to his house and constrained me to remain overnight though the Lord spoke to me, giving a premonition of trouble. I had already written to a friend when first arriving in May friend and told him that I had come to the place in safety but had no hopes of remaining long before the arch enemy were upon me. I was still in good heart. But I cannot think but that even though I referred to the friends of the Covenant in the letter by their code numbers of 331 and 334, also D. and L. as our enemies, yet it may have been through the missive that they found a clue to my whereabouts, if it fell into the wrong hands. But I suspect otherwise. I certainly did warn Hugh Ferguson that it would be a dear night's quarters to us both. So it proved. Hugh, whose guest I was, is only a bonnet laird, nae mair than a farmer, but the Council fined him a thousand merks for reset and harbour of me. Puir man, he was brought to the Edinburgh Tolbooth like me, but on payment of his fine, was set at liberty I'm glad to say. The blood money was divided among my captors, fifty pounds sterling to Major Cockburn who was to divide further twenty five pounds between the soldiers who apprehended me."

Brea's countenance was even darker with anger, "They should have given it to the Judas who betrayed your sanctuary! God knows there are enough of them! Sir John Maxwell of Pollok was held at Haggs Castle for harbouring some hunted bodies and having Conventicles in the Castle, naething more than some prayer, psalm singing and a bit preaching from the Book. It could not be construed of a treasonable nature unless it be to worship their God, and King Charles puts himself above the Almighty. The Privy Council fined Sir John Maxwell £8000 sterling or sixteen months in the Tolbooth. Anything is better than that hellhole. But it was a price designed to ruin him and was a King's ransom. He's been in and out of the prison more times than a cuckoo's chick's mouth opens at feeding time. Lady Maxwell is trying desperately to raise the money."

"It wid be better if they were to make it guid Scots pounds and then we could divide it by twelve!"

"No such fortune. John Hamilton of Silvertonhill who is the tenant of the Provan Hall in the Prebentary of Barlanark near Glasgow, holds Conventicles for the faithful in the Provan. Before they took me to this Rock, he did tell me his fears that the Secret Council were so incensed against the town of Glasgow for suffering these meetings that they made the Glasgow Town Council eject Hamilton from the Provan Hall with all his goods and plenishings. There is a local bully boy there who was only too ready to vent his spleen on John Hamilton whom he hated, a John Barnes, Baillie of the Provand. As you know, there are plenty of ruffians in Glasgow without any allegiance or religion but their own avarice and interests, whom he could hire for a pittance if he could gain the necessary warrant for the keys to the Hall."

"We're no the only ones wi' a cross to bear, Fraser, right enough. We're lucky we even have the chance to converse together."

"Fortunate we are to be allowed this. Normally we are not allowed to converse, diet and even worship together, except on few occasions when we are conducted out by twos once in the day. I envy these geese their freedom but we are close shut up day and night to hear only the sighs and groans of our fellow prisoners."

"I heard from a young dragoon coming over that they are eatin' these young solans."

"Dainty eating indeed, as much as two shillings a piece, paid by the epicures, I'm thinking. One guard was telling me that even the Curate of North Berwick is paid partly for his stipend in solan geese! These false preachers are like the birds droppings that paint the great crags seeming as a morning frost. They are a blemish and cold and lifeless. God knows too these Curates are gluttons whose God is their belly."

A rattle is heard without and a guard thrusts his flintlock in through the bars. "Wheesht, you canting rebels! You get enough chance of whining and preaching when outside. Any more and you'll get reported to the Governor, and then you'll be buzzard bait, forsooth! Now here's the Governor's dochters, so haud yer tongues." He withdrew and continued his measured tread on the pavement without. Peden silently prayed for him, for he knew many of these soldiers were not wholly willing servants of the State and served their masters because they knew no other.

Just then a young girl of about fourteen years, suddenly and naturally unexpectedly, came skipping up with loud and mocking laughter. Her very movements spoke of a spoilt upbringing and the resultant selfwill of a rich man's only daughter.

"Let's hear you prophesy, Mr. Prophet Peden! I might even coax my father to let you out for a wee bit whiles if you do some prophesying for me. My father's the Governor, you know? My father tells me that you are as wild as a peat hag, fearsome to look at, and fearsome to hear, and your voice dinnless in folk's lugs. I don't think you look so fearsome, Mr. Prophet Man."

James Fraser of Brea, angry at this disrespect spoke out, "Silence, girl! in the presence of your elders and show respect as befits your age!"

"I think you're just two funny old men and you're in such a dirty state that your God will be sore displeased. This is the Sabbath morn. You'll have to have a wash before you say your prayers, Mr. Peden. And get your hair cut too." She turned skipping over her rope towards the nearby soldier and they both laughed.

There was a moment's silence as if in dread anticipation and Peden spoke gravely with no hint of anger, his dark eyes fixed on the girl. "Poor thing, poor thing! I hear you skirl and laugh but the Lord has a deid shot prepared for you, and at that surprising judgement ye shall skirl by the ae time! Poor thing, you mock and laugh at the worship of God but your sudden judgement shall stay your laughing, and you shall not escape it. A sad ending to a young life it is. There might still be a place for repenting, pray God."

A frozen stillness had fallen as the girl cringed, pale with fear for a moment, and recovering, she mocked again, "You dirty old prophet man', but her voice trilled and trembled and she hastily retreated no longer skipping but the rope gathered up.

"Kennel up, there, kennel up, you dogs of the Covenant. Or I'll see ye shipped like the curs ye are."

"Guard your tongue, my mannie. Ye never ken when fortune micht turn her fickle mind and reveal her other side wi' the tables reversed. Then whaur would ye be? Cast withoot an anchor in the storm that will sweep Scotland, and there will be nowhere to turn." The prophetic fire in Peden was deeply roused now. His normally kindly eye blazed.

The guard, shocked, answered with relief, "Here's some comrades of mine come to change the guard. Glad am I that I can get away from your mad prophesyings, with your Bible texting, and that gleam in your eye." The latter he spoke under his breath. "I have noticed the uncanny way you have of stopping your speech in full flow, casting your ear and een to the skies as if your God has something to say to you specially, you crazy fool. Hey, Tam, come and take charge of these Covenanting hypocrites!"

The newcomer had the look of a man whose emotions were straightforward and uncomplicated. Tam Dale was a local Lothians man and not too happy in his task. He much preferred farming back at his father's steading in East Withensgate by East Linton village. But when Tam Dalzell of Binns called for recruits for the Scots Grey Dragoons, then one did not dare deny him. Tam spoke out with a bravado not felt, "The Devil take him, that Peden. The Governor says he's as wild as a peat hag with a voice like a solans that dinnless in folks lugs." It seemed he was repeating the girl's words and heading for the same judgement.

Peden overhearing him, addressed the erstwhile dragoon, "Fy, fy, the poor fool. Ye know not what you're saying but ye'll repent that 'Deil hae ye, an' I see the deil at your oxter. I may have a voice like a solans but it is the voice of judgement, Tam Dale."

"Tis the voice of judgement! How does he ken my name?"

"The Lord reveals the secret things. As the Psalmist says 'The secret of the Lord is with them that fear Him; and He will show them His Covenant.' The Proverbs of Solomon tell us that the froward is an abomination to the Lord; but his secret is with the righteous."

"Och, someone told you. old man. Your threats are no gonna scare a soldier of the King. You're just an antiquated dreamer"

"Remember, Tam Dale, that God's servant, Daniel, had the secret of the night vision revealed to him concerning King Nebuchadnezzar that was denied to all the wise men of the East. The God of Heaven shows the deep and secret things. Beware!"

In a dead panic Tam Dale stood transfixed, and then rushed off to his companions of the guard who were still mocking. But Tam's spirit was affected and he cried out in a strangled voice, "Bring me Mr. Peden, for the Devil is coming to take me away immediately."

"We'll take you away, you fool. You'll find the Devil preferable to the Governor if you keep this up."

When the young former farmer continued to writhe as if torn by internal torture so that he clawed at the stonework of the prison walls, the sergeant had Peden brought from the cell. "You wizard, undo this sorcery from my fine trooper or your magic will be ended forever."

Sandy answered nothing but knelt over Tam Dale, who was now rolling about on the flagstones and whispered inaudibly in his ear. His great hands rested gently on Tam's temples. The paroxysms ceased slowly to be replaced by a vacant look. Peden told the officer to let him see Tam again the next morning. Just then a despairing scream was heard in the gusting wind and shortly a dragoon guard ran needlessly across the herb garden to gasp, "The Governors dochter has gone and fallen fae the cliff edge. A blast of wind swept her off into the sea. She is lost for I spied her sink like a wheen weight. Her skirts have been the end of her. The Captain maun tell the Governor. His anger and grief will be mixed with his cups and be something terrible."

The unco thing was that the Governor of the Bass was so subdued in his gloom that he scarce seemed to comprehend the event and distractedly permitted Sandy to see the young soldier on the morn. He spoke words of comfort to the mute man who had not spoken since the previous happenings. Suddenly his empty face lit up. Staring at the Covenanter, he said meekly, "I pray in Christ's great Name, that you forgive me all the wrong I have done you and the people of God. I cannot for the life of me explain the sorrow and happiness I feel at the one time."

"Now you are well again, take up your arms, Tam Dale," said Peden quietly, knowing the response.

"Never shall I lift arms against Jesus Christ, His cause, and people. I have done that too long."

Dale, shackled between the guard with whom he was due on duty, was marched to the Governor. The latter, deep in his cups now, was torn between his superstitious awe of Peden and an apoplectic drunkenness. "You will be shot by ten o' clock the morn's morn, an you don't relinquish this madness and do your duty. This wild wizard has addled your brain, Dale. I'm considering an extra ration of spirits for the garrison. The climate on this rock is gey cold." The

Captain attending looked aside to conceal his grue. They were obliged to drink the twopenny ale of the Governor's brewing, and thought it scarcely worth a halfpenny the pint.

"Though you tear me in pieces, I shall never lift arms in that way," answered the young man confidently and repeated himself again twice as if to save the Governor further entreaty or threat. Nothing shifted him and no alternative was found to removing Dale three days later to the mainland. Standing high on the sugar loaf Bass, Sandy saw the boat draw into North Berwick three and a half miles away, and Tam being greeted by his wife and two bairns. He smiled happily as they hurried away to East Withensgate by East Linton. A devoted Christian service and hard farming life lay ahead of Tam. The Rock had a grand view of the noble estuary of the Forth with its many islets, its waters mingling with the German Ocean, on one side the varied coast of Fife with its succession of little fishing villages, and on the other the rich verdure and spacious fields of East Lothian, overlooked by the isolated cone of North Berwick Law . . . on its summit, he knew many a beacon fire had glared over the deep in the warlike times of our ancestors. Opposite the Bass stood the magnificent Tantallon Castle and he recalled the impossible legend.

"They say, 'Ding doon Tantallon Castle, and mak' a brig to the Bass' James." He called over to Fraser of Brea, exercising his legs briskly on the plateau of naked red rocks. He was glad that it had been permitted for the prisoners to have the liberty of the isle betwixt sunrise and sunset, provided that none but two have freedom at once, and they be shut up before the other two come out. "It's as sure as Irish Finn MacCool taking the high road from the giants causeway on Antrim's coast to the cave of Fingal."

"Legends abound where Tantallon's dizzy steep hangs over the margin of the deep. Where the far projecting battlements leans over the booming ocean and the half breeze, half spray, whistles by them; dark deeds have been done and the castle's enemies were subjected to an unwholesome death. Cast into the sea, floating with corks and a bit caller herring tied to their skulls brought swarms of seabirds to peck the fish and the brains out of their heads."

"An unwholesome death indeed, James, and unwholesome are the appearance of these pink tree plants that grow so much here. I have never seen their like anywhere on the mainland. Are they a plant or a tree?"

"That's where you are mistaken, for the dried leaves of these pink mallow herbs turn dark blue and provide an odourless drug which is a softening lotion that reduces inflammation. I have studied herbal medicine a little as well as languages, and it contains mucilage. As you can see, they do grow tall to a luxuriant height of six and eight feet, Brea pointed to a clump of the weird plant, "and are known as tree mallow but they are a herb."

They are a strange and alien plant to my eye which I have never seen elsewhere on the mainland."

"Yes, the mallow comes from the southern Mediterranean. Either the soil of this volcanic Rock of the Bass is specially suitable for its growth or spores of its seeds were brought by the Solan Geese. Marsh mallows are also to be found in boggy land. Dead leaves killed by rust must always be knocked off." Brea stetched his hand to skite some brown leaves from a clump of the giant plants as they passed.

They came on dead gannets and rabbits in all stages of decay. Myriads of solan geese, and seagulls wheeled in the sunshine to land and whiten the cliffs, where sat cormorants, shags and guillemots and mergansers, silent sentinels, save to dive headlong for their sustenance.

"Aye, Lauderdale bought a fragment of a former world passed on when he purchased the Bass, in the name of the Government, to become a State prison.

"True, Rev. Peden. The castle of the Bass could never be taken by storm and the waters round it are full forty fathoms deep."

But it was a great joy for the two to be permitted to walk together for a few hours on the island. They were able to strengthen one another, and encourage one another to hold fast the principles for which they suffered. The cool, fresh sea breeze revived their health and spirits, and made them better able to endure the unwholesome dungeon.

"I am heart sick sorry for James Mitchell who is not permitted the liberty of the island like the rest, for the attempt on the life of Archbishop Sharpe in the Blackfriar's Wynd of Edinburgh. I could almost wish his aim had been better, for Sharpe will not rest until his death is achieved," Sandy sighed wearily.

Though their letters to and from relatives and friends were often opened and the writings mocked, one day Sandy was delighted to receive a parcel from the Rev. Patrick Simpson of Kilmacolm. It contained money and a supply of food from Christian friends. Fare had been scanty as the boat had not dared to put out for ten days by reason of the stormy weather. The food had been mainly dried fish but their chief suffering had been lack of pure water since the Bass had no springs and the only alternative was to collect rainwater in cavities. In winter they procured it by melting snow though such water soon became putrid and oatmeal was sprinkled on it to make it palatable. But Peden's massive build was as yet unaffected by the unhealthy dungeons. His wanderings, escapes and long days' flights before pursuing dragoons had hardened his great physical strength. His fifty one years seemed like a youngster's and he eagerly shared the gift from Patrick Simpson with James Fraser. His ingenuity easily found ways to leave some also in places frequented by other prisoners. The guards awe of his prophetic powers left Sandy well alone on his walks. They even supplied him with writing materials to pen a short letter of grateful thanks to Patrick Simpson. It was a pithy note from a brother to another, that he envied reverently the birds their freedom, but that Christ's cross is whatever service is done, in prison or freedom, and when it was darkest, there would be light. His faith remained unabated, with hope ever present in his heart.

10

To Be Transported

His four years and three months on the Bass had taken a demanding toll of Sandy Peden. His constitution, though robust through a life of continual pursuit and abiding in the fastness of the Lowland moors, the Border hills, and the glens of Ulster, had been worn thin. His very breath had been freedom and this incarceration in the diminutive cell was claustrophobic in the extreme. Light and air were almost excluded so that dampness and cold prevailed. The slop he was served was scarce but the agony of hunger was almost equalled by the sickness brought on by the maggot-ridden mutton, green moulded bread, and water, he was sure, mixed with the brine. Taken in any degree, the potion would have driven the Covenanting prisoners mad, had not Sandy in anger called for the Governor in such authority that the normally brutal guards were so taken aback that they passed on the request and that gentleman whose character was of a weak nature, taken up with the practice of gambling, gave a surly assent to provide fresh water regularly from North Berwick. He had already been shaken by the prophets foreknowledge of his gambling habit. Peden had condemned his weakness on three occasions as sinful. Such a judgement he would have dismissed as of a madman as it was part of his being to get thrills from the fall of a dice and turn of a card, but the seeming omniscience of the man scared his superstitious mind. His was a mind reached only by feelings of self interest and it had penetrated his brain clouded by alcohol and the insensitivity of the gambling instinct, that Peden had friends in high places.

After eighteen months Rev. Peden had written to the Earl of Leven and Melville a petition to be passed on to the Privy Council.

In a mood of gentle persuasion he had sat down to pen this cry for mercy and appeal to their humanity. Depression of a kind had settled on his spirit and the impression that the spirit was weak, but the weakness of the flesh was stronger. But always mingled with the emotions of his heart, in which sadness and joy continually chased one another across his soul, was the ever optimistic regard for the best in his fellow beings. In John Graham he saw the gallantry of a royalist and even in Dalzell a bull-like leadership. So one day he had requested a quill and ink. With no feeling of obseqiousness Sandy had written the appeal to the clergy of the magistrates, many of whom were unwilling servants of the Stewarts. 'Unto the right honourable, the Lords of His Majesty's Privy Council, the petition of Mr. Alexander Peden.'

'That your Lordships' petitioner has been, by your Lordships' order, detained prisoner in the Bass eighteen months past, during which time he has been through sickness and great infirmity of body, and want of maintenance, reduced unto great extremity, so that his present lot is exceeding sad and lamentable.

'May it therefore please your lordships, in Christian compassion and tenderness, to commiserate his deplorable condition, and to grant him such enlargement as your Lordships, in your wisdom and goodness, shall think fit, and your Lordships petitioner shall ever humbly pray.' — Peathine.

Sandy often spelt his surname thus, though he knew that some were trying to standardise spelling and make everyone write according to their stiff rules. But what was good enough for his father Hugh was worthy to be respected, though he accepted with equanimity when most others addressed him as Peden. He smiled to himself as he thought that at forty eight years of age it was a bit late to change. His smile of gentleness had become the weapon that turned away many a harsh word and harsher action. So it was that his epistle of appeal to their humanity bore fruit again, for friends were allowed to minister to some of his necesities at a distance. The Cunninghams of Craigends sent him subscriptions which would pay the garrison to provide healthier food which Peden insisted be distributed amongst his fellow prisoners. James Fraser of Brea was surviving very doggedly through it all, like for all as a wiry terrior, but Thomas Hog of Kiltearn from Tain in the county of Ross, because of the stale air and confinement, lost health rapidly and fell into a bloody flux. A physician was called who said his opinion was that unless Thomas Hog was liberated immediately he would enter death's gate. Alexander loved Thomas Hog dearly even though he came from the strange and distant lands of the Highlands, to his lowland mind a land which to him might have been of another planet. But there was about Pastor Hog that aura of the mystic which others observed quietly around Peden. The story of Kiltearn's remarkable recovery owed nothing to Sandy's attempt to help and a fullness of joy overflowed, so that he laughed out loud in his cell one night and the guards shook with fright, thinking that this gangrel body of a Covenanting minister was in league with the Devil. They could not distinguish between an eldritch mocking and the pure laughter of God. As Thomas had told him, the physician, conscientious to his profession, had, without Hog's knowledge, given in a petition to the Council, in the strongest terms he could devise "For in no circumstances would I address that mongrel court," he told Sandy one evening when on a rare occasion they were allowed to walk in the little herb garden where a few cherry trees grew which they took the opportunity to pick. Unfortunately just beneath the garden was what had been the chapel but was now profaned by the soldiery to be a storehouse for their ammunition.

"Aye, that I agree. For they are a mixed group. But you maun always remember that among the mongrel breed you get both the curs and those whose true strain make them faithful dogs to their master. They did agree somewhat to my petition to help my ageing bones."

"Tis true. Some of the Lords interceded for me. They told the rest of the Council that I lived more quietly and travelled less round the country than other Presbyterians." Hog of Kiltearn chuckled, amused by the thought. "Little do some of the enemies of God know that a light can shine just as easily and effectively in a bottle as in a crystal chandelier and a voice can be heard in a cockleshell as much as the blowing of a trumpet. But that traitor Sharpe, with the cunning of his breed, saw this, and told them that I could do them more hurt, sitting in my elbow-chair than twenty others could by travelling through the country. The serpent was always wiser than all the other animals. The hypocrisy of our Archbishop was exposed in all its rottenness in his words to the Privy Council that if the justice of God were pursuing me to take me off the stage of our great fight, the clemency of the Government should not interpose to hinder it. The justice of God is something he knows nought about. But pretence in mankind is as old as Judas' claim to be interested in the poor on whom the value of the spikenard from the alabaster box should be spent. Sharpe told them that if there was any place in the Bass prison worse than another, I should be put there. When the keeper informed me, it was as if Satan had been the penman as, though being cribbed and cabbined in an atmosphere so thick with smoke my lungs were coughing blood, yet I did not want to crawl before such men. My servant William Bulloch helped carry me down to a dismal cell by a subterranean alley. It is a hideous cavern, Sandy, arched overhead, deep in the bowels of the Bass, dark and dripping, and with an opening towards the sea which dashes within a few feet below. It wasn't a place for any self respecting rat and my poor man Bulloch started weeping. He clearly thought my death was imminent. But as I told him it was when men show no mercy, then that's just the time that the Lord will show Himself merciful. Praise the Lord, it was from the moment that I entered into that black stink hole that I date my recovery. My lungs began to heal and it was as if that stank putrescent air was the very air of Heaven and my lungs gulped it in eagerly."

"Twas a miracle indeed" Sandy smiled, as if his face could not express fully what his soul was feeling. He stared fixedly up at the blue vastness of the clear summer sky with white wisps of cloud trailing.

"As I said of his grace of St. Andrews often afterwards, 'Commend him to me for a good physician,'" Hog added laughingly. "Yes, many are the wonders that our reason cannot explain, hidebound as she is by her logic."

"Tell me of some" mused Sandy. This was like the elixir of life to him.

"Well then, Sandy, one little happening took place after I was put in my charge at Kiltearn by the Synod of Ross, and the laird of Park called me to Morayshire and the parish of Knockgoudy near Auldearn. The presence of the Spirit was so rich and full and free that I adventured to give the sacrament there. Now a man of the West from Rosshire, one MacLeod, came to it who knew no English. But since I spoke the Gaelic, MacLeod told me that he came there directly guided by the spirit and understood every word preached in English as if it was the Gaelic. It was a wonder and I cannot but think that it was of such a gift of tongues that took place on the day of Pentecost when Peter described it as the fulfilment of the prophecy of Joel. Parthians, Medes, Elamites, Arabians and Cretes, those from Egypt, Cappadocia and many other places, all heard the message in their own tongue. Whether it was the tongues of men or angels, I know not."

"We run out of English words to say what our heart wishes, Thomas, and I have on occasion spoken to the Lord in tongues which are unknown. It is then that we are speaking not to men but to God. The winds and the creatures have their own language also. The cry of the pee-wee is God's alarm cry to me."

"My healing is following many wondrous healings which took place in my ministry. A David Dunbar was healed and restored to his right mind from a mad frenzy. Some of his friends were for letting blood to relieve the lad's agony of spirit but I told them that the prelates had deprived us of enough money to pay physicians and we should employ Him who cures freely. To be honest, I asked Mr. Fraser to pray but he put it back on me. Likewise the daughter of the laird of Park, my brother-in-law, had a high fever, with little hope of life left. I loved that child dearly and would have been heart broken if she had had her young life snapped. After deep prayer with her parents, acknowledging the sins of us all, including the child, God marvellously intervened. Another dear lady, who was in extreme distress in both her mind and her body, was given relief through prayer. But be assured that I am always watchful amd aware of delusions from the Devil. We can be deceived in thinking we have achieved healings by a miracle. Yet I believe the body and mind are inextricably entwined. The Lord gives the power of a sound mind."

"Yes, Hog of Kiltearn, I have found the dividing line between the supernatural experiences of God and the Devil sometimes misty, and mystical deceptions abound. At times the leanings of the body have the upper hand. My moorland fastings can bring me close to ending this grey valley of life."

"However, I am sure that God would have us advance in knowledge about the workings of the human body. It has been said that Michael Servetus had discovered facts about the circulation of the blood, especially that it coursed through the lungs before going through the heart, and this was not palatable to the Church which has always, in the Roman See, been hostile to change. How sad to remember that it was our own John Calvin of Geneva who had Servetus burned at the stake!"

"But wasn't that for heresy against the Trinity?"

"Does it matter whether it was for doctrinal impurity or trying to advance in knowledge? It is ever a stain on Calvin's great memory. Yet he in natural knowledge was one of the fathers of the Reformation."

"We are all cracked pots even in our mighty moments." said Sandy sadly. "Zwingli took up the sword in the same Switzerland and died by it. I do confess to my little musket bayonet and that muckle horse pistol, but never have I done harm with them. My defence is their purpose."

"I'm afraid I would fault even that, Sandy. The world of God's power has always been my resort. As you know, many hae the superstitious idea that burial in the Kirk's churchyard itself has some special blessing and the General Assembly banned this. Now a William Munro, a strong, hectoring fellow, once tried to force his way into the churchyard along with supporters to bury a corpse. So like Baalim's ass, I stood in his way at the Kirk door and with a sudden grab wrenched the key from Munro. My words were no less from the Lord than those of the ass. If God can use a stupid donkey, much more can he a man. I prophesised that unless he repented, William Munro would have a sudden judgement shortly. A few months later this violent man attacked another who, as they grappled, pulled out Munro's dagger and thrust him through. Violence brings her own prompt reward."

The scene swam across Peden's mind's eye as he looked out over the waves as they pulled away from the Bass. He heard clearly the sobbing and surging as if the sough was calling him back to that island Patmos. He thought of the old Celtic Saint Baldred whose hermitage still mouldered on the Rock's face. He must have found it a refuge. Sandy had written his name and many psalm words on the dank walls. It was then that the deception of sound over time and place was imposed on his spirits with that old melancholy, as Sandy realised that the crash of the waves he now felt with a jar through his tired frame, was that which hammered against the bowels of the sailing vessel, the "Saint Michael" of Scarborough, in which he was shackled with sixty other Covenanting prisoners, in the Leith Roads, Edinburgh. Their future was decided — a life of slavery in the plantations of the Americas.

The feeling of life's circular character was unavoidable as the Privy Council pronounced the cruel sentence. "On this day of December, 1678, we do sentence these Covenanting traitors, all sixty one, to a lifelong banishment to the Plantations of the Americas as slaves to the owners, never to return to Scotland on pain of death. This is their due punishment for their treachery to his Royal Highness, King Charles II".

The four and a half years on the rocky isle of Bass seemed like yeaterday while the fifteen months which had followed in the Tolbooth prison of Edinburgh had been an age of uncertainty, punctuated only by educated companionship. The entry into the capital had been a procession of jeering from the mocking populace who were fickle enough to switch their opinions in accordance with those in power. Walking behind the dragoon's horse, manacled to the saddle, along woth other prisoners, they had endured the ribaldry of the guttersnipe crowd while the sympathetic and merely curious kept their gabs clamped.

Edinburgh in the latter half of the seventeenth century was densely populated, closely constricted between natural barriers and the narrow boundaries of her own walls. The Castle Rock rose above the swampy valleys that was to become an elegant thoroughfare, and the northern limits of the town were sealed in turn by this marsh, the Nor Loch, which drained it ineffectually, and north-east, by the crags of Calton Hill. In the south beyond the city walls few buildings as yet encroached on the open fields. The main thoroughfare was the mile long High Street and Canongate that ran through from the Castle in the West to the Abbey and Palace of Holyrood in the east. A secondary street, the Cowgate, stretched the same distance, scarcely two hundred yards away to the south, while connecting the Cowgate to the High Street, were the countless closes and wynds in which almost the entire population had their dwellings, with little or no distinction of class or status. Dark and narrow stairs climbing often to ten of even twelve storeys, gave entry to low ceilinged, ill-lit flats, for the most part of little architectural value, and differing only from one another in the number of their rooms and closets. It was from these precarious tenements and rabbit warren wynds that countless faces grinned and glared their spite at beings worse off than themselves. Forgetful of glorious events in the Churchyard of the Greyfriars forty years before and the great tradition handed down, the mob made their progress to the Tolbooth a dolorous way. Handfuls of mud and garbage of unmentionable slop were hurled. Few concessions were made, even in the capital, to comfort and sanitation. The High Street in whose centre stood the Tolbooth, served only to act as the city's drain into which the inhabitants daily cast the ordure of each household and the flowers of Edinburgh, as the more charitable referred to the resulting mess, had never known a garden.

Accompanying the missiles came cries of derision. "Where is your God noo? Has he deserted you for the noo. Maybe He's changed sides!"

"The Iron Maiden's in a humour for guid company the day! Besides, you'll find her a bonnie lass. The Grassmarket's in need of some fine entertainment forby farming carts, the swinging kind!"

The Tolbooth finally loomed up and grateful they passed dragged into its mass, eager to swallow whatever sacrifices. The ancient Tolbooth was built by the citizens in 1561 and destined for the accommodation of Parliament as well as the High Courts of justice;

and at the same time for the confinement of prisoners for debt or on criminal charges. Since 1640 when the Parliament House was erected, the Tolbooth was occupied as a prison only. Gloomy and dismal as it was, the situation in the High Street rendered it so particularly well-aired, and that when the plague laid waste the city in 1645, it affected none within these melancholy precincts. On the south of the Tolbooth into which the prison opened was a narrow lane and Sandy glimpsed the famous Luckenbooths, a veritable heap of small stalls, nestling under the lane's Gothic arches, which sold every kind of clothes, hats, gloves, children's toys and trinkets from Holland.

It was there in the Tolbooth prison that he was to meet Alan Gregory, a man of urbanity and sophistication, such as he did not encounter in the country districts. Intellectual pursuits had been notoriously lacking in his rural haunts. The mental stimulus of a keen brain who was in touch with the intelligentsia that still existed in troubled Scotland, was a challenge to Sandy, though he was to discover Gregory more in prison for his humanitarian political views which baulked at a repressive government and clergy, than any sympathy with the religious faith of the Covenant.

"My, they are a more ignorant crowd, these Edinburgh folk, like a cur that can't be trusted. They are only concerned with feeding time." Peden was not impressed with his welcome. "It's an unworthy capital."

The high forehead of the academic was clearly seen in Gregory and his firm, emotionless, blue eyes indicated more of the pragmatist than the visionary. Despite his dusty surroundings, his ruffles were still fresh, brown great coat merely a little wine stained, and neatly tied fair hair giving off a powder.

"Do not judge her by the filth in the streets and stairs. It is a picturesque enough town with no less colourful inhabitants, especially when augmented in the years since the Union of the Crowns when the nobility and the retainers periodically descend on our capital in attendance on the nation's business. Many claim this is Edinburgh's most glorious age. I would not agree with this but her social structure is fairly settled and a shopkeeper here thinks nothing of sharing a common stair with a noble customer and a judge of being a neighbour to clerks and artisans. This is what I dream of, a classless society where her citizens are valued for their achievements."

"You have a dream too, as I have of when God's Kingdom here on earth shall be established with just rulers. I have seen a rosebud in the East and it is coming soon."

"No, no, none of your mystic for me. But I am concerned with equality for humanity, wherever in the world that right is abused. You Covenanters are too parochial, as if you are the only martyrs for truth, and the truth of your God at that! There is a world of truth, the truth of healing and medicine, of art, philosophy and music. My cousin, Dr. Gregory, is flighting close to being Professor of Mathematics at our University. But healing is my profession. My heart is sore for the medical art is sadly decadent. At the University, apart from the barrier added to learning by the fact that all instruction is imparted in Latin, for which few students are adequately prepared, training in the professions of law and medicine are totally excluded. The Incorporation of Surgeons and Barbers is gaining respect. As you know, sir Covenanting minister, the Barbers both shave and perform operations. But their techniques haven't advanced for a century and a half and have remained primitive. A few years ago the Surgeons and Barbers separated and a new profession in Scotland was formed of Chirurgeon-Apothecary to act as general practitioners. The Barbers were left to their mundane craft. Yet apprenticeship is still haphazard, I'm afraid. After a three year period it is incredible that he is not allowed to attend any professor of medicine, anatomy, surgery or materia medica for other than his own Master for the first two years. At the end the Incorporation give a slipshod examination and almost never withhold a license. But the ordinary physicians are worse if possible. The concoctions they prescribe are barbaric, and old wife's tales. The bubonic plague cure, in the case of a boil for instance, was to wrap up in a woollen cloth, and compel the sick party to sweat, and, if he does, keep him moderately there till the sore begins to rise, then apply a half-live pigeon, cut up into two or a plaster from an egg yolk, honey herb of grace, chopped exceedingly small, and wheaten flour. It is no wonder they died. Six years ago I organised a census of some fair accuracy with the Universities of Glasgow and St. Andrews and estimated that three hundred children died of smallpox."

"Many's the time I have overseen the burial of infants whose life is a flimsy thread," said Peden sadly. "But love is stronger than death."

"Other prescriptions include spider's webs, gizzard of hen, spawn of frogs, and juice of woodlice. Even the great Professor Pitcairne, previously Professor at Leiden, the greatest of the European medical schools, recommends mercury and broth, with earthworms and powder of human skull added! But out of this sea of ignorance has come the gentle study of botany, here in the centre of Edinburgh. The strange thing is that it is two young Edinburgh physician friends of mine who have advanced both the cause of medicine and botany. Andrew Balfour, though he is from Denmiln in Fife, and Robert Sibbald, have set up a medical practice, and have added a botanic garden where exotic herbs and plants are grown from seed received from Oxford, London, Paris Leiden and even Tangiers. Balfour spent fifteen years travelling abroad, observing the natural history of the European countries and has brought back antique medals, pictures, arms, mathematical instruments, and of course surgical instruments with which he has performed dissections in surgery previously unknown in Scotland. He built up a collection it has been my privilege to inspect, of plants, animals and fossils, but it has been Robert Sibbald, a very prodigy of learning, appalled by the number of quacks and mountebanks he sees, who, set up the study of plants indigenous to Scotland, and established a private garden to cultivate medical herbs. Eight years ago they obtained from John Brown, gardener at North Yards in Holyrood Abbey, the lease of an enclosure at St. Anne's Yards. It has been the pratice of the hereditary Keeper of Holyrood House to let the area of St. Anne's Yards to market gardeners. There Sibbald and Balfour have established the most wonderful collection of something between eight and nine hundred plants despite the stiff opposition of the Cirurgeon Apothecaries, jealous of the possible establishment of a College of Physicians. May I say, my dear Peden, that many of the plants were obtained from the garden of Patrick Murray, the Laird of West Lothian, showing that not all of our gentry are grasping and ignorant."

"I'm right glad to see the advance o' knowledge, but touching your last point, it's the head that wags the tail, Mr. Gregory. Charles II has produced vile gentry. He has neither consulted the interests of England or Scotland, or followed the advice of his Parliament. But he never cared for the country, for Parliaments, nor for Protestants. He kept no faith with his people but just after they had restored him with so much joy, was bargaining with his brother Louis for 10,000 dragoons from France to enslave them. He shut up the Exchequer, contrary to all faith and common honesty, and robbed his subjects of near £1,500,000, I have heard, which they had placed there for safety. The man is an absolute rogue and to him we owe our troubles. He only pretended to show toleration to Protestant dissenters that he might give favour to the other dissenters, his brethren the Roman Catholics. He has sold Dunkirk to the French, instituting a nest of pirates to destroy England's trade, as well as involving her in his Dutch wars. Our suffering in Scotland is only a reflection of what is happening in England, only worse because of his hatred for Presbyterianism." Sandy stopped short a little ashamed of his tirade against the monarch he had never seen. "Forgive me, I have however appreciated your words of learning."

Just then their talk was sharply interrupted by a voice filled with groaning misery from among the shackled prisoners nearby.

"There is no return from the living hell of the canebrakes of Barbados and Virginia. Next to death in the Grassmarket or a meeting with the Iron Maiden, this banishment to the Plantations is the worst. In these death traps they call ships our chances of even reaching the shores of the Americas or the Indies, are sma'. I've heard tell that they plan to batten down the hatches if a storm overtakes us." The speaker's face was as haggard as his despairing tones.

Peden leant over in the semi darkness and kindly said, "Wheesht, man. Whaur is it you dwell, James Law? Is it no round the Water of Leith?"

"Aye it is, Rev. Peden. And never again will my eyes feast on the kye grazing on the pastures or the ewes wandering on a braeside. Never again will I guddle speckled brown trout in the stony burns wi my bairns. Aye, they'll batten doon all the hatches." The panic rose in his throat once more. "We'll a' be drowned ."

"Quiet, James Law, I say! Is your guid wife due to come on board? I have a word from the Lord for you both. I tell you, the ship's no' been built that will take old Sandy to the Indies."

Gregory spoke up with a reprimand in his manner. "You are living in a fantasy land. When the Plantations were originated, as their name betokens, they were just colonial settlements, where men and women were planted or settled in distant parts of the earth, and with numerous grants and privileges, left to fight their way to success or failure. A beginning was made by Queen Elizabeth, but since the beginning of this century a serious difficulty has affected the success or failure of the plantations. The difficulty has been that of providing a sufficient supply of labourers for the new annexed countries, so vast and so thinly populated. Various solutions have been attempted. Two years ago the Royal African Company, whose head was your good friend, the Duke of York," — Dr. Alan Gregory's cynicism was not concealed and jarred on Sandy's nerves — "received a charter for the exclusive supply of slaves to Jamaica and the other West Indian islands. Prisoners-of-war have also frequently been disposed of in this way and, let me say," again his lip curled in bitterness, "where men and even women have become obnoxious to those in power, either for their political or religious opinions, a ready market is always at hand, and a twofold purpose gained by ridding the country of troublesome people, and supplying a clamant want. At a time, also, when truth has fallen in the street and equity cannot enter, there is too much reason to fear that the representatives of law and order are not indifferent to bribes. There is a lurid light about the legal proceedings of our country. Believe me, your fate has been sealed from the beginning."

Another shadowy figure leant over and wearily held up his chains, "How can you say these words of false comfort, Rev. Peden? Ten years sin' after the Pentland Rising, dear friends of mine who refused to accept the Act of Indemnity were banished by the Privy Council. John Bryce, William Ferguson, William Adam, James Anderson, John Wright and Robert Grier have never been seen in their homeland again. I am destined to exchange the bonnie fields of Fife for the heathen darkness of the Americas where, if we do not die of exhaustion in heat of the sugar-cane plantations, we shall certainly end up murdered by some savage. I hear they are red in the Americas but it matters not the colour. Forby they are going to send down the thumbkins to keep us from rebelling. There is no comfort in the thumbkins or the boot, Rev. Peden. They would certes make one confess to anything, sir."

"But why are you all so discouraged? You need not fear, for there will neither thumbkins nor the boot come here; lift up your hearts for the day of your redemption draws near. If we come to London, we will all be set at liberty. So, James Pride, you will see soon the stately towers of St. Andrews University and the Palace of Falkland, with its cluster of homes, where Richie Cameron was born."

"We are heading for London in this vessel, the 'Saint Michael' out of Scarborough, for a place cried Gravesend. I heared through the grating the Captain issuing his instructions. God send some of our Huguenot allies or our Dutch friends to intercept us. Rotterdam and Groningen have been havens of refuge to the Covenanting folk and a seat of learning, for our Ministers have even been ordained there?"

"This is well known, Mr. Pride. There is no need of prophetic insight. There is a close bond between Holland and Scotland. Both nations are Protestant and have their struggles for liberty. Holland is only repaying the debt she has so long owed to Scotland. In the reign of David I, a considerable number of the industrious and enterprising inhabitants of the Netherlands had already settled in

Scotland and carried on trade in its eastern ports. When the Flemings were expelled from England we took them in. Under the hated Spanish Philip II and the vicious Duke of Alba many thousands died, but this reign of terror at length came to an end, and, having broken the yoke of Spanish and Popish tyranny, Holland has been able to stretch forth a helping hand to the oppressed of every creed and nation. The Jews, who have been despised and hated everywhere, even have found in Holland an asylum, and helped to increase her wealth. The Jansenists, driven from France by their enemies, the Jesuits, were recognised there when recognition was a dangerous offence."

"Our Dutch brethren have indeed been so kind that a Scots church has been established in Rotterdam. Rev. Robert McWard, once of the Outer High Church in, Glasgow, was appointed minister of it. He was ordered into banishment for treasonable preaching but was free to choose the place of his exile. His sermon was from Amos, 'You only have I chosen of all the families of the earth; therefore will I punish you for all your sins.' I think he was a wheen too personal with his application." James Pride was now forgetful of his earlier bitterness and allowed himself a wry chuckle.

"There's nae need to be mungin when the Lord has provided sic a cave of Addullam, even for indiscreet preachers, eh?" Sandy smiled that affectionate smile. "As for the English crew who man this vessel, they seem like honest chiels who are simply employed in their duty as sailors and know little of the religious struggles of Scotland. Cromwell was an easier master than such unworthy fellow countrymen as Claverhouse, Dalzell of Binns and Grierson of Lag."

James Law interrupted, "The Lord have mercy on us. I feel the ship moving. We are all undone! We have not even the chance of a farewell sight of our Scottish shores."

"How long will you disbelieve the Word of the Lord? Let us get to our knees in prayer. 'Sweet Lord our God, such is the hatred of the enemy for us that they will not let us stay in our own land to serve You, though some of us have nothing but the canopy of the Heavens above and your earth below; but Lord, cut short our voyage, and frustrate their wicked designs and some of us shall go home richer than when we came from home'." A scraping sound caused Sandy to break off from his intercession with the Almighty, and he turned to see a prisoner pulling and gabbling in high emotion to some of the others. "I see you are excited about something, Robert Pounton. I know you have been a worthy and respected burgess of the parish of Dalmeny by Queensferry. It must take some little matter to arouse you."

A serious faced man under the strain of an unaccustomed emotion pulled at Peden's arm violently, "They are loosening the hatches and little do they ken but I've loosened my own chains. When the guard enters with the food we can overpower him, turn all free and commandeer the ship. These sailors are mercenary scum who work solely for blood money. I ken Malloch, that wicked merchant in Edinburgh gets £10 for each of the slaves he transports to the Indies, and I'm sure that Captain Johnstone gets the lion's share of the payment to the St. Michael. I've heard that the crew are disgruntled. They are a different cattle to the professional dragoons and will be no match for some bonnie Covenanting lads." Robert Pounton to any casual observer was in a mood of high fervour, and not responsible for his words, irrespective of any truth in them. His enthusiam was infectious to the others, desperate for any lifeline in their hopeless plight. But they would not venture on it without Peden's advice.

"What's your word, Sandy?" It was a quiet and attentive James Law from the Water o' Leith who spoke. "You have been wonderful encouragement to my wife and myself that we shall see one another again. Bide by the Minister's word, I say, men."

"Let all well alone. For the Lord will set us at liberty in a way more conducive to his glory and our safety." Gradually he ministered patience and hope to the hearts roused by a false hope.

Sure enough the turbulent seas and vicious east coast winds continued to throw the St. Michael around like a cork and sickness affected not only the ill fed and shackled prisoners but also the experienced crew. Their resulting temper made life even more difficult for the human cargo.

Even when they arrived at Gravesend, where a Ralph Williamson of London had given security that he would transport them to Virginia and sell them to the best advantage, the prisoners sensed that all was not well above. The passage from Leith to Gravesend was five days longer than Williamson had expected, and when the ship arrived he was not to be found. Confusion reigned above decks, where Captain Johnstone was enraged at the expense of waiting and feeding the prisoners. He had done his part, and for all Johnstone's perverted heart was concerned, the Covenanters could all be tipped into the ocean, complete with shackles. He waited on for some time, and, just when provisions were running low, Ralph Williamson's arrival was announced. The honest faced London merchant sailor was greeted in surly fashion by Johnstone, who could barely restrain an oath.

"Whaur hae ye been, man?" demanded the Leith sailor, who had but bought the vessel in Scarborough.

"Ah, my dear Captain, when you did not arrive in time, I waited four days and concluded there had been a mistake in the missive. You know, writing has come to a pretty pass these days. Alternatively they had changed their minds up in Edinburgh. I decided to return from London to check if you had been delayed. However, all's well, so let us inspect the condition of the cargo."

"Aye, it was foul weather, so let me be gone while things are fair and the tide is running," snarled Johnstone, leading Williamson and his party to the hatches.

"I brought a platoon of merchant seamen in case these convicts are troublesome." Johnstone blinked but did not say anything. A sailor threw open a hatch and Williamson stared down into the darkness.

"I can't see them clearly. I've undertaken to transport sixty seven, no less, no more. Will you light a taper?"

Reluctantly now, Johnstone assented and they clambered below with a guard. The flickering light shone dully on the grey parchment faces, filled with strain and fatigue, but also an integrity, obvious to all but the most jaundiced eye.

"They don't look like thieves and felons to me," said the Londoner. "You, sir, your name, station and crime?"

"James Millar, souter in Kirkaldy, and we are all honest Christians banished for our Presbyterian principles.

Williamson was aghast and had the taper swung round the crowded quarters. "You two there, speak up."

"Adam Abercorn, chaplain. 'Tis true, we are persecuted Covenanting Christians."

"The Rev. Alexander Peden. Some call me the Prophet of the Covenant."

Williamson swung round in angry protest. "I will sail the seas with none such as these grave and sober Christians. This was not the contract to transport criminals."

"What do I care for about contracts?" snapped Johnstone, "I just do what I'm paid for. They are your responsibility. I'll keep them no longer." There was now tension in the air as they returned to the deck to clear the confusion. The honest Williamson would not be moved and a stalemate was reached. Sailors fingered their weapons nervously. Breaking point was near when a halloo was heard from the dockside and a tall imperious figure could be seen accompanied by a band of tough looking men. "It is Anthony Ashley Cooper, Lord Shaftesbury!" said Williamson, slightly awed.

"I hear you have some good Presbyterians aboard. I have come to set them free. Give us no trouble, for these here are the Brisk Boys of Wapping, a finer mob not to be found in all of London town."

"How did he know?" gasped Johnstone, now totally confused. Sandy listened below with a quiet confidence of the outcome.

"Tis simple. My Lord Shaftesbury has an elaborate Whig Party organisation, based on the famous Green Ribbon Club, and he even exercises some control over elections. He has spies everywhere and a genius for propaganda and publicity. Lord Shaftesbury is not one to cross at all."

His warning was not necessary, so shaken was the Captain of the St. Michael, who signalled them to board.

A tall gentleman with long brown ringlets, Anthony Ashley Cooper had rather sad watery eyes, a long thin nose, a wispy moustache, and high pencil eyebrows, the last of which gave him a look of deceptive innocence. But there was nothing deceptive nor innocent about the Brisk Boys, the offscourings of dockland, knowing nothing but a life of cut and thrust.

"Ah, Ralph Williamson, how delightful! You should know, sir," Turning to Captain Johnstone, "that the London merchants as well as the London mob support me."

By this stage Johnstone was in a haste to set sail, and stuttered, "Y...o...ur! Your Grace!"

"So I desire that these honest Christians below be not punished merely because they adhere to Presbyterian views, but be liberated without any bond or imposition." He waved a cursory hand to a rough looking leader of the Wapping gang. "Get the key. I want our Scotch friends to see that London is not a hotbed of Romish tyranny, despite the King's policy." The last phrase was added under his breath, and the watery eyes narrowed and hardened.

When the amazed and overjoyed Covenanters were brought loosed on deck, Shaftesbury asked for their leader. Adam Abercorn and Robert Meikle pushed Sandy Peden forward.

"You will be pleased at your deliverance from a living death on the Plantations of Virginia. You cold Scots would shrivel in the heat." Shaftesbury had a condescending air.

"I knew that the ship had not been built that would take me over the sea to the Plantations." Peden answered quietly.

"Quite," the nobleman answered curtly. "Anyway, I wish the goodwill of all Presbyterians, on both sides of the border. You, sir, will dine with me. You will all be shown kindness before your journey home. Ralph Williamson, you will be reimbursed for your loss if you call at my city address."

"There is no need, my Lord," said that honest merchant with a bow, and took his leave.

Alexander Peden was taken in the luxurious carriage of their liberator to his mansion within the sound of Bow Bells. He was grateful, but felt that this man was governed more by political expediency alone, and that his kindness was not unalloyed. For a while this was put in the corner of his mind, as he was overwhelmed by the mass of novelty, carriages, sedan chairs carried by black liveried servants, perfumed ladies of fashion peeping out, fisherwomen plying their trade, hot chestnuts burning on braziers, horseguards proudly clattering through the throngs. All was bustle. As for the great buildings closing in on him, this was the New London, rising from the ashes of the Great Fire. Still in the process of construction by Christopher Wren, the many company houses, Customs House at the docks and magnificent spires of St. Mary-le-Bow, and St. Clement Danes, were most impressive to him.

Seated at a table laden with exotic fruits, some curved and yellow, some orange in segments with foliage growing from them, and huge yellow ones like balloons, roast peacocks and hog, and various wines, Peden felt his stomach turn and yearn for Scots brose, bannocks and tuppenny ale. Without offence, he requested simple fare, and was brought a huge china basin of potatoes in a tarty sauce, buttered, toasted scones, and milk. Shaftesbury eyed him with curiosity.

"Where is your parish, sir?"

"The hills, moors and glens of Scotland, my Lord. They are sufficient for me."

"Have you never sought a position of authority with a church of your own and influence over Lords, Ladies and Politicians? I have been Chancellor of England for 11 years and earned high praise but, King Charles disliked me as he says I always have an excuse for my actions. Therefore I was dismissed so that he could appoint his Roman Catholic minions."

"But we must always have reasons for our actions."

"Yes, so called responsible men have regarded me with disfavour because they say I have made frequent changes of policy and have inclined to extreme courses, but I have always had a reason and it's because I did not want extreme actions. I only supported Cromwell with reservations. Regicide was not my desire. So after being imprisoned for a year, I was freed at the Restoration and made Privy Councillor. But neither was I an extreme Royalist and with reason."

Here Shaftesbury lowered his voice. "Are you aware, sir Covenanter, of the crypto-Roman Catholic policy of the King?"

"I know the Roman Church are a danger to Presbyterian Scotland, but so is the rule of Bishops." Sandy felt he must tread guardedly with this experienced politician, who clearly still had so much influence despite royal disfavour.

"The good Protestant Duke of Monmouth, natural son to Charles by Lucy Walters, would subject you to neither if he was once enthroned. I stand for civil and religious liberty, Rev. Peden. Already I have composed the basis for a Habeas Corpus Act under which if any one has another in custody, he must produce the prisoner and state the reason for his detention, so that the judge may decide if it is just. By the law of England in the Magna Carta no freeman can be imprisoned except for a crime of which he has been found guilty by his peers. Some of them would take away these liberties. Have you not heard of Titus Oates and the Popish Plot? Ah, talk of the Devil, here's the man himself, and John Locke, gentlemen forsooth! You amaze me that you have come in each other's company!"

"We met by accident, I assure you, my Lord, if that should be necessary," said a frail looking gentleman with an asthmatic voice, but the high forehead and bearing of an intellectual. His companion, by contrast, was in high spirits but was shifty eyed in a way that gave the lie to his exuberance. The flushed colour and feverish look of the fanatic betrayed Titus Oates to the Rev. Alexander Peden. His gift of discernment revealed an intrigue about the other.

Shaftesbury was playing the genial host. "Rev. Peden, Covenanter prophet, may I introduce two of my friends, the best and the worst, but still my friends." He smiled as if joking. "I'll let you decide which is which. This is Mr. Titus Oates, one time naval chaplain, expelled student of a Jesuit seminary, son of a Norwich ribbon weaver, and here is Mr. John Locke, distinguished philosopher, from the Westminster School of Puritan divines and Calvinist theology, he prefers facts to words and persons to books."

Peden immediately preferred Locke to Oates, especially the natural, easy and unaffected piety he displayed. For all his high qualifications as a philosopher, there was a simple friendliness about John Locke. Titus Oates, on the other hand, exuded an air of deviousness, which when Sandy heard what he had been involved in, made his actions quite consistent with his character.

"Mr. Locke and Mr. Oates are both engaged in research of their own kind, though slightly different to one another. John discusses philosophical, religious, and scientific problems, as well as encouraging trade with the Americas, especially the southern Plantations. In fact you very nearly became part of that trade, Mr. Peden." Shaftesbury laughed mirthlessly. "At the same time Titus here is busy ferreting out Jesuit plots and apprehending Roman Catholic conspirators. He is the hero of the day here in London town." Oates looked as pleased as punch but Shaftesbury's words sounded hollow and mocking.

"What Jesuit Plot?" Alexander Peden had no love for Rome but he dealt in facts.

"Why, the Popish Plot, of course," responded Titus Oates at once. "Where have you been? Have you not heard of the plot to assassinate the King and perpetrate a general massacre of Protestants?"

"I have been far away, sir, beyond the Scottish Border, and . . ." Before he could finish Sandy Peden was interrupted by Locke the philosopher, who turned angrily on Oates, "The testimony of Bedloe, Dangerfield, and other such wretches who came forward to witness to the charges, is scarcely reliable, and when Sir Edmund Berry Godfrey, the Magistrate to whom you had sworn to the truth of the charge, was found dead in a ditch, it was all too convenient. All London went wild with fear and rage."

"How dare you insinuate, sir, that my integrity is suspect. Already thirty five Catholics have been executed and many cast into prison, Even the Queen herself is not above suspicion, as I and my good friend Rev. Israel Tonge delved out."

"Now, now, gentlemen, in these hectic years we need all the men with courage and skill to ride the storm!"

Locke turned away with disgust from Oates, and with interest alive in his pale, rather ascetic features, he said to the Covenanting Minister, "So you are of the Presbyterian Church of Scotland? What do you think of Platonism and Latitudinarianism?"

"I prefer the Bible to Greek philosophy, and lang words are a plague to our faith. You maun explain yourself, man. The Athenian philosophers got short shrift from God's servant, Paul."

Locke was surprising unruffled. "Essentially, my friend, they emphasise practical conduct as part of the religious life, and that if a man confesses Christ, then conformity in non-essentials should not be demanded."

"Tis true, Mr. Locke, that they strain at a gnat and swallow a camel. If a man does what is important, he will know how to do what is unimportant. A'body must ken for themselves what is important and not be forced by others. Bishops may be for England but not for Scotland. The Church of Scotland acknowledge no authority save God Himself. In the years before 1560 it was the Pope and worldly priests who stood between a man and the rightful worship of his chosen God. Now under the Stewart monarchs it is the dangerous doctrine of the Divine Right of Kings. You will hear before our Scottish Communion Service these words solemnly spoken, '. . . in the Name of Our Lord Jesus Christ, King and Head of the Church . . .' "

"Our philosophies are parallel, Mr. Peden. No man has such complete wisdom and knowledge that he can dictate the form of another man's religion. Each individual is a moral being, responsible before God, and this presupposes freedom. No compulsion that is contrary to the will of the individual can secure more than an outward conformity." Here Locke became bent double as his voice broke into a hoarse wracking cough. "After four years abroad in Paris and Montpellier, it only takes two weeks back to bring out my asthma again. It's this London air, that's so damp." He sounded bitter.

"My body still shivers from the soakings on the mosses and hags of Scotland forced on me by your English Government, Mr. Locke."

"Government is a trust and its purpose is the security of the citizen's person and property. The subject has the right to withdraw his confidence in the ruler when the latter fails in his task. Government and politics are necessary, but so is the liberty of the citizen."

Sandy warmed to Mr. Locke, and this helped to make him more comfortable as he recognised in Anthony Ashley Cooper, Lord Shaftesbury, an extremist like Oates, but unlike him, a more calculating extremist, who had skillfully fanned the excitement roused by Oates' wild rumours, so that when the London population had become filled with fear and rage, Shaftesbury was regarded as the only man with the courage and leadership to deliver the people from the Popish Plot. Just then Titus Oates broke into whistling a lively tune with great cheerfulness. "Ah, you're whistling again that ballad everyone is starting to like," said Shaftesbury amusedly.

"What is that melody known as?" asked the Scotsman. "I'm afraid I'm no' familiar with it."

Here Titus Oates sang a chorus of the ditty.

"It's called 'Lilliburlero' by most and its a fine marching song isn't it? It treats the Papists and the Irish Catholics in particular to the ridicule they deserve."

"Is it right to scorn those you disagree with?" asked Sandy pointedly.

"I would remind you, Scotsman, the Lilliburlero was the watchword used by the Catholic Irish in the massacre of their Protestant countrymen in forty one," answered Oates angrily, his face contorted. "The word of the Papists was nothing when they promised a safe passage to the Protestants."

"Seldom has so slight a thing had so great an effect," intervened the nobleman, again trying to sooth the atmosphere. "The whole army, and the people both in the city and the country are singing it."

"Let me sing the Psalms of David on Cairntable's heights. You will excuse me, your Lordship, if I retire. It's been a long journey with a happy result, for which I wish to thank my Lord in a privacy unsullied by external disturbance." Sandy looked pointedly at Titus Oates, who answered insolently with further strains of Liliburlero. "Lilliburlero, bullen a la, liero, lero, Lilliburlero, lero, lero, bullen a la."

After a few days Alexander Peden thanked the nobleman sincerely for his kindness and help in the deliverance of the Covenanters. Only now did he realise how close a thing it had been, despite the word of knowledge which God had given him beforehand. In conversation with his host he gathered that the transportation of prisoners, introduced by Cromwell, had during the past several years reached the stage where licenses were given in frequent succession to many vessels to carry off idlers, vagrants, and entirely innocent people. One ship engaged in the kidnapping service and which bore the hypocritical appellation of "The Ewe and the Lamb" seemed to have been particularly active. There had been complaints that the master and merchants of the ship Hercules, bound for the Plantations, had apprehended some free persons upon pretext that they were vagabonds. The Lords had therefore commissioned two of their number to go abroad and liberate any persons improperly detained.

It was with a thankful heart that Peden took his leave, assuring the philosopher, economist, and physician, John Locke, that he would step off the stage of life in God's time and not the enemy's Significantly he made no such predictions to my Lord Ashley nor Titus Oates, the rabble rouser, as Sandy recognised him as. Stepping into the London street, he was narrowly missed by a Hackney

Carriage which, along with Stage Coaches and Sedan Chairs, seemed everywhere. In Scotland there were no Stage Coaches at this time and in Edinburgh itself only a few Hackneys which one could hire into the country on urgent occasions. Edinburgh being packed into the space of a mile in length and half a mile in breadth, upon irregular ground, had very few streets fit for the passage of wheeled vehicles. London town was a world apart in its myriad of streets and fine avenues from the heather and bracken clad hills and moorlands of Scotland which were Alexander Peden's familiar home.

11
Return To Redesdale

On his miraculous deliverance from a future of slavery in the Virginia Plantations by a combination of good fortune, human kindness, political expediency, and he believed, the overruling power of a sovereign God, Sandy remained for a while in the great metropolis, which really overawed the hill preacher. His home was where he wandered over the trackless wildernesses of Ayrshire, Galloway and Wigtown. Here he wandered through the streets, narrow and congested with squabbling people of the Tower Bridge area, and the parish of St. Paul's, he felt as a lost soul. Even the pigeons were different from their delicately hued country cousins, the cushat. London had not yet recovered from the Great Plague in 1665 and the Great Fire, a year later. Before the embers had died down, Christopher Wren, an architect from near Tisbury in Wiltshire, and son of a well known clergyman, Dean of Windsor, as virtual surveyor general, had felt it his duty to prepare a scheme for the rebuilding of the city.

Wren had also been elected as Professor of Astronomy at Oxford but architecture was his greatest achievement. The fire had raged from the second of September till the eighth, and on the twelfth he laid before the King a sketch plan of his designs for the restoration of the city. It was a plan which would now have made a magnificent city but the magnificent spirit was lacking and a more hand to mouth expedient was adopted, still a record to Wren's genius. It meant the building of a Cathedral in the parish of St. Paul's greater than before, more than fifty parish churches, thirty six of the Companies Halls, the Customs House, and several private houses and provincial works, all for an extremely small remuneration.

In St, Paul's, Wren had the central tower removed and the formation made of a cupola covering a wide area as a proper place in which a vast auditory would be possible for sermons to be preached in future. Though St. Paul's was still not finished when Sandy stood on the old Blackfriar's Bridge, he realised the loftiness which Christopher Wren had adopted for his churches, such as St. Mary-le-Bow, St. Clement Danes and St. Stephen Wallbrook. The open and appreciative spirit of the Covenanters, though accustomed to the plainness of the Presbyterian Churches style, and even more to the open air Cathedral of the moorlands, could yet admire the magnificent architecture of one man. The Monument commemorating the Great Fire was a Roman Doric column, beautifully tall and impressive in its classical style, while less appreciated by the Covenanter, was the equestrian statue of Charles I at Charing Cross.

If the Great Plague had caused much misery with a seventh of the population within the walls dying, the Great Fire destroyed thirteen thousand houses and left eighty thousand homeless. Rebuilding had to go on apace since, with the country at war, the taxes were high, and therefore, the port, commerce and finances had to be restored. Wider, better drained streets with no stalls had been built, lined by flat fronted, well constructed brick houses. Fleet River was canalized and non flooding quays established at intervals along the Thames. The New Commission of Sewers drained the Fleet Street and Chancery Lane houses and helped ensure that there would be no more plagues. London had become one of the healthiest cities in Europe. Money was flowing in from the Hudson's Bay Company which developed London's world fur market.

Peden remained for a few days at the home of an old Scots widow in Cheapside Street. A week was enough to expose the magnetism of his own Scottish hills and he set off north on a steed given by friends of Shaftesbury. A week took him to Derbyshire as heavy rain made the roads a quagmire. Taking then to the backbone of England, formed by the Pennine ridge, he passed by Keighley, and the ancient town and Cathedral of Ripon. Then he came to the Yorkshire dales, scenting the atmosphere of home. From Barnard Castle, careful to avoid the garrison, and the lonely hills round high Alston, a short tramp led to the timeless Roman Hadrian's Wall, impervious to the vicissitudes and changing fortunes of history. The Roman Wall in all its seventy two miles was neutral in allegiance to the Royalist or Covenanting party. It was the evidence however of the attempt of an imperialist power to subjugate a free people. Covenanter and

Caledonian tribesman both had their common bond. He almost assumed the personality of a Roman legionary after walking ten miles along the Wall following the undulating contours of the land from its fifteen foot height. From there the remote hill country and woodlands of Wark and Keilder took him into Northumberland until at last he entered Redesdale, a familiar scene for William Veitch, himself and other Covenanting ministers who had crossed the border on a number of occasions to preach.

Peden had baptised the child of a Redesdale reaver, Robson of Emmethaugh in a natural springwell at the foot of Birdhopecraig beside Rochester, a dozen miles from the Carter Bar on the Scottish border. The locals had hallowed it ever since, if that was meant by their everyday use for domestic purposes. Most of all he longed to see that Pike, a rounded hill with a gradual slope, four miles from Otterburn, where from a panoramic view of Redesdale, he had preached the eternal word to the Borderers. In those days reavers, the border thieves and plunderers, owned the valley and things were very wild. Even the King had sent officials to check on Redesdale, and found they knew no Prince but Percy, hereditary rulers from their seat in Alnwick Castle. A Warden of the Rede was tolerated in the Peel Tower in Otterburn village. There was an overpopulation in the village since primogeniture was not yet in operation and so the whole family tended to stay around. Lawlessness resulted since there was not enough family property to go round.

It was a glorious sun scorching day in Redesdale and the heat hung in the air like a blanket of haze. Even the birds were drowsy. It was wonderful for March to skip in like a lamb, but the sun had not penetrated the thick heather tufts to dry up the rain soaked moorland. Sandy strode off the Pennine range. Whin greys zipped and zoomed ahead and some blackcocks broke from cover, roused from their sleep. What a haven this had been in thrilling past. The memories flooded back.

After the Battle of the Pentlands several of the Covenanting ministers had taken refuge on this side of the border, and once when William Veitch was being searched for, he lay in a hut, near the Carter Bar, covered with heather tufts as if they had been growing. These English nonconformist Presbyterians had welcomed them as brothers, despite the feuds of the reavers of old and the memory of that moonlit night at Otterburn when Sir Henry "Hotspur" Percy had mistakenly attacked the area occupied by the Scots camp followers, and James Earl of Douglas, had seized the chance to slaughter the English force, with almost 3,000 killed to the Scots

100. But the past was laid aside in the common bond of Christ. John Hall of Otterburn was reported for holding Conventicles in his home ten years before. Secrecy had been tried with Veitch assuming the name of Johnson, though the house of Martin, John's son, called Martin o' the Bog affectionately, was well kent as a resort for the Covenanters and Nonconformists.

There were various places in the neighbourhood where worship was frequently held by some of the fugitive ministers long before they dared to gather a congregation in a Meeting House. The Hool Kirk or Haly Kirk, was situated among the rocks up the Sills Burn, half a mile from Birdhopecraig. Deadwood Kirk and Babswood of Chattelhope Kirk were one mile and six miles respectively from Birdhopecraig.

His old preaching spot was one which afforded a panoramic view of the countryside with the communities of Otterburn, Elsden and Old Town, and the farmlands of Dargues, Garret Shiels, High Green Manor and Tofts strung out at varying angles of his vision. Clear at the foot of the pike was Dargues Farm about three hundred yards distant, and still he could make out the massive outline of the ancient Roman camp with the ditch, massive rampart and gates built for Rome's all powerful cohorts. The military genius of the legions was stamped everywhere. Sandy's classical education gave correct interpretation of Bremenium Fort by Rochester village further north with some ballistae stones still remaining, and the Roman highway of Dere Street running nearby, almost straight as an arrow. As he glanced round behind him he felt these legionaires could have driven their roads through the Pennine range wilderness if they had minded and would not have been surprised to find milestones there.

Having savoured his memories, the pilgrim descended the gentle slope of the Pike to Dargues Farm and its overflowing sheep pens, suggesting that the owner did really a hard dargue of a day's work. Passing Garret Shiels, he crossed some fields into the village of Otterburn, nestling on the river Otter. Elsden was the chief town of Redesdale being a market town with a weekly market on Tuesdays and an annual fair in August. It had a castle, an Inn for the refreshment of Scotch carriers and cattle traders, and the riding of the bounds brought hundreds from the surrounding countryside. But picturesque Otterburn was growing rapidly with substantial stone houses and the Mill ground excellent corn, so valuable that it was guarded nightly against marauding Scots. The Scottish raids had been a cause of decline after the Battle of Bannockburn. Elsden had been the heart of the system of drove roads and border tracks. Now the road leading up by the Otter to the Carter Bar was much improved on ten years ago and Otterburn would come again. He saw, as he crossed over the bridge, the old pele-tower presented itself as a relic of the medieval glory when the Manor of Otterburn possessed many acres of demesne lands and the Tower was so strong, situated among the marshes, that the Scots before the famous battle wearied of attacking it. The Norman Umphrevilles had passed the lordship on to the Halls, the most powerful clan in Redesdale. A fish plopped below the arch and he remembered the sweet salmon served him by his host John Hall in the vast dining room with its glowing polished rosewood panelling and how he admired the painted frieze of the Battle of Otterburn above the fireplace when they retired to the library. The son of the Manor had been a plump and precocious youngster, nicknamed Martin o' the Bog, which he delighted in. Sandy had equally delighted in joshing the prickly young man about his unusual haunts and his father had rarely enjoyed his son's embarrasment.

Few folks were abroad but those stared at the northener askance. Peden had forgotten the weird figure he must have displayed. Imprisonment had ravaged his virile freshness. Along with his height, which was beyond the ordinary, his hair fell upon his shoulders and his beard, grey now, descended upon his chest. His high cheeks, once russet with health, were more gaunt and yellow. The inward look of his wide set eyes frightened the villagers who hurried by, and Sandy, somewhat bewildered and sad, felt a loneliness where he had been welcome once. Suddenly he spied a muscular figure tending to beefiness. Even from the rear there was no mistaking the thick neck and shoulders as he staulked across the little square. His heavy hand fell on him, causing the borderer to whirl round in alarm, bayonet sword drawn.

"What ho, Martin o' the Bog? A strange greeting for an old respected friend. A time there was you could not depart my speiring banter quick enough." The broad rubicund face scanned this gangrel body quizzically, at a loss. No doubt he was a travelling mendicant or a tinker out to tell his fortune.

"Ye have got me at a decided disadvantage, and one to you, as I have not a plack to spare for soothsaying. Everyone kens my name. So that proves nothing."

"Look ye closer, Martin, and recall the days of yore when the Covenant was fresh and hearts were keen on the hill preaching, though prophecy from the Lord is still my gift."

A slow dawning recognition seized Martin o' the Bog and his voice choked in a whisper, "Peden the Prophet! You're no mortal. We heard you were dead and a' Redesdale mourned lang. They've ever ca'd yon hill Peden's Pike."

"Ye do me honour. I find it still a fine outstanding hill, and I have been a thousand times hunted like a partridge upon a thousand hills, Martin. A hundred times I have been in the net but have ever escaped. The Lord has recently delivered me as He promised with the others from slavery in the Plantations of Virginia. Once the ship had left Gravesend my rickle bones would have occupied a tomb in the American wilderness. Tell me of the folk o' the Rede and their faith."

"I'm fair dooncast at your failing, Rev. Peden. I maun say that we're no a canny bit better in the Rede than the Gallowa'. They are times o' rugging and riving throughout the hale country, when its ilka ane for himself, and God for us, so they believe." His north country twang was softer than the Scots with the dialect almost the same. "Nae man wants property if an he has the strength to tak' it, or has it langer than he has the power to tak' it. Its one o'er anither whichever wins upmaist."

"I live as I can and am content to die when I am ca'd upon. Never envy another Lord his mansion, either in his sleeping or his waking moments. Be not concerned about my health. I have a hardy frame."

"Its you and your preaching we are in sair need of. You brought a godly fame to Otterburn. Elsdon has again become the spiritual capital of the Middle Marches, and the clans have their common burial, religious rites, market and assembly place there. In it all there is a heathen touch. The Midsummer Bonfires, through which the cattle are driven to protect them from disease, are lit."

"Baal worship, and its evil companions!" Peden groaned barely audibly. "Whats more the cruelty to God's creatures is openly practised. A Bull-ring and cock fighting pit in the Green sees animals driven mad to distraction and birds torn to shreds." He had scarce uttered this when a terror stricken scream reached the square presently filled for market.

"A bull has broken free of the ring in Elsdon and is heading this way trampling all in its path!" A man had ridden poste-haste from Elsdon and even his beast had the froth of madness. Their own mothers child was everyone's concern and soon the square was deserted but for the two reunited friends.

"Hurry, Rev. Peden, and dinna be loth to take shelter. Enraged bulls are no' particular whom they tear and toss."

But too late was their departure for a snorting and tatoo of hooves heralded the creature's arrival as its black shape stampeded in a cloud of dust down the hill into Otterburn. Sandy had shown no sign of movement, and stood transfixed, his head held high and straight black walking stick pointed in the bull's direction. The red animal eyes rolled wildly as it sought release from its own panic and an object to vent its anger on. Moving or still, it mattered not to this veteran who had sired countless heifers in the valley of Redesdale. Sandy and Martin were clear targets, but as he charged there was a certain hesitation which was more marked as the powerful bull drew to within twenty yards of its victims. His wicked horns had already gored a young woman badly and trampled on an old man fatally in Elsdon.

Sandy Peden had meanwhile stood fixing the great bull with his eye and, slithering to a halt, the animal shied away in fear from the stare. A stare absent of panic. A twisting and turning brought the bull to some five yards away as he pawed the cobbles surrounding the central village well, as if fighting some influence. Finally, to the amazement of Martin o' the Bog, the magnificent head went down, and he stepped up gently to the Covenanter, defeated in spirit. Peden's hand stroked the quivering hot nostrils as he whispered something inaudible.

"Man, I've ne'er spied the like o' yon. That was a canny bit work!" Martin's incredulity was no less than the villagers who crept cautiously from their steadings.

"God gave man dominion over his Creatures, and they are but his vassals until tampered by sin in Man. Fear breeds fear and they must meet their Master.

The bull but needed compassion. I've sweated more over quiet evil in traitorous men. Now, I am famished and would relish a whole kebbock of cheese and a bicker o' rich steaming brose with a lump of butter floating in the middle."

"Na, na!" laughed the Redesdale laird. "None o' your Scotch fare but a good lump of English beef and aiblins some honey mead after this morning. A trim for that growth would not go amiss either. The folks ken who ye are. So your disguise has gone." Arm in arm they made for the Peel Tower and the people followed the Scotsman like the pied piper to cheer, and some few embraced him as memories of Peden's hill preachings cut the ten years away.

He stayed for a week, renewing them in the spirit, and administering communion from the Hill they had named after him. A thousand gathered from the valley and many from Elsdon were converted from their half pagan ways. The call of home syne grew too strong and, renewed in his own spirit, he headed north for the Carter Bar. The land rose gradually as he approached the Scottish border and the air grew sharper and colder. The great forest of Keilder stood eternal over on his far left as he passed Byrness and the Druid's circle. This area of Redesdale was studded with prehistoric remains and, at Catcleugh, the Covenanter paused by the eight fallen stones called the Border Line and the circle of three stones, The Three Kings. If the Three Kings could speak, what tales would be told. Diverging to see the famous waterfall of the Chattlehope Spout, falling seventy five feet, he was disappointed to find it dry because of the hot summer. However, nature compensated somewhat by revealing the beautiful jasper stone polished by the water's action. The colours were good, yellow, red, and a bluish white chalcedony, spotted with red. Sandy, attracted by natural beauty, gathered a handful, determined to pass them on to his btother Hugh on Ten Shillingside Farm near Auchincloich. Hugh had the artistic streak to fashion them into a polished Celtic cross.

Two miles further and with a high heart, he came to the Carter Bar, over one thousand feet above the sea. Sandy felt how bleak and windy it was as he shivered under his long cloak, now threadbare. When asked what he thought of the weather up there, an old carrier had replied, "Hoot, man, hoot; the very de'il himself wadna bide there half an hour unless he was tethered." Carter Bar was a neck of land, connecting Catleugh Shin and Arks Edge. Sandy leapt across the neck of land joyfully. His months away had made him sick with longing for Scotland which, if his enemies had got their way, he would never have seen again. He hoped all the rest of the sixty had made their way home safe. Their fears of a life in the canebrake of the heathen Americas, slaving under a pitiless sun had been unfulfiled as he had foreseen.

Though he had no place to truly call his home, yet Lowland Scotland was his parish and in it many preaching stations like the Shotts Moor and on the banks of the Tigg by Colmonell, but his familiar scenes in the Borders were Gameshope, a wild glen adjoining a small loch and burn in the Tweedsmuir parish of Peebleshire, and Ruberslaw, a rugged range six miles east of Hawick where there were many recesses and chambers and he had preached to large congregations. He would make for Gameshope, the highest tarn in the southern highlands, an ideal hiding place, and, if all was clear, on to Ruberslaw. It was good to be home.

12
A Judas Come To Judgement

A group of nine horsemen were gathered, clearly disconsolate, on the moors near the village of Ceres in Fife. Their heads hung almost as low as those of their horses. Their quarry had obviously escaped their search, and anger and frustration were mixed with weariness. One who was clearly a leader was giving vent to the feelings of the group. John Balfour, a little man, squint eyed and of a very fierce aspect, was not known as the Jehu of the Covenant for nothing. Like Jehu, son of Jehoshaphat, anointed King of Israel by the word of Elisha the Prophet, he drove his chariot furiously. John Balfour regarded himself as an avenging angel against the enemies of the Covenant and it was not difficult to imagine him answering when asked by Jeram, son of Ahab, if it was peace, "What peace is there, so long as the whoredom of his mother, Jezebel, and her witchcrafts are so many?" Balfour had been invested with his nickname of "Burley" because in physical appearance he was "laigh and broad".

"That instrument of Satan has escaped out of our hands again this day. It seems our chastisement of William Carmichael must wait till another time. When Archbishop Sharpe appointed William Carmichael, that drunken insolvent, as the Sheriff-Depute of Fife, he did give it to one of his own evil spawn indeed. He has not only been a persecutor but gone on from robbery to rape." Balfour's squint became more pronounced and he almost leered, belying his words.

"Our scheme of revenge has been planned for weeks and we even sent away that friend of yours, Andrew Gillan. We could not be certain of his Covenanted faith, and even his credentials. Remember that your enemies are even those of your own camp. And then, when we heard that Carmichael was in the area of Cupar, our chance was ripe. The Lord even proved a good night's sleep in the barn of Baldinnie Farm."

"Aye" interrupted Andrew Gillan, "the farmer, Robert Black, was a wise and wary man, to absent himself from his own homestead and leave us his guests in possession. Word has got around what we are about, and they ken our mettle."

"Dinna interrupt, Gillan" Balfour answered testily. "Glad we were, Willie Daniel, after sending you on a mission to find Carmichael's whereabouts, you returned at seven in this Saturday morning to encourage our souls that our hated quarry was to spend the day with three or four friends, out hunting hares with his dogs on the hillsides."

William Daniel, a thin stick of a man, responded with the speed of a man eager to please. "Aye, Burley, I hastened back at crack o' dawn from Cupar when I overheard one of these drunken dragoons in his cups at the Hangingshaw Inn in Cupar Town. He didnae think muckle of Sheriff Carmichael himself, and observed that the man couldnae hit a hare wi' a musket ball at a yard's range even if the hare sat up and begged."

"The Lord has indeed delivered the ungodly into the hands of his servants. Like the web I used to weave on my handloom in Dundee." There was anger in Andrew Gillan's voice. "The Lord weaves His own wonderful patterns in our lives and the tapestry of that traitor Sharpe has come to its last thread. I can't wait to get my loof on him after what I suffered for refusing to listen to their false curates in Dundee town."

A tall dark-haired man, with a sombre but compassionate countenance, as if marked by the knowledge of man's inhumanity, and filled with the desire somehow to banish that evil, entered into the conversation. David Hackston of Rathillet in the beautiful parish of Kilmany there in Fifeshire, was the brother in law to John Balfour but there the affinity ended. Hackston was a man of God to satisfy the extremest zealot of the Cause. He was also a leader in his own right and not to be led like a sheep by some hill collie.

"Hold there. Gillan! We had decided that it would be enough to succeed in frightening Carmichael from the district."

Balfour's face was screwed up in anger as he sought to control his emotions. "Silence, you fool Gillan! Don't you realise that the man we seek has almost certainly evaded our grasp? Did not James Russell of Kettle sight Sheriff Carmichael hastening to Cupar with all speed. Some hint must have reached him of the risks by which he was beset. As for you, Hackston of Rathillet, your sentiments seem to me to savour of the Preacher Peden of Sorn, who is forever harping on about peace and agin violence and for turning the other cheek. His weapons of the Spirit have done nothing for us this far. The sword of the Lord and Gideon, say I! I don't care if you are my brother in law. This is something greater than blood. And, Rathillet, remember it was your horse that stumbled, then took fright and fled. The time we took in recapturing the nervous creature could have been just the delay that let our enemy escape. Any man that controls his horse properly will not see it lose its footing!"

"How dare you question either my courage or my skill as a soldier of the Covenant." David Hackston's normally calm and reasoning tone was swept aside in the anger of the moment. "In my younger years I was indeed a roughneck without the least notion of anything religious, until it pleased the Lord in His infinite goodness, to incline me to go out and attend to the Gospel in the fields as it was preached in power. There I was caught in the Lord's net. Nor do you cast libels on the famous Sandy Peden, the Prophet of the Covenant, a man of God in whose presence none of us can stand comparison. For all your reputation and nickname of Burley, I doubt if you would have the courage to look the Rev. Peden in the eye with your own squint one."

"**Beware, Rathillet, Peden may be the Prophet of the Covenant but I am the Jehu of the Covenant and drive my chariot furiously!**"

"Horses are even at their best God's silly creatures and so beware lest your's stumble and fall like mine in its weakness."

James Russel of Kettle broke in quickly before things could develop. "Peace, brethren. Remember that our time was delayed further by myself and others of the brethren chasing for miles a rider we sighted and mistook for Carmichael, only to find it was a harmless laird of our acquaintance. God has remarkably kept us back and him out of our hand. But, who's this that is running up over the moors?. It's none other than the farm boy from Baldinnie! Do you remember how he could not stop touching our weapons in admiration and hanging on our every word. He could not do enough to make our stay yesternight in the barn a comfortable one. One could see he had been reared in the Covenanting truths and principles."

A young farm lad with long hair swirling and half hiding his face, came rushing breathlessly up to them. Excitement was in his tremulous voice. The thrill of adventure was in his whole being. Life at Baldinnie Farm was at the best of times a wearisome ritual of hoeing at early morning, ploughing the acid soil, and finally reaping a meagre harvest of barley, oats and a little corn.

"Sirs, I thocht ye wid want to ken that the carriage of Archbishop Sharpe will pass in a few minutes. A traveller passing Baldinnie telt us that he is journeying from Edinburgh to St. Andrews before going to London to get the King's signature to his new law against the Coventicles. He said it gave liberty to kill any man who went armed to or from a meeting in the fields. No trial wid be needed. Onyway, he stayed last night at Kennoway with Captain Seatoun and was a while at Ceres the morn wi' the Curate. Then he bided a wee at Lord Crawford's."

"We had planned to castigate a subordinate but the Lord has delivered into our hands the prime author of our troubles!" Burley was exultant now with the smell of blood at hand. "Think of what this new edict could mean! The meanest Officer who wears the Kings uniform might shoot the suspected person on the spot."

"With more than ordinary outlettings of the Spirit for two weeks now while staying at Leslie it has been borne in upon me that the Lord would employ me in some piece of service, and that there would be some great man in the land, who was an enemy of the Kirk of God, cut off from the living. I cannot be quit of the thought of Nero. Where can I find that Scripture for it escapes me?" The others were staring at James Russel of Kettle as at a dreamer. The spirit was upon him and Elijah could not have commanded a more obedient audience. Even the thin ascetic profile of the man stamped him as one with the enduement as far as the Covenanting mind was governed.

To murmurs of approval, Burley continued, "What need we proof more? Mount and let us with all speed to the moorland road to St. Andrews."

William Daniel was a man of reason still. "Hold fast! Let us first select a commander. Otherwise we shall lack decision at the right time like the Covenanting army at Dunbar when faced with the chance of crushing Cromwell's Ironsides; they listened to the unwise cant of some of the Ministers who foolishly took the place of generals and lost the God given advantage of their high position on the hills. It was Cromwell's crowning mercy but our most abject defeat as a result of our crowning conceit. I vote David Hackston of Rathillet as leader for he is a man of principle, honour, both fearless and compassionate."

The tall figure of Hackston who had remained quietly apart, now came forward and responded with a shake of his head, "Nay, I decline it my friends, The Lord is my witness, that I am willing to venture all that I have for the cause of Christ; yet I dare not lead you on to this action. For there is a known quarrel betwixt the Bishop and me, so that's what I should do, would be imputed to my personal revenge and would mar my testimony. I have been wronged by the Primate Sharpe in a civil process, but I would not give the world ground to think it was rather out of personel revenge and pique. But as you are determined to go forward, I will not leave you."

"Gentlemen, follow me!" With this, Balfour spurred his steed and galloped madly across the flat moorland with the rest in a slightly less mad hurry.

Meanwhile, the object of their renewed energies was riding securely content in his carriage of State, drawn by six horses and accompanied by his eldest daughter. He had an escort of five servants. His daughter, who loved him in the way that only a daughter can of a man who had not gone out of his way to be known among his fellows for the milk of human kindness, was engaged in animated conversation with her father.

"I am worried, father, because a strange foreboding that makes me shiver and my bones to tremble has taken me these past two days. I remember that terrible message too clearly the boy servant at the Palace brought back from the preaching at Boulter Hall in the parish of Forgan, where he heard that wicked man, John Wellwood give sermon and after he gave him a fearful message — O Father! He said 'Tell him that from me his wicked life is now near to an end, and that his death shall be sudden, surprising and bloody'."

The Archbishop's pale lifeless skin seemed to take on a darker hue for a passing moment, and his watery blue eyes shrink. But with a shrug he cast off the fears. "Wheesht ye, child. Do not fret over the raving of those wild madmen, ranting hypocrites that they are. They see visions and prophecies in every dream, even drunken ones which they probably have in secret." He guffawed like a man accustomed to cheap jokes. "Just wait till I get King Charles' signature in London for my new law against the Conventicles. I will deal with that lying and insolent Wellwood — the nerve to tell me that my wicked life was near to an end and that my death would be sudden and surprising and bloody. I'll see him by the thumbscrew, and maybe even after, the Boot, and finally the Iron Maiden. The good Bishop Paterson who invented the thumbkins is a most close friend of mine." These last words were uttered in an undertone as even Sharpe knew there was a limit to his daughter's shame. But his mockery was open.

"Father, don't talk like that please. You're not really so cruel as these Covenanters' lies say. I remember when as a little girl, you used to support the Covenant even."

"Silence, girl. A man learns the error of his ways as he grows older. Now that was a good pipe I smoked with the Episcopal incumbent of Ceres, good, satisfying tobacco, from the plantations in Virginia, where some of these Covenanting dogs are paying for their treason to King Charles, slaving away out there in the sun. At least the dogs should be grateful for the sunshine. There's gey few rays reach our sodden hills and frozen Fifelands. But that was a bonnie wee place Ceres and the quaintest of old brigs. I might even take some time from the affairs of State to paint its ancient arches. One needs a channel for cultural pursuits, eh, daughter. You'll see enough o' that in London town. His Highness is a dandy and his beaus will flutter like moths round a candle when your fresh Scottish bloom strikes their hearts." A sudden commotion breaks out and the carriage jolts to an increased speed. "What's going on there, driver?"

The driver bent his head and shoulders to screw his words into the coach. "There are men chasing us, your Lordship! They're coming over the high ground of Magus Moor".

Sharpe became as a demented being "Drive on! Drive!" But it was in vain as the Covenanting force had come from nowhere it seemed, like dark avenging angels, and Russel, riding alongside, fired in but the ball struck the lining of the carriage. Russel realising his miss, shouted in "Judas, be taken. Remember James Mitchell, you pledge-breaker."

Balfour surged up and grasping the reins shouted, "Hold the servants. Cut the traces and let the horses go free. We don't want help to halt this day's good work. Russel, open the door. Come out, Sharpe. We mean no harm to your daughter but your end is come."

"No, no, mercy." All disdain and scorn for the Covenant was gone as he cowered in the corner, an object figure of fear.

"Fire into the coach, men, you Fleming and George Balfour. Thrust him through if need be." These two pushed their pistols in the window and discharged the contents. The carriage was now filled with smoke from the blasts.

After they had fired several pistols at Sharp, he was pulled out of the coach, and Balfour of Kinloch, having a blunderbuss charged with several bullets, fired it so near his breast, that his gown, clothes and shirt were burnt, and he fell flat on his face. Thinking a window had been made through the Archbishop's body, his assailants went off, but, Andrew Gillan, stopping to tighten his horse's girth, heard Sharpe's daughter call to the coachman for help.

"He must be dead. Let us begone. The deed is done." Balfour was satisfied. But there were muffled cries from inside and the girls' screaming made out. "There's life yet."

With a snarl Balfour turned swiftly. "Back! He is still alive. Recall, Sharpe before you die, how you have shed the blood of the saints like water and how you promised with the full agreement of the Privy Council to send James Mitchell to the Bass Rock. And you promised to preserve his life if he confessed to having attempted to shoot you in the streets of Edinburgh these ten years ago. But your lying tongue brought an indelible stain upon the ermine of Scottish justice and poor James Mitchell was sent to glorify God in the Grassmarket. Aye, and Mitchell was but a fey, gangrel body who was affected by all the sufferings of our land. Nae true Court of Justice wid have held him accountable for his actions."

"Gentlemen, gentlemen, save my life and I will see to the saving of yours."

"Nothing can shake our resolve. We are spokesmen and swordsmen of God this day."

"I will give you money,"

"Your money perish with you." Kinloch's patience was at breaking point. "Shoot him! Stab him." Steel flashed in the afternoon sun as in Caesar's assassination each vied to get the first blow in. But still it seemed that Archbishop Sharpe refused to die, either kept alive by the evil power that had animated his actions for the decade past, or as if God was not willing to lay this dark act to the account of the Covenanters, however justified they felt. Sharpe crawled out of the recesses of the coach, wounded badly and seeing Hackston sitting mounted apart, wrapped silently with his cloak around his mouth, forcibly restraining his own tongue from words he might regret, crawled over towards Rathillet and clawed at him beseechingly, "Sir, you are a gentleman! You will protect me!"

"I will not lay my hand on you." Answered the other enigmatically. Kinloch had reached his tether and ruthlessly grasped the Archbishop's white locks. "If you are not going to pray, it is time for you to die at last. I think Satan does protect you from our bullets and a silver one is needful as with that other spawn of Satan, Dalzell, that mad beast of a Muscovite. Cold steel is enough." The swords flash, cut and stab. Hackston galloped over with a despairing cry, "Spare those grey hairs" but it was too late. "Tis done at last, a wound for every Covenanted man in our band." Said James Russel, wiping his Andrea Ferrara on the grass. "Search him. He was intent on further mischief and may have a document of ill intent on his person. So what have we here? A tobacco-box, a Bible, and a few papers."

Having searched his pockets, he found the King's letter for executing more cruelties, as also a little purse with two pistol bullets, a little ball made up of all colours of silk, a bit of parchment, a finger breadth in length, with two long words written upon it which none could read, though the characters were like Hebrew or Chaldean. These they took but meddled with neither money nor watch.

"And what is this that flies out of the baccy box, a live humming bee!" Balfour of Kinloch showed how thin a veneer of religion hid the deep rooted superstition in his life and beliefs. His little eyes had a frozen look of genuine fear of the unknown. "It must be his familiar. The odour of wizardry hangs around the man to the close." Superstition was rife in Scotland of the 17th century. The belief was widespread that good and evil spirits haunted everywhere, especially the abode of the dead. The old pagan customs had not been rooted out from the dark side of people's minds, and strange rituals went on in deep woodland groves where headless cocks were discovered. Covenanting ministers could not always tell when a bland expression on the face of the most respected elder hid a darker mind, clouded by witchcraft and superstition. Sprites and kelpies inhabited every stream and dell. Balfour of Kinloch was a man of his times, among those whom the Gospel of the Lord was not reaching and changing.

"There are also a pair of pistol balls, pairings of nails, some worsit silk, and a paper with some characters. What's a familiar, Burley? Sounds like a devil. Go!" Russel turned in threatening gesture to the servants who were standing in a fearful group for comfort, liveried lackeys of the Archbishop. "Take your priest and begone!"

The terrified servants with the daughter in dead faint, whipped the carriage away across the moors towards St. Andrews to report of the horrific butchery of their master. For this deed none were responsible except those who were there, and seven of the nine, notably Balfour of Burleigh, had no misgivings at the heinous crime. But many were to be brought to trouble afterwards for it, and some, who were perfectly innocent, chose deliberately to suffer rather than to brand it as murder and condemn the perpetrators.

13
A Glasgow Baillie

Baillie George MacPhail stood idly under the group of elm and ash trees, which clustered at regular intervals along the Low Green as it bordered on the banks of the Clyde, meandering its broad way to the sea. He was glad that Baillie Campbell and the Dean of Guild had recommended that more trees be planted on the Green and to consider the overture made by William Cumming, the Magistrate, that, as one tree had been cut down in the Old Kirk-yard, twelve trees should be planted elsewhere. It maintained the characteristic feature of the Magistrates of his time, to protect the trees of the city. Ash and elm trees, he observed, seemed to have been especially favoured. But it was only right, as the Low Green had at one time been part of the Bishop's Forest which extended for several miles to the east. James II had made a grant of it to the Church and Bishop Turnbull 200 years before. Bishop Turnbull had presented it to the town and it had become the common grazing land of the Burgh. The cows of the citizens were pastured on the Green, the Gallowmuir, and the Cowcaddens, and driven by the town herd to the North-West Common, in the vicinity of Port Dundas Road, for milking. Personally, Baillie MacPhail thought it stupid that these beasts should be driven up the High Street which was, even without that, not in the best state of cleanliness. They could easily be milked at the foot of Saltmarket. That would come, if his plans for the city came to fruition.

But he experienced a deep sigh of satisfaction and his thumbs pressed against the swell of his stomach through his purple velvet waistcoat pockets, as he gazed over the recent additions made to the Green by the purchasing of the Linen Haugh, the lands of Peat Bog,

Daisie Green, Kinclaith, and Craignestock, the last three of which had gone to make up the High Green. There had always been a danger of flooding, with the broad waters of the Clyde constantly encroaching. The Provosts Haugh which was still separate from the Public Green was continually being flooded. They would have to raise the level of much of the Low Green in the future. Some twenty years before, in 1659, the Glasgow Burgh had recommended to the Dean of Guild to fill up the open cast mine made in the Meikle Green by the monks of St. Mungo's Church and make that part level with the rest of the Green. Mining for smiddy coals was certainly important but that could be better done out in the Monklands of the county of Lanark than disfiguring the Green. When all was said, it had a name to live up to as the Dear Green Place.

But as the Baillie's attention was drawn to Arn's Well on the Braeface of the Green, he agreed that there was much to be gained from a group of alders, also called arn trees, which grew near the spring. But the water from this well was considered the purest and best in the city and was in great demand for the making of specially good tea and punch. George MacPhail liked his tea and punch, especially hot and bitter, but he was very partial to this new coffee craze which was coming in with the trade from the West Indies and, in fact, was waiting on his friend and fellow Baillie, Andrew Spreull, to accompany him to the first Coffee-House which had been established in the Candleriggs with a monopoly in the Candleriggs. There were actually several mineral wells on the banks of the Clyde which possessed special characteristics from their chemical ingredients. Robin's Well was known for its bleaching qualities, and even now several women were passing his stance, in the shade of the trees, without noticing him as they hurried, with their carts piled high with grimy clothes, towards Robin's Well, as it stood at the bend of the river. Eager they were to eat into their washing mountains before the morning sun rose high in the sky.

The women of Glasgow were tough and resolute and folk still recounted the story to him of how, over forty years ago, the gentler sex had been rather unceremonious in their treatment of turncoat Ministers. When the Rev. William Annan, the Minister of Ayr and traitor to the Presbyterian cause, had preached in Glasgow, on his exit from the church, he found thirty or forty of the most honest ladies of the town fall upon him and even the magistrates, with railing, cursing, scolding and screamed threats. Two of the poorer women among his assailants were taken to the Tolbooth prison. But all day long, wherever Annan went, up and down the High Street, along the Trongate, or sneaking up Baxter's Wynd, he was terrified by the aggressive words and looks from the windows and closes of the enshrouding tenement Lands. These Lands were buildings with a good number of stories which seemed to overhang the narrow streets. After supper when he went to visit the Bishop and started out on the causeway with four other Ministers at nine o' clock, hundreds of enraged women assaulted them with neaves, staves, and peats but fortunately for their lives, no stones were used. However they were sore with the beating they took, and his cloak, ruff and hat were badly torn. Mr Annan and his companions only escaped bloodshed by many windows being thrown open and candles lighting up the scene. MacPhail would certainly give much to avoid the scorn and wrath of Glasgow ladies, who were normally given to a working and consientious domesticity which cared first and foremost for their spouses and bairns. The last of the group hastening to Robins Well over the grass glanced up and smiled as if reading his thoughts and reassuring him that he was in no immediate danger, while the first had already reached the much desired waters and were either beating their garments on the rocky shore, looking out at the island in the middle of the Clyde, or strenuously hauling up heavy buckets of the mineral laden water.

A salmon plopped quietly, causing his palate to water in anticipation. It wasn't the Sabbath and if he had had a line of cowgut, Baillie MacPhail felt very inclined to try his fortune in the shallow waters of the Clutha, the old name which he preferred to use, and even pluck off his silver buckled shoes and yellow hosen to guddle for salmon and trout when the tide was out. The Calvinistic prohibition of taking salmon from the Clyde on the Sunday was equally obnoxious to George as was the prohibition on holding Christmas Day. From the Middle Ages the Clyde had rich herring. But, for commerce, it was still not much better than a shallow canal which silted up on occasion. It was frustrating the enterprising merchants of Glasgow like George and Andrew who, sensing that opportunity was knocking at their door, saw the great opportunity of opening the river to shipping with the new trade to the plantations of the West Indies and Virginia. Even the tiny sea going vessels could scarcely get beyond Dumbarton, sixteen miles away. A gallant but vain attempt had been made to cut a navigable channel through one of the worst sandbanks at Dumbuck, but as one of the exasperated citizens had expressed it, the river was still in a state of nature. It had been allowed to expand too much in width. Nothing larger than barges and small craft could make their way up the Clyde. His gossip, Baillie Spreull, had been one of the farsighted thinkers who suggested that a harbour be located near the mouth of the river but clear of interference from people in the royal burghs of Dumbarton and Renfrew. The Council had agreed, 13 acres had been purchased near Greenock, and Port Glasgow come into existence with the first engraving dock.

Shaking himself out of this reverie, annoyed that Andrew Spreull had still not arrived, he looked up and over his shoulder towards the town and the Water Port, which had been built at the bottom of Stockwell Street by the Covenanting townspeople as a defence against Charles I and the royalists. MacPhail was less interested in the religious aspect of the question than in the advance of the commercial interests and growth of this city he loved deeply. While decidedly on the Covenanting side, he wished devoutly that the extremists on both sides would come to their senses and stop continuing the destructive strife so that peace could give the country, and Glasgow of course, a chance to do the important thing in life, make money. His eyes lit up as the burly figure of Andrew Spreull rolled out of the great oaken port, studded with its shining iron nails. There had never been any continuous wall around Glasgow, but each street was terminated by a Port. Westwards from the Cross of Glasgow was St. Thenaw's gait, sometimes known as St. Enoch's gait, which was spanned by the West Port of course, St. Mungo's gait defended the north side, the Nether Barass Yett at the end of the Saltmarket.

As George MacPhail was tall and spare, so Andrew Spreull was rotund and had more to spare than most of Glasgow's citizens when the Poor Law was too inadequate to provide for the needy among the vagrants from the Highlands, local Gaberlunzies, and numerous waifs. But to these two such things were inevitable in life and business though, if their work prospered, then such features would be reduced considerably. Meanwhile the Coffee House was waiting for their custom.

"Good morning, Baillie, and ye maun forgive me my tardiness but I was gathering the news that there's been a bit of a skirmish out by Strathaven, Drumclog near the Loudon Hill, I'm told. Remember that some of our Covenanter extremists posted a bold and foolhardy declaration at Rutherglen Toon the other day. It could be expected of those two fanatics, Balfour of Burley and Russel, who were among the murderers who assassinated Archbishop Sharpe; but Sir Robert Hamilton should have known there was nothing to be gained by precipitate action, especially on the Kings Restoration Day. Everyone in the town was there round the celebration bonfire. Eighty Covenanters rode in, put out the fire, marched to the Cross, and burnt all the Acts of the Parliament during the last nineteen years against the Covenanted Reformation. Of course it wasn't long before John Graham was on their trail, hiking over from Falkirk, and heading for Strathaven. But the news is so confused. It says they have sustained a defeat. I can scarce believe that."

"Listen Andrew, don't get carried away with the excesses of the Covenanting cause. What's the latest in the dispute with the Fleshers over the supply of tallow to our candleworks?"

"Good news, Geordie. The Council are preparing a declaration, prohibiting any freemen from transporting quantities of tallow out of the city without a special licence, otherwise it will be seized. There will be no lack of information because the informer gets a quarter, and there is a parcel of rogues round Glasgow's vennels."

"That will deal with that other parcel of rogues, the Fleshers."

"Aye, that's another thing. The Council is going to ordain that the Fleshers make up the tallow without any flesh, with no pieces of greater bulk than 6 stone. They've also to deliver tallow at least once a week to our candleworks."

"Wonderful, just all I desired. This calls for a celebration. Straight for Colonel Whiteford's Coffee House. Walter is a close crony of mine and assures me that the monopoly he has on the Coffee House will continue for a long time, nineteen years I think. So he'll raise the prices no doubt but you may have noticed, Andrew, that our charges are no great weight." Baillie MacPhail chuckled privately. "I give him free soap and candles. Peter Gemmel of the Wester Sugar Works supplies Colonel Whiteford with cheap sugar too. I hear Peter has got himself a Dutchman as Master Boiler."

By this time the two, arm in arm, had entered the Water Port and were purposely heading up the crown of the causeway which was Stockwell Street, as if to challenge any obstruction or opposing traffic. Merchants were the gentry of Glasgow, with their scarlet cloaks and silver nobbed canes, and they knew it. However they soon encountered an obstacle they couldn't avoid, groups of children playing in the street with loud halloos and antics. One group were in a chain of boys holding each other by the hands. The one standing steadily at one end was the pin round whom the others coiled, like a watch chain round the cylinder till the winding finished. They were crying "Rowity, chowity, bacco" and hugged each other. The tobacco trade was influencing the Glasgow customs to its roots. But others were amusing themselves in the traditional blind man's palmie, pulling, pinching and buffetting the blind man after three twirls. Thread the needle almost caught the two worthy baillies up in the thread as the circle of children wove under the arms of every second, back and forth, repeating a rhyme. The Baillies felt their memories revive of past simple delights but there was no valid reason to brook delay. Dinner was between twelve and one o'clock while shops were locked up, and merchants and traders sat down to their meal accompanied by the apprentices. No great hurry was taken over opening the shops and warehouses again after dinner for they would not be closed till eight o'clock. Throwing a bawbee to a few of the rowity, chowity bacco bairns who pleased him most, MacPhail hastened his fellow on.

The Coffee House was on the west of the Saltmarket on the south west corner of the Trongate, belonging to the Merchants Hospital. It had been built by the merchant and Provost of Glasgow, Walter Gibson, stood on eighteen stately pillars and was admired by foreigners and strangers alike. Entering the shadowy porticos, they soom came into the restaurant area which, despite the smoky atmosphere of pipe fumes, was brightly lit with oil lamps installed by Sir George Maxwell of Pollok and some distinguished merchant friends. Their fleet of five ships brought the blubber in a great trade from the Davis Straits and the Greenland Fisheries, risking life and limb in mountainous seas.

"There's Captain John Anderson, commander of the Providence. He tells me that the ship, the Lion, has just been built at Belfast, Ireland, with a burden of 700 tons and 40 pieces of ordnance. Graham of Douglaston and John Campbell of Woodside are getting a rich bounty for their £1,500."

"MacPhail, you never fail meal times." A strident voice rose from the raucous din. The clientele of the Glasgow Coffee House were refreshingly boisterous and witty, hearty and outspoken, rough but frank. It was one of the more boisterous members who claimed their attention, an imposing figure, lounging in a corner, swinging a white stick with an obvious sense of importance.

"That's Johnnie Dempster, the Bumbeadle. Shall we join him?"

"Dinna tell me. The whole toon knows him. I'm glad to say that Mr. Dempster comes off second best in his attempts to evangelise the Philistines. What right has he to go around arresting people walking about during the hours of Kirk service and compelling them to go to the Kirk?"

"Let's join him whatever, Dempster's always good for a wag."

So, esconsed with the Bumbeadle, they called for broth of barley and green vegetables. Scotland's agriculture as yet provided few root crops. Fowl, boiled salted meat, with haggis or silver grilse from the Clyde was to follow.

"There's one I would like to see end up in the Tolbooth," said Spreull, as a figure entered importantly.

"But that's Walter Gibson, who had this very Coffee House built. Some call him the father of trade of all the west coasts, a famous man. He has projected the first quay at the Broomielaw." protested the Bumbeadle.

"I don't care if he has quays built from here all the way to Dumbarton. I don't like the fellow. There is something deep down uncaring about him. There is something revulses me about him. He is driven on by money but he doesn't care how he gets it."

"Ah but I relish his cured red herrings! They're a tasty morsel! The fish sellers ca' them Glasgow Magistrates, and they're more popular than most of the real Magistrates!"

"Aye," interrupted George MacPhail, "you must admit that it took a lot of initiative to use the great shoals of herring that come up the Firth of Clyde, when Gibson started the first curing factory for red herrings in the country down at Gourock."

"I still don't care, George. That man would sell his grandmother. I feel it in my bones. He's no friend of the Covenanters either."

"I know what you mean, Andrew. The St. Agatha trades not only barrels of herring for brandy and salt but has human cargo, Covenanting prisoners."

"Let's forget about him. There's no point in getting involved," Johnny Dempster hastily added as Walter Gibson passed nearby to sit down."

"Now, here's a different kettle of fish. Ho, what say my humour, gentlemen? Hello there, Doctor Wingate. How are you faring?"

"The students at the Grammar School are still as reluctant to take to the Classics as ever, Mr. Dempster, as in French and formal dancing. Also our mistress of manners is having a problem instilling good breeding into the young women of the town. But the classes in Arithmetic, Navigation, Music and Fencing are very popular."

"Come now, sir, you are the only one entitled to the address of Mr. as a graduate of our esteemed University of Glasgow. But you cannot be happy with the miserable stipend of £100 per annum."

"But the Town Council have granted me an augmentation of £20 and the Grammar School doctors can count on additions from feu-duties, scholars fees, and Candlemas gifts. Don't forget that we get free daily peats brought into the town for firing, and for those over particular, some 'fugies' from the cock-fights. Bumbeadle, Dempster, you'll ken what 'fugies' are?"

"You mean the beaten cocks killed in the cock-fights. I'm surprised at you, Mr. Wingate, with the bird all bloody, torn and dirty. I wouldnae touch them."

"Tschaw, Dempster. You counted yourself a friend of Thomas Hutcheson, who was humble enough to establish the Hutchesons' School to educate ten orphan boys as well as the Hospital for the aged. A 'fugie' has as good flesh as the next to the hungry. Are you too proud to take a bet wager?" MacPhail suddenly changed to a banter again. "The Council has not only provided a prize of twenty shillings for the foot-race three times round the New Green, but has set a goldsmith to making prize cups for the occasion. What say we choose our winner for a wager of £5."

But before there was any response from a startled Beadle, a dramatic interruption took place.

A barefoot servant lass brought their broth, red faced with exertion, rather than self consciousness, as she had but a minute before carried the water for cooking and domestic uses from a public well, the Lady Well up by the Drygait, more than likely. The appearance of the worthy Baillies and of their erstwhile companion, the Bumbeadle, was seen under the oil lamps to be that of men of sallow, pockmarked, complexion, with a grossness to them. Tuberculosis and smallpox had taken their toll, inevitable when infant mortality was often the only alternative to being marked for life. Their table manners were very basic, but handkerchiefs tucked in sleeves were in operation with gusto, as the hot prepared soup brought colds to the surface. For the great part of Glasgow's population knew no such thing as kerchiefs.

"And how's work, Johnnie? Methinks you have some what changed masters."

"Discipline is discipline, no matter Presbytery or Episcopacy. I still eject screaming children, and women, who have secretly smuggled in a plaid for sleeping during the time of prayer, get the edge of my cane." Here he swished it menacingly and glared pompously round the Coffee House. His bulbous eyes told of a debauchery, inconsistent with his profession. "Things have become too lax in Glasgow and the sanctity and solemnity of the Sabbath must be preserved. I have even heard the playing of bagpipes on the Sunday. This deserves severe censure."

"Come, come, Johnnie. Would you also abolish the town herd

from his musical march along Trongait and up that slough of despond they call the Cow Loan. How would we know when to turn out our cows?" Baillie MacPhail delighted in bantering and exposing the hypocrisy of the stout Bumbeadle.

"I'd put all lawbreakers in the Tolbooth. They all end up there if they break the law of the church, Presbyterian or Episcopalian."

Andrew Spreull glanced out through the obscure light, penetrating by a mullioned window at the grim front of the Tolbooth with its grated cell windows. Many a conversation was carried on by signs with parties in the streets. Executions and pillories took place on a platform which projected from the steeple. There was a small door in the side of the prison opening out on the platform by which the parties were ushered out. He smiled wryly as he spoke, "Do you recall the unfortunate wretch who wanted to see what other people were like and got himself pilloried in the sight of hundreds. The poor fellow wasn't extricated for several hours, till some of the gratings had been sawn through."

"Aye, I fair enjoyed that." Johnnie Dempster lived on the discomfiture of others.

"For me it was more amusing to see the opportunism of the Covenanting faction in our city when the great fire broke out and a hundred and thirty houses and shops on both sides of the Saltmarket were burned down and more than six hundred families made homeless."

"Some rascally little smith's apprentice started it out of revenge when he was beaten by his master. I have it on good authority from another of that breed whom I let off for a moral misdemeanour. But it couldn't be proved." growled the Bumbeadle.

"As I was saying," Spreull continued, ignoring the interruption, "using the pretext that as the clock of the Tolbooth was set alight the whole prison was in danger, a Covenanting mob broke open the doors. Was it no amusing to see the magistrates discomfited as they could not deny there was danger to the lives of the prisoners who were nearly all Covenanters. Their friends seemed to have right long ladders just at hand. They all escaped including Kerr, Laird of Kersland, after eight years in prison and he has found safe residence in Utrecht. It was a welcome fire, George."

"The only welcome thing to come from that fire was that the Council ordered that no more houses should be built of wood but stone should be used for front, back and gables. It's time this city made progress." Dempster the beadle was not without legitimate desires.

"Don't forget Gibson's Wynd was built as a result, to give an access in case of another fire."

Just then an almighty hullaballoo broke out in the High Street nearby. Something very dramatic was happening and Glasgow's population was intent on being involved. George and his cronies were subject to like passions as the rest and they rushed out, leaving the boiled capon and fried silver grilse untouched.

Red gowned students were rushing down from the University College where its five quadrangles, covering at least four acres, housed the four hundred or so students who came from different parts of England and Ireland as well as the homeland, since rigid restrictions there had been put on the education of dissenters at University. Not only did the College Steeple stand out, almost one hundred and fifty feet high, but its library was outstanding, with liberal endowments from Thomas Hutcheson who founded Hutcheson's Hospital in Ingram Street and even from the Rev. Zachary Boyd, minister of the Cathedral, though he never did get expounding on his special theology to the students, much to their relief. The students' potency had already been seen one year ago, Baillie MacPhail mused, as the red gowned mass flooded by him, heading for the Tolbooth and Glasgow Cross. When the Highland Host, that army of uncivilised Celts, had been brought to the city to force the recalcitrant Glaswegians to renounce their Presbyterianism, they had plundered the townsfolk right and left, bringing spades and sacks to carry it away, and lived at free quarters for five days. The northern raiders then transfered their uncouth attentions to Ayrshire to ravage the countryside to the tune of over a hundred thousand pounds Scots. But retribution was awaiting on returning through Glasgow. A large concourse of students and other Glasgow keelies were barring the old bridge which the Highlanders had to cross as the river was high. Fantastic as it may seem to relate, these resolute young men had made these fierce Highlanders relinquish their booty, and made them leave by the West Port, all two thousand of them, in parties of forty. Now the object of their wrath was the troop of dragoons who were riding furiously into the city bedraggled and clearly panic stricken. They had met an unexpected foe. Battle no longer meant foregone victory. Frustration chased fear across their features as they careered along the Gallowgate. Suddenly there came the anguished cry of love choked in the throat. A child, barely more than an infant, had begun to run across the slippery cobbles of the Gallowgate to the welcome arms of his mammy, but his tiny feet had been betrayed by the wet surface. A dragoon's horse could not be checked and the small life was obliterated by a cruel second of flying hooves. A moment of pity showed in the soldier's face to be replaced by an oath directed at what he considered a careless mother. The woman's horrified screams further inflamed the frenzied students who had come to jeer and hiss. From shouts of "puppet soldiers" they changed to "Murderers". But my Lord Ross's regiment came out in force from their quarters just short of the Cross and had the effect of blunting any attack from the students and ushered Claverhouse's two hundred troops into stabling. For it was Claverhouse, his handsome face suffused with fury and an ill hidden humiliation, who led the flight on a steed, clearly not his own as he savagely wrenched at its bit. As it happened, his own sorrel had had its belly opened by a pitchfork.

Claverhouse violently grasped the ruffled neckpiece of Lord George Ross of Hawkhead, a noble who fished best in troubled waters, and no friend of the hill folk.

"Corporal Crawford, Captain Blyth and my own dearest nephew, the Cornet Robert Graham, have all been cut down in their glorious colour by a traitorous mishmash of a Covenanter mob, damn their rebellious hides. They caught us at a disadvantege. Who was to know they had received armaments from the Low Countries? Usually these bumpkins carry antiquated halberts. One of them ripped my sorrel, so that his guts hung out half an ell, and yet he carried me off for a mile. They pursued us so hotly that we had no time to rally. I saved the standards from what would have been unbearable shame but we lost about ten men, besides wounded; but the dragoons lost many more."

Lord Ross was accustomed to play the sycophant to this gay cavalier favourite of the King. "You'll be pleased to hear that we raided the house of a Simon Pickerscalls here in Glasgow, which he has made in the form of a church to hold a conventicle, with public collections even. The concessions offered by our over gentle Bishop Leighton have been taken by the extremists for signs of weakness on the part of our Government and the number of armed conventicles have increased. They are nothing but seminaries of rebellion."

"Pesht to your troubles, Ross. Our pursuers are close on our retreat, certainly as we rode through Strathaven. Their canticler of a crack-brained preacher cried me to stay for the afternoon sermon." Humour creased his smooth, olive skin and the luminous eyes crinkled. "Now to the defences, man! Erect barricades of carts, timber, furniture and any other materials available in each of these four streets converging on the Cross and make half of your troops stand to their arms all night. Station musketeers at every vantage point and tell them to watch for the approach of the enemy. Glasgow is a prize worth their making an effort to win, and they have too many allies within the walls. So drive these pestilent students off the streets. Cargill and Peden have been sowing rebellion among them. Some of these bloated, power seeking, merchant-baillies need shooting." He looked pointedly across the Gallowgate at where George MacPhail and Andrew Spreull were smirking openly at Claverhouse's angry bellowing. But John Graham knew the danger of jeopardizing the influential merchant faction of Glasgow, and strode off fuming into the garrison quarters.

But Lord Ross had no such compunctions and immediately accosted MacPhail and Spreull along with other colleagues and spectators to lead his soldiers to their mansions and more wealthy tenement lands to collect materials for the barricade. The two worthies had no option but to obey with ill grace. Both their villas in Shawfield were ransacked of the heavy furniture with their wives mute and helpless. Soon a formidable barrier was erected around the Cross, Town house and Tolbooth. That night all was silent.

Next day shortly after the neb of the morning, Captain Creighton and six troopers quietly trotted out of the Water Port, heading for Ruthergen way. About ten o'clock the Captain raced in across the old bridge ahead of his soldiers.

"The Covenanters are in sight. They are divided into two groups. One is marching along the Gallowgate and the other is trying to take our position in the flank, going the circuitous route by the Drygate and the College."

There was instant preparation but it was scarcely needed. The two attacks were badly timed. When the force that came at Creighton's heels along the Gallowgate, reached the barricade, it was met with a volley which at once threw it into confusion, and the soldiers, leaping the obstruction, had no difficulty in driving their Covenanting assailants out of the town. Their withering fire from the barricades and the house windows killed eight and wounded many. They had time to do this before returning to the station and facing the force descending the High Street. It also was made to retreat but in some order to rally in a field behind the Cathedral. They remained there till five o'clock before retiring to Tollcross Moor and then retreated to Hamilton with Claverhouse in pursuit.

Claverhouse refused to allow the citizens to remove the bodies of the slain and they lay on the street. Baillie MacPhail was outraged, despite his pragmatic views of the religious struggle. He urged the other burgesses to protest but they were sufficiently cowed for their consciences to take second place to their fears. As the soldiers kept back the encroaching crowds, whose angry humour was now ill concealed so that the officers were worried, Claverhouse bellowed across the Gallowgate, "Leave these bodies where they are and let the dogs devour them. If anyone touches them, he will be answerable to me." Neither the troops nor the citizenry were inclined to doubt his word. With reluctance MacPhail and the others dispersed the people, but George took the opportunity to swing his boot at Walter Gibson, the traitor in their midst, who would be willing to sell his soul for lucre. MacPhail and Spreull, for all their commercial ambitions and interests, were essentially men of heart.

"Away and sell your Glasgow Magistrates, Gibson. There's nae profit here like in herrings. I'm sure you cannae sell dead bodies."

Gibson was enraged but knew he could do nothing. If he called the dragoons in, MacPhail would slip into the crowd with whom the Baillie was really popluar. Despite the Town Council, Glasgow at grass roots was a Covenanting city.

Later that night George MacPhail led a small group of his workers out to the scene of the skirmish and they carried the dead Covenanters into nearby houses. But a guard had spied them and so the rapacious rushed across in a half drunken mood to the houses where the bodies had already been wrapped in linen, but unfortunately there was no sense of reverence in these men and the linen could be sold. MacPhail protested in vain. The women in the houses had even constructed biers to carry the bodies on poles and started to march through the streets. But the drunken enemy had not finished their work and when the procession started, they seized the poles and even the plaids that the ladies tried to use. It was as they were passing the Alms House near the High Church that the attack upon the defenceless women took place. So they were compelled to leave the coffins in the Alms House until proper internment was allowed. God was to grant them this favour sooner than expected-

My Lord Ross, finding the gathering of the country people growing, and fearing that every day considerable numbers would be added, so that they couldn't withstand a second attack, thought it advisable to retire eastward. The rebellion was now becoming rapidly formidable. Encouraged by success at Drumclog, and taking it as a sign that the Lord had at last bared his right arm for the destruction of the Amalekites, the disaffected folk in Lanarkshire, Ayrshire and Renfrew, flocked to join the little army in such numbers that in a day or two there were five thousand men in the field. Wild rumours were deliberately spread amongst the militia so that Claverhouse and my Lord Ross felt they had no option but to retreat and, as they did, the populace of Glasgow showed their thinly veiled delight. A stone or two thrown by street urchins at the rearguard troops only symbolised their antagonism. As the Presbyterians were encamped at Hamilton it was towards Stirling that the Royalist troops made a hurried departure. Little did they know that the Covenanting force was in most cases an inexperienced, undisciplined, and scarcely half-armed peasantry, while among the better classes there were few good officers who had been tried in actual warfare. They were also grievously defective in ammunition and artillery, those essentials which now constituted the strength of an army, and of which the Royalists had an unlimited command.

But still worse were the divisions in their opinions about religion. The leaders of the Covenanters spent their time in useless disputations and made no attempt to organise their followers into military discipline. Robert Hamilton, the commander-in-chief, held that position because his doctrines were more extreme than those of anyone else. He had no military experience, but some of the insurgent Covenanters gloried in the conviction that their reliance was placed, not in any arm of the flesh, but in a higher power. Prophet Sandy had often remonstrated with them over the madness of taking to the weapon which could only end one way. But Peden's wise words of advice were lacking with his absence at a Meeting in the Borders in the great mass of Ruberslaw, six miles from Hawick. Even there his prophetic spirit was strained within him as he felt the powers of disaster flooding like a black tide over the gallant men of the Covenant. But the Devil was to have his day, a day of mourning for the Presbyterian people of Scotland.

John Welsh, the great-grandson of John Knox brought a body of followers from Ayrshire, and also dissension since he desired to bring about a compromise with the indulged Ministers, which, in the eyes of the fanatical extremists, was a sin sufficient to bring the curse of Heaven upon the whole undertaking. As they lay camped on the south side of the Clyde at Bothwell Bridge, these two parties devoted themselves to totally destructive mutual recrimination. Under the two Ministers, Rev. Donald Cargill and a Rev. Douglas, and Hamilton, the commander of the Covenanting army, as well as a great number of the lay officers, believed King Charles had forfeited their allegiance by his attempt to dominate the Church. They absolutely refused to condemn the Indulgence. Before marching to the camp on the Clyde on the green quiet banks at Bothwell Bridge, they had taken possession of Glasgow for a short time. It was then that Baillie MacPhail, by now caught up from the neutral position to which his commercial desires for Glasgow's growth had held him, blazed in anger at the factious leaders, foreseeing clearly how their blindness was leading them. A day of darkness lay ahead. Unity was no optional extra at all but vital for victory.

Hamilton received him grudgingly in the Provands Lordship, Glasgow's oldest building and the one time residence of the Canon of Glasgow Cathedral. It was a three-storied building, with crow-stepped gables, and looked across the square to the twelfth century Cathedral of St. Mungo. It's oldest part had housed the clergy of St. Nicholas's Hospital which had stood nearby and had once housed twelve poor men as an almshouse. But charity was the last sentiment in either of the hearts of these two men as they confronted one another like human bulldogs.

"What's your pleasure, Baillie? Time is short and we must be about the Lord's business." Hamilton was peremptory and rude, distrusting merchants who made safe profits, while soldiers were shedding their heart's blood.

"What's the Lord's business is mine too, Commander. You seem to forget that we Glasgow Baillies have crossed our Rubicon and will suffer if you don't succeed."

"Don't talk in riddles. I'm a plain soldier and you don't play games with soldiers. We are already rooting out the half-hearted and I believe that it will be only those who have disclaimed that false pervert and truce breaker Charles who will stand firm on the day of testing upon us."

"Man do you know what you are marching into, certain death. The army will not abide traitors to the Crown. As long as it was a religious disputation, there is hope. To be divided courts disaster, and for foolish reasons when we are all Presbyterians."

"Foolish reasons, you merchant adventurer! What do you know about the doctrines of double predestination and the calumny of the Laodicean crew who would associate with the Erastian heresy?"

MacPhail sighed with frustration born of long experience of circular arguments in religious matters. People ended up entrenched even more rigorously than if they were separated by a moat.

To George, God was practical if anything. Such people tried to put the thatch in order when the foundations were burning down. They even excluded one another for not being exclusive enough. They, no doubt to his mind, were persons of precision in their own way but they fought over fitches and left the corn to the crows."

"We must unite in what's important," he exclaimed, throwing diplomacy to the winds. "When Cromwell was in control of Glasgow, and attended the Cathedral service, we discovered then that the only difference between the Covenanters and the Independents was that, while the Covenanters groaned in agreement with the preacher, the Independents made a distinctly humming sound. I wouldn't say it was much of a thological difference, would you, Commander Hamilton?"

"Get on with what you have to say, merchant. "You are close to blasphemy." The soldier was becoming clearly angry at MacPhail's banter.

"Cromwell must have been a man of good sense. When Zachary Boyd attacked him from the Cathedral pulpit, his answer must have given God a rare laugh instead of our continual solemnity, when he made him endure a three hour grace on bended knee as his guest at the evening meal. Zachary was a great deal more open to theological persuasion thereafter."

Hamilton was beside himself with rage as his neck veins swelled, and an apoplectic fit seemed imminent. But visibly he survived, to snarl what remained of the storm on his emotion at Baillie MacPhail.

"MacPhail, you stick with your candles, soap, and whatever other greasy things you deal in, and leave the soldiering to me of God's army. I have fought on fields you never heard of. We already have servants of God, like Mr. Cargill." He lowered his fanatical eye, and turned his broad leather jerkinned back. George MacPhail knew he was dismissed.

As he walked pensively down the High Street, he admitted to himself that Donald Cargill, one time minister of the Barony Church, was indeed a godly person. Cargill and Cameron, whom many were now calling the Lion of the Covenant, had lately joined company. When Cargill had been caught ten years before, it had in fact been through his own intervention and other persons of quality and especially his wife's relations, that Donald had been released. He had continued with what to George was the extremist party. If he was a man of peace and of the cloth, why was he joining himself to fighting and blood letting? There had been a man, Alexander Peden, a mysterious man, who had come preaching around Cathcart and Williamwood the Gospel of peace, wherever possible, a man to whom he had been strangely attracted. Why could all preachers not be as him? A dark cloud of forboding descended on the honest Baillie, as he surprised some common street hawkers of snuff by stepping out of their path on the narrow plainstanes.

14
Dark Disaster

With their return to Hamilton and the nearby Bothwell Brig, news reached the Covenanters on the 22nd of June that the Govenment forces were at hand. To meet the menace and put an end to the insurrection as speedily and humanely as possible, the Government in London had got together an effective army. They had displayed great alacrity and judgement, sadly for the men of the Covenant. The militia in the well affected counties were called out, also the landed gentlemen who came on horseback, with as many followers as they could muster. An express was also sent to London for a body from the English forces. The passages on the Forth were seized and secured from any whose loyalty was questioned or were wavering on the brink of decision. Military stores were seized for the use of the Government, and Edinburgh and Stirling Castles were supplied and fortified. King Charles, on the advice of his Council in London, named as Commander his natural son, the Duke of Monmouth, but who was known to the Scots as the Duke of Buccleuch, from his marriage to the heiress of the Scotts, the Border family. On being appointed, he left the metropolis immediately on the 15th June and three days later arrived at Edinburgh, where, after a day he joined his army to move eastwards, through Livingston and Bathgate. So it was on the 21st they came up with the Covenanting forces and confronted an army of religious men who, in their view, were rebels.

But in the leadership of the Covenanters Sir Robert Hamilton continued to row his bigoted course. That very morning of the Saturday he stood by his pavilion, and satisfaction and anticipation gleamed in his mein as he shouted to the men who were erecting what was clearly a large gibbet on the riverbank. "Build her high, my lads. She has a job to do, though the persecutors would deny her so. Vengeance is mine upon the enemy about to be delivered into our hands. Don't be short in the rope. Short shrift doesnae mean short rope." He laughed ignorantly as cart loads of rope were rolled underneath. The men who carried out his instructions did so with a fearful hesitancy, as if afraid of Gods wrath, if they obeyed or disobeyed. Many of the scattered forces of the Covenant had not roused themselves fully, and at that moment James Ure of Shargarten in Perthshire was mustering his troop of volunteers from the northern counties under the Blue Banner. As Ure had his sleep filled eyes horror struck by the sight of the hangman's noose, he was enraged and his face shocked white. Turning to Commander Hamilton he asked, "What in Heaven's name is the meaning of this instrument, Commander? Surely none of our troops have committed a crime?"

"Shargarten, you have been too long among the red grouse of Perthshire. Maybe you would prefer to hunt them than the enemies of the Covenant, the Amalekites, cursed of the Lord? No, this is for them, as they will be delivered into our hands. They will glorify their master on the banks of the Clyde."

"You are taken up more with other men's sins than with your own. That is our duty first, to begin with ourselves."

Hamilton scorned him with a scathing curl of the lips and pointed across the river. "We have not come here to fight among ourselves. While you have been sleeping and indulging the concourse of the Amalekites has arrived. While we were halting between two opinions last night, and Welsh of Irongray and his Indulgence-lovers were shaming the memory of the great John Knox, their host of dragoons and Highlanders have crept up unawares almost to our tents gates." The dark skin tents of the Government stretched like some Arab host over the Clyde slopes. The smaller starting force of five thousand, with the Highland militia and Scots dragoons added to the English, now amounted to 15,000 men, well equipped and provided for. The Covenanting army were facing an army three times their size. Ure of Shargarten voiced both their thoughts.

"I don't care their size but we can sweep them all before the wind. Union and enthusiasm have done greater things. But our camp is as agitated as ever with disputes and no preparations have been made to receive the foe whom we knew were coming, Commander Hamilton. Yet no one has even gone through the army to see if we wanted powder or ball. I'm convinced that there are few who have both powder and ball to shoot twice."

"While you are bleating here, Shargarten, that Bridge of Bothwell lies there an open unguarded avenue for the enemy." He gesticulated angrily towards the twelve foot wide bridge, old, steep and narrow, which stretched across the placid waters of the Clyde. A guardhouse stood in the centre. It was as if Hamilton was reading the mind of the young Duke of Monmouth, the King's son, who the day before faced his general officers to lay out the campaign.

"The army should march directly through the river, and attack the enemy without mercy, sire," advocated Claverhouse harshly. "The river is here fordable."

"No, Sir John, you were ever an impetuous one. These are my good English lads and I'd fain not lose them drowned before coming to grips with the opposition. Early in the morning of tomorrow's Sabbath we shall quietly approach the Bridge of Bothwell, and drag our cannon there. Perhaps we may even get these unfortunate wretches to surrender. Their grievances have not been adequately dealt with, I believe."

Claverhouse, persecutor to the end, and feeling his killer instinct in danger of being frustrated, gripped his sabre basket hilt till his knuckles were as white as his face which was full of suppressed anger. He dared say nothing. For this was the King's son and handsome favourite.

Back in the Covenanting camp, Donald Cargill, one time minister of the Barony in Glasgow, was entreating the wavering Covenanters, still rent by division, to form into rank.

"See, the flag of the Covenant!" The blue and white insignia was billowing in the breeze off the Clyde. "See the motto in letters of gold, 'Christ's Crown and Covenant.' Hear the voice of your country, your weeping country. Do away with this discord and let us, as a band of brothers, present a bold front to the foe." Donald Cargill's lips trembled and his eyes filled with tears of emotion. Timid and shrinking though he was by nature and disposition, he could do things as audacious as the young Lion of the Covenant from Falkland, Richard Cameron, whom he admired so much. In vain however Cargill entreated.

Yet amidst this confusion and idiotic folly there were three true and vigilant officers. All the day and all the night previous to the engagement, that old bridge of Bothwell, which was the key of the defence, was watched by David Hackston of Rathillet, Henry Hall and a man Turnbull. There they stood firm and steadfast, afterwards joined by Ure of Shargarten and John Fowler, the one time servant of Commander Hamilton who had made him a

Captain. Captain Paton of Meadowhead had been promoted to Colonel, and as such, he had to remain with the principal body, though he thirsted to be down at the bridge with Hackston, his comrade. They had in command three hundred good men of Galloway but only one cannon, as likely to burst in their faces as kill the enemy dragoons. They were alert when about three o'clock in the morning of that June Sabbath, the advance guard of the Royal forces crept in the half light up to the opposite side of the bridge, breath steaming in the cold air, as they dragged up the cannon.

The attack was begun and vigorously resisted by the gallant three hundred, to all appearance like the Spartans at Thermopylae, though Hackston, unlike the Leonidas tradition in the face of the Persian host, had no time to comb his hair. They returned fire for fire, taking shelter behind a fortification of boulders from the river banks, and fallen logs from the Duchess of Hamilton's woods nearby. Monmouth's forces were exposed and suffered quite heavy casualties. The powder smoke was still hanging thick when the bugle sounded from the Government side for a parley. The enemy came right to the bridge end with a white flag. Their spokesman called over, strident and harsh.

"Send over an envoy and we'll not harm him. We would speak with your Commander."

Daylight had fully come when two Covenanters were sent over, not Hamilton, who feared a trap, but David Hume, who had been Minister at Coldingham, and Welsh's right hand man, and a Galloway landlord, named Murdoch. The soft faced Duke received them kindly enough in his red silk pavillion with its golden tassels. Claverhouse hovered in the shadows like a hawk, waiting to pounce. General Tam Dalzell's commission was late in arriving from London, much to his annoyance, and he did not get to the scene of action until everything was over. When the Covenanters' Declaration Manifesto had been read, the Duke pursed his lips slightly.

"Your Grace, will you prevent the effusion of further blood, we beg you?" Hume was a gentleman to the core without any false diplomacy.

"Your petition for Presbyterianism should have been more humbly worded. Lay down your arms and come in to my mercy. You will be favourably dealt with. That is my last word, Reverend Covenanter." Monmouth was patronising but gentle, sure that resistance would end.

Hume returned to report to Hamilton who snorted proudly, "And hang next?"

Hume was concerned to fling out one more lifeline. "Maybe they have terms from England, sire?"

"Well, ask, man, before I change my mind." Hamilton was impatient for battle.

A Major crossed over from the King's lines in answer to Hume's signal with the white flag. His impatience was as equally obvious as the Covenanter commander, being of Claverhouse's dragoon troop.

"Did His Grace the Duke not bring terms from England? We insist on knowing what they are?"

The Major, crimson with emotion, reined in his prancing steed. "The parleyings are over. The time for action has arrived. The die has been cast and you must prepare for the King's justice." The words rang mockingly in Hume's ears as the Major galloped back over the bridge. He had barely reached its end when Hamilton flung the white flag down into the river Clyde.

The three hundred under Hackston renewed their struggle and even repulsed their assailants from the guns. For three hours into early afternoon these weary and overtaxed men bore the brunt of the attack. They were not supported by the reserves from behind who ought to have crossed the bridge, taken the initiative, and pursued the flying troops. Victory had been within their grasp to crown Drumclog, but controversy between the moderates and the extremists still raged. Even when they asked for more ammunition as their store failed, the answer came back that it was exhausted.

"How can this be? They have not even engaged Monmouth." David Hackston's honest heart was torn with anguish. "There is a traitor in our midst."

"Nay, sir, Commander Hamilton orders you to fall back upon the main body. You cannot maintain your position. We shall fight the enemy with hand strokes on the moor."

Hackston swallowed his bitter retort with difficulty. "Let it be known that we do so with sore hearts, for the fate of the battle is sealed. This is the last folly."

So the gallant three hundred withdrew and the Royal artillery and army remorselessly crept over the Bothwell Bridge and gathered at leisure on the same bank as the Covenanter army. Strangely enough at that point the Covenanters were in high spirits. All of a sudden however a panic cry ran through their ranks.

"Our leaders have fled! The maniacs have betrayed us. We have clutched treachery to our bosoms!" The normally discreet voice of young David Hume had cast aside any semblance of discipline. It was not Commander Hamilton who had valiantly driven back the impetuous charges of his well-armed assailants. For all his fanatical hatred, Hamilton was a brave man. If there had been union, he felt sure they could have inflicted a complete defeat on the superior enemy, but when his subordinate officers and some extremist Ministers began to flee, sadly he could no longer dare to expose his forces to threatened slaughter.

Chaos reigned. The cavalry escaped through the ranks of the confused infantry, trampling them into disorder. By ten o' clock in the morning it was a torrent of retreat apart from David Hackston of Rathillet and his troop of horse who let the rest retreat to see whom they could help. Eventually they too retired, gloomy and sullenly silent, trying to maintain a cold and tight lipped dignity in the disgrace. In contrast, a joyful messenger, horse and rider gaily caparisoned in crimson plume, was dispatched to Edinburgh to prepare for the triumphant entrance. Sadly for the Covenanters, Peden, preaching down by Hawick, could have foretold a procession of misery and scorn.

John Paton, who abandoned his short lived title of Colonel, ashamed of the disgrace of Bothwell Brig, made his way back to Meadowhead, on a fine harnessed horse given by the Sheriff of Ayr, a Covenanter. Unfortunately the man he trusted to return it to the Sheriff, stole the quality mountings. In addition to him being declared a rebel and a round sum being offered for his head, a stain was cast on the character of the honest Covenanting Captain.

Like mastiffs straining at the taut lease, the Royal Army sprung upon the helpless crowd in what became a death-chase. Running along the banks of the Clyde and through the woods of Hamilton, about four hundred were cut to pieces by the brutal soldiery. No quarter was given or prisoners taken. Twelve hundred had no choice but to throw down their arms and surrender. Their trust in mercy would have been totally betrayed and massacre was on the cards but for the intervention of the kindly Duke of Monmouth. With trumpeting herald he rode up, as bloody Claverhouse was intent on drawing up his dragoons for a fusilade.

"We must show mercy! No killing of prisoners. Their blood will only haunt our victory. Nor must you pursue the others into Hamilton Park there because the Duchess Anne has refused entrance in case we disturb the game. We must pay respect to her deer," he said with a whimsical smile. Claverhouse clearly did not share the joke and scowled viciously. But he determined to quietly satiate his barbarity when Monmouth departed the field. His dragoons, Mar's Highlanders and Mulligan's Irish, roamed like a pack of wolves through the streets of Hamilton and the neighbourhood, slaughtering at will. As for the prisoners, Clavers and his ilk had special treatment planned.

"Strip them of any armed accoutrements, their pathetic blue bonnets and whatever they call a uniform. They'll no be needing them more. Then lie them flat on the field and, if any raise their heads untold, shoot them like vermin for attempting to escape. We shall soon see what their gumption is. Oh, and they're not to be given water till I command." The veneer of gallantry had been stripped totally from his manners.

The time passed tortuously for the prisoners and thirst and cramp caused them to try to change postures, forgetful of the threat. But the cruel soldiery were as good as Clavers' word and pistol shot laid many lifeless for the least movement. Some gentle country women braved the brutality and ventured forward with stone pitchers of water.

"Hey, maybe its brandy in thae pitchers? They're clever chiels, thae Whigs, and pretty ones, b'God!" A rough dragoon and a hairy unkempt Highland soldier accosted the compassionate women, farmers' daughters in the prime of their beauty, and wrenched the vessels from their clutch.

"Och, its nothin' but the river water, and puir Lowland mixture at that, nae usquebagh! Awa' with the rubbish!" The crude Highlander smashed it on the bank rocks, scorning the parched prisoners. "Now, ye lassies are much more appetising." He made a smatch at the strings of a girls mutch and ripped her blouse. She screamed and huddled back with her friends, her modesty outraged, her spirit afraid. The gathered soldiers laughed uproariously and poked at the cowering group of lassies. The pitchers were all broken.

But this was but the beginning for the prisoners. Two by two, they were dragged eastwards in disgusting triumph to Edinburgh. On the road no one was allowed to attend to their basic toilet necessities purposely. All along the long weary way no one dared to help them, because those men who had started to were seized and added to the train of prisoners. When women tried to feed them, the food was thrown away. On reaching the capital at last their welcome was as that to Sandy when he was being hauled to the Tolbooth. Like pagan savages, the Edinburgh mob exulted over them with mockery and laughter. Accompanied by twisted grimaces and hoots came the cries of "Where's your God now? Where's your Covenanting God?"

At the time of the defeat Peden was forty miles away from the scene. His heart had been full of fear for his friends in arms. Knowing that the Covenanting force could ill cope with the Royalist troops, he had dreaded the worst. He retired to a small cottage outside Hawick until noon. It was so hard to pray even. He kenned that dark disaster had happened. A sound outside called his attention and an elder entered respectfully to say that a small knot had gathered outside to hear him preach.

"Let the people go to their prayers." Sandy answered sadly. "As for me, I neither am able to, nor will preach any today. For your friends and mine have fallen and are fleeing before the enemy at Hamilton. The enemy are hagging and bashing them down and their blood is running like water. If they use powder and shot they only further strengthen the tyrants' arm." All strength had drained from his tired frame through sorrow. Sandy's visions and dreams carried a heavy burden. Turning to the small group, he said with tears close, "Pray more. Prayer will do more good than preaching. An awful curse has to be removed from Scotland, and prayer alone will do it. It is praying folk who will win through the storm. I'm afraid, like Richie Cameron, that the Frenchies will yet land on British soil. King Charles is assisted by French gold and the power of the French King is at his back. Pray that the French Monzies will not march over the length and breadth of Scotland up to their bridle reins in our blood. Now please allow me to retire and be alone." The Hawick folk shocked by the news and seeing his depression, retired silently to their steadings. Standing alone, he spoke to the dark skies in great weariness. "The extremists among the Covenanters have often scorned my counsel, but now they are sadly regretting they did not listen."

Meanwhile, in the capital, the wicked climax of the Bothwell Bridge defeat was reached with the execution at the Mercat Cross of two ministers, John Kid and John King, who had escaped from and laughed at Claverhouse after Drumclog's defeat. Five innocent Covenanters were taken out onto Magus Moor to be hanged for the murder of Archbishop Sharpe, and not least, the conversion took place of Greyfriars Churchyard into a prison as the crowd, now over a thousand, could not be held in the existing gaols. The terrible irony that this prison was Greyfriars Churchyard, where forty years before the National Covenant had been signed, seemed to bow their spirits and shoulders as they were herded in, like sheep. Sentinels were stationed over them day and night. The seasons of autumn and winter brought both sun and rain, wind and weather. All night they had to lie on the bare hard ground with very scanty clothing. Insufficient food was allocated and when some more charitable Edinburgh citizens came to supply some food or any little gift, either access was denied or they had to bribe the sentries. Often whatever was brought in was plundered in some way in the passing. A James Corson from Lanark had received a parcel from his distraught wife who had hurried with a little money from their souter's shop to the capital.

"It's from your wife, James Corson. She's been troubling us for the past week. She maun think a wheen o' ye to gie ye sic bonnie cheese." The guard laughed mockingly as he threw it through the gate separating the Covenanters prison from the main churchyard. The other men nearby in the cramped situation looked on enviously at their companion's good fortune.

"We'll eat the kebbock of cheese tonight. I would like you all to see what grand cheese my wife can make. Coorie roon sin' the rain will spoil it otherwise."

A hasty exclamation from Corson startled them as he removed the damp cloth wrapping, "Dod! Strange cheeses they're making in the Lanark mill these days. He held up a filthy smelling cabbage, though admittedly the scrapings of a once huge cheese round remained.

"What more can ye expect from a pig but some of his usual fare. That guard is like an animal and kicked old Johnnie here the ither night and robbed him of the few placks and bawbees he had, even the velveteen waistcoat, a family heirloom." The man pointed to a huddled figure in the corner.

"God curse them for false Scotsmen. Four months we have been penned in till this freezing October time and they boast they have done us a great favour by erecting some wooden huts. We're not allowed to raise our heads from the ground at night without being shot at by the guards."

"Yet there's a lot more room since the faint hearted submitted to subscribe the bond agreeing to take up arms against the King no more and were set free."

"Much more to be commended are the brave fellows who escaped that cloudy night, disguised as women in the clothes smuggled in with the men's garments we requested. But mostly I admire our Minister, Mr. Kid, who has gone to glory with Mr. King at the Mercat Cross. Did you hear that he joked to Mr. King as they walked hand in hand to the hanging that he had often heard and read of a kid sacrifice?"

By November they were reduced in number to 257, those who had failed to escape, who had no friends at headquarters, and who stoutly refused to take the bond. Without any previous intimation to themselves or their friends, early on a cold, raw morning, they were conveyed by a party of soldiers from Greyfriars to a vessel, the Crown, lying in Leith Roads, for the purpose, as it was given out, of being transported to the American plantations, and sold as slaves. The Privy Council had agreed that the prisoners, including James Corson, should be banished to the West Indies. His heart was anguished as he in vain appealed to the lieutenant to pass a message to his wife in the Cowgate Vennel. A sympathetic trooper overhearing, mentally resolved to look out the address.

They were crowded under deck in a space, not sufficient to hold one hundred people. Those with some little health left were forced to continue standing, that the sick and dying might lie down on the hard boards. Hour after hour the old ship lurched on, low in the water, and many fainted in the poisonous air. Thirty already had been suffering from flux, bronchitis and pleurisy. Meat and water were doled out in niggardly fashion. Fortunately James Corson's work as a Lanark cobbler had stood him in good stead. His whipcord muscles resisted the strain and restrained a few, maddened by thirst, from drinking their own urine. He set up such uproar that the Skipper, though a hardened ruffian, sent down fresh water.

James managed to gain a small piece of parchment to inscribe a letter to his wife and friends. Some returning ship might take it but his own return to Scotland was remote. Hope strove in his breast as he wrote, "All the troubles we have met since Bothwell are not to be compared with the present circumstances. Our uneasiness about the future is beyond words. Yet the Lord consoles us and this overbalances everything else. I hope we are near our port and heaven is open for us."

He broke off as the vessel lurched violently. The Crown had been encountering great tempests in the North Seas for the last three days but this seemed serious trouble.

"Yon's the Orkneys. Set for shore!" The cry was heard above the storm.

"Chain and batten down the hatches! Cast anchor by these lights!"

Corson rushed to the hatch and shouted desperately through the grating, "I beg you in Heaven's name, to land us and lodge us in any prison to await the further orders of the Government."

But already a sailor was winding a great chain between the grating. His boot ground viciously into Corson's hands as he pushed upward with full force. He fell backward among his panic stricken fellow Covenanters. The darkness falling rapidly further increased their confusion and fears. About ten o' clock a fearful swell broke over the Crown, and dashed her against the rocks. She was cleft right down the middle. The sailors, lowering the mast, laid it between the sinking vessel and the rock on which she had split, providing a bridge for their own escape. All was wild chaos on deck as well as below. The Skipper still refused to open the hatches, notwithstanding the agonising cries and entreaties of the prisoners.

However, when the vessel was torn asunder on the Orkney's rocks, James Corson saw their last opportunity and led all the fittest onto the flooded deck as the storm raged. Hope lit a flame in about sixty hearts and they heeded Corson when he bellowed, "Tear up the deck. The ship has no more need of it. We can drift ashore on the wreckage! The Lord will take us or leave us. We have but one choice here!" He looked with a strained face and deep pity on the poor wretches too weak to do anything, stumbling drunkenly in the lashing rain. With a lunge Corson threw himself into the brine and in ten minutes lay half drowned on the Orkney shore. Almost sixty others were similarly saved. Two hundred Covenanters were swallowed up in the raging deep, some welcoming this death to the persecution in their native land and slavery aboad.

The fate of the survivors was nothing now to the sailors, their being no profit, and James Corson and his friends found kind refuge with the Nordic Orcadians who had little interest in the issues of King and Covenant. The Privy Council were more concerned with public executions at the Grassmarket to attest the Government in London that they were doing something. So it was that, after many weeks wandering, James Corson arrived back in Lanark, to his souter's last and his wife's arms.

All this had been foretold by Sandy Peden when preaching on the moors of Galloway. Suddenly, halting again in the middle of a prayer as the vision came, he told the Conventicle of hill folk, "Our dear friends, the prisoners at Edinburgh, have done something to try to save their lives, but, as the Lord lives, that shall not do for them, but many shall have the sea-billows as their winding sheet. A few shall escape, who shall be useful for God in dear old Scotland."

15
The Devil's Pride

The meeting which took place in the great banqueting room of Deane Castle, the ancient seat of the Boyds of the estates of Deane and Asloss, was a union of kindred spirits, kindred in evil. Deane Castle, situated on the edge of Kilmarnock, and in a sheltered spot just west of Fenwick Water, belonged to an unbending Royalist family, and could not be a more suitable meeting place. Not many miles away was Loudon Castle, where lived my Lord the Earl, whose eldest son, Lord Mauchline, had been tutored by the Minister of the Covenant, the Rev. William Guthrie of Fenwick. This Minister was known abroad as a man of deep merriment and spiritual humour, who sometimes mixed among the people of Fenwick Parish, disguised in the dress of a traveller. He was known once, in disguise, to have given a man two shillings to make him go to his church. But the two men who met that day were of a different kind. There was about them both an atmosphere of evil, only in one raw and blatant, while the other a subtler more refined and dangerous quality. General Tam Dalzell of the Binns was as he appeared, a wild and bloody man of crude manner and bestial humour. Such men are found in every land and are equally at home among the soldiers of the Russian steppes as among the Scots Dragoon Greys, which Dalzell formed for his beloved master King Charles. The cruelty of barbaric Muscovy, where he was promoted to General in the Czar's army, was said to have perverted Dalzell's nature since in that vast land, so shrouded as yet in a semi-oriental mystery, it was known that people were serfs and the Covenanting spirit of freedom unheard of. The exquisite instruments of the Boot to torture the shin bones and the thumbscrews for the other extremity were sources of delight to Dalzell.

A strange figure indeed he presented and astonished even his soldiers, who were in mortal dread of his temper. Though of immoral nature, he would not tolerate it in others and hung two soldiers who had stolen saddle gear. It was known that his life seemed to bear a charmed existence, as if the Devil protected his own and the only effective means of ending it was a silver bullet which Captain Paton had attempted at Rullion Green, when the forces of the Covenant met with disaster. In appearance he presented a mighty figure, his head almost bald and often covered with a beaver hat, his beard long and bushy and almost to his girdle. The features of Dalzell were of a man born for war, with fierce blue eyes and beak like nose, cheeks marked with deep merciless furrows, no gentle crinkles apparent. A casing of blue black armour covered his brawny chest. His coarse habits were a source of amusement at the court of the King, as he washed only on dire occasions and was on some occasions bare footed. A jockey coat close to his frame with tight sleeves of home spun wool was his usual dress, even on state visits to his beloved Sovereign who tried to get Dalzell to attire like some of his dandies, complaining that he attracted a rabble of urchins when he visited London. But when the General complied and came replete in ruffles, lace, buckled shoes and powdered wig, King Charles, a man not unaccustomed to mockery of others, laughed at his loyal subject so much that he reverted to his antique habits, his temper only in control from his deep love for King Charles, who never felt the deep affection of courtiers who fawned on him and paunced off the royal resources, and had an intimate trust in this bear of a man. The London ragamuffins were pleased also, as they had missed Dalzell as the dandy.

As for his companion in Dean Castle great hall, there was portrayed a contrast in appearance to the world, though not to the Whigs of the south west, as they knew to their cost. John Graham of Claverhouse was a gentleman and soldier whose private life was of a higher sphere than most of his royalist comperes. Not a tall man but of mid between five and six feet, his complexion was unusually dark and eyes large, dark and full. A kind of womanly loveliness seemed to haunt his smooth skinned boyish face and the frizzly long red love locks had obviously had the small lead weights attached at night to his tress ends to keep them in place. There was high breeding in every line.

But this John Graham of Claverhouse was a terror, at the mention of whose name intending conventiclers disappeared, and called Bloody Clavers for good reason. This John Graham, eldest son of Sir

William, Laird of Claverhouse and Claypotts Castle, near Dundee, and of Lady Magdalene Carnegie, fifth daughter of John, Earl of Ethie, afterwards first Earl of Northesk, was of aristocratic lineage. Born in 1648, ten years after that historic scene among Greyfriars tombs, he was left fatherless at five. This high birth contributed to the comparative influence of Claverhouse at his majority. Like Turner, Bruce of Earlshall, Grierson of Lag, and others who harried Sandy Peden, John Paton and those of the Covenant, he had a University education, though no one could conjecture this from his compositions which he sent to Sir George McKenzie, the Lord Advocate. His thoughts were expressed in a rude, vulgar and curiously spelt dialect, not employed by other students at St. Andrews. With £600 annually from his property, he had no need to become a mercenary like Turner, fighting for daily bread. Yet Claverhouse had gone to, and returned from, France and Holland, with the reputation of a dashing officer, whose white plume had marked the track of his gallantry at the battle of Seneffe. At this encounter in the Low Countries, Claverhouse was reputed to have saved the life of William, Prince of Orange, when his horse stuck in the mud and the forces of Louis XIV threatened his death. Such are the ironic quirks of fate and history, had they but known the future. But Peden's prophetic gift is not the common possession of man, for throughout the land were men with eyes who could not see and ears but could not hear. Prejudice, hatred, fear and violence had shrouded men's vision.

On returning to Scotland, at the instance of the King and his brother, the hated Duke of York, an open and avowed Catholic in a supposedly Protestant monarchy, Claverhouse was gazetted Captain of a new troop of horse on the 23rd September 1678. His duty in patrolling troublesome Dumfriesshire that winter animated him with a zeal and delight. He came to have within himself a peculiar view of soldiering in his homeland. It was not unique for such men, considering himself to be an armed high priest, commissioned to sacrifice the enemies of the Crown, as much for their own sake as for that of his employer the King, for whom, like Dalzell, he had a consuming loyalty. He had become an Episcopal Crusader, inspired to do battle with dissent and cleanse away the gangrene likely to infect and destroy divine Episcopacy. Though he had made many enemies, including the Marquis of Queensberry, a powerful landowner in the borders, he had written frequently to the Marquis and confessed that, for his own part, he looked on himself as a cleanser. He could cure people guilty of the plague of Presbytery even in conversing with them but could not be affected. Such then was the crusading angel of darkness to the Covenanters.

He now came forward eagerly, with manicured hand outstretched and a triumphant smile wreathing his lips in which there was a hint of condescension. Dalzell's mighty hands enclosed it in crushing style, as if in answer to the other's superior smile.

"By the Lord God, I am pleased right heartily to meet thee, Tam Dalzell, Master of Binns, Your reputation went far and wide during the Civil War in England when you fought with great constancy against that regicide Cromwell and his Ironsides. Their square cropped heads would please you, Tam, since you havenae much hair yourself." Claverhouse grinned sardonically and Dalzell laughed a dangerous laugh like a bear growling. "But they were a fair army, these Ironsides, but too canting and psalm singing for my liking. I believe you had many adventures over the country and even in Ireland, you old fire eater."

"Aye thae croppies offered £200 and a free pardon to any who would deliver me dead or alive to that wart faced toad Cromwell! But none daur betray General Tam Dalzell. The mad beast of Muscovy is what these prick eared Whigs crie me!" His great beard shook.

"Yes, I heard that soon after you had followed the soldier-gentleman's path abroad to offer your services and sword to the highest bidder and did enter the army of the Czar of all the Russians. May I congratulate you on being raised to the rank of General for distinguished service. It is a great honour for I hear they're bonnie fechters there with less of our refinements of chivalry. Be assured we have need of that service here. These Covenanting dogs are on the increase. There's as many elephants and giraffes in Galloway as loyal citizens!" This time they laughed together as they warmed to their common hatred. The fascination of evil had created a common bond, comparable almost to the love of the Covenanting brethren.

"Twas rare sport indeed, fechtin agin' the Poles, Turks, and Tartars! They fought furiously for their freedom for which I like it all the more. I can't stomach soldiers that turn and flee at the first sign of bloodshed. These Tartars presented difficult opponents. Their horsemanship would make your hillmen and their garrons look like elephants for clumsiness. Aye, I've seen that strange monstrous creature brought into Scotland last year. They rode and wheeled almost with the speed of the arrows they so expertly fired. Only when you got near and fought hand to hand or surprised their camp, could they be defeated. Aye, the Czar promoted me to the position of General, which I found to my liking. I'd rather be his General than his subject who, if truth be told, is more his serf. Mother Russia taught me some glorious ways of dealing with her enemies. Even these hard Cossacks were broken."

"Fine it would be if you used some of these glorious ways against these Covenanter rebels. Their obstinate canting wills need some breaking."

"I'm the very man to deal with them. On leaving Russia in 1665 the Czar did furnish me with a letter testifying that I was a man of 'virtue and honour and great experience in military matters.' All of this I am!" Dalzell was clearly enjoying this meeting more than at first and his coarse bombastic nature took full advantage. "I have brought a new and improved thumbkins. I just love this Scots nickname for thumbscrews. It shows true affection." He reached over down into a dark corner of the hall to which he had walked while saying this last. "See here, Captain Graham, these thumbkins would make even you confess to being a Whiggish Covenanter!"

"Never! They even call me 'Bloody Clavers' because of my faithful pursuance of these rebels. It has been reported that they talk of me as Clavers in a' my pride, they with their hypocritical humility. They have been a continual source of annoyance. When I was first appointed as Captain and after you had formed your Dragoon Guard in '78, my dear General, my orders confined me to Dumfries and Annandale, and I had to complain to Lord Linlithgow with great embarrassment that the other end of the bridge was in Galloway and so there was nothing to prevent the disaffected from holding coventicles across the river under our nose if they do chose. Such an insult as that did not please me and yet on the other hand I did not want to exceed orders. The offending meeting house was demolished by my good friend, Sir Robert Grierson of Lag, Ye ken Sir Robert?"

"I do that! A real firebrand! Like me, he has withstood the Covenant from the first flush of its traitorous popularity. The whole country it seemed was aflame with this fanatical zeal and even Montrose had signed their damned National Covenant. But I have remained throughout my life constantly averse to every type of Covenant and Covenanter. I wrote to Lauderdale as Secretary of State that these sedition mongers should be deported to the sugar and tobacco plantations of Barbados, Jamaica, Virginia and the Carolinas, never to return. I have found that many of those who profess much for His Majesty are far too mercifully inclined towards that damned crew!"

"Well spoken, my friend and comrade."

"This land will never be quiet till all the Nonconformist Ministers be banished and the Puritan ladies sent to bear them company! Though I be not betrothed and never had a spouse legal wise, yet I have never lacked female company. They find my beard catches their fancy and my habits strange but fascinating. But I would not take all the fish in the Baltic nor all the tobacco in the Americas for an association of intimacy with one of your Puritan ladies. They do know the Bible backwards and their nagging tongues repeat nought else. As for men I doubt they know them."

Claverhouse, whose moral life was of a higher quality than the Muscovite mercenary, answered not but returned to his point. "If I be suffered to stay any time here, I expect to see this the best settled part of the Kingdom this side of the Tay. The south west of Scotland will become truly loyal to King Charles. But in the end there will be a need to make examples of the stubborn that will not comply. Nor will there be any danger in this after we have gained the great body of the people to whom I am become acceptable enough. We'll soon make them loyal citizens of His Majesty. Incidentally, General, is it true that you have undertaken a vow not to shave that beard since the murder of King Charles I?"

"Aye, that I did, God bless His Majesty's memory! But since I'm bald and don't wear a peruke anyway then I have to make up for the lack elsewhere! Once or twice a year I go to London, only to kiss the hand of his worthy son, who has a great esteem for my worth and valour."

"Otherwise he could not have appointed you Commander-in-Chief of His Majesty's forces in Scotland."

"But, my good Claverhouse, His Majesty is none too pleased when we go walking in the Park of St. James. He bids me go to the Devil for bringing such a rabble of boys with me. This crowd of boys always were accustomed to follow me when I attended at Court. They are attracted by my long beard and antique dress. I never wear boots nor above one coat with close sleeves and tight on the body. These urchins love my beaver skin hat which I gained in Muscovia. King Charles did once request me to shave and dress like other Christians. And so going to Court in the height of fashion, he then laughed so much at my strange figure that I donned my old habit. All the boys methinks were pleased no end as I had escaped their weasel eyes in my gentleman's garb."

"Maybe they think you the Devil in human disguise, Tam! These Covenanting breed have superstitious minds clouded over with too much religion. They see the Devil in everything. They believe I am the Devil's spawn and can only be killed by a silver bullet. They call my black stallion Satan because it can negotiate the steepest of hillsides. They'll no forget quickly that time I rode my Satan along the face of the Stey Gail down Enterkin Pass, and gey precipitous it was. Don't you have any Devil's stories?"

"Mine are not stories. Everyone knows of the great occasion that I played cards with the Devil at the House of Binns and I lost. He was devilish good, you know, aha! So I threw the card table at him and missed. It flew through the window and into the Loch beside the Binns. If one were ever to drag and drain it I could prove it by the evidence."

"I'm not going to try, General Tam. I prefer my feet in the stirrups. The Graham crest is a Phoenix bird arising from the flames, but this Graham is not going to rise from the dead if I am to meet my Maker."

"Would that be God or the Devil?"

"Take your choice. As I told John Brown's widow out at Priesthill Farm by Muirkirk, 'To man I can be answerable, but as for God, I shall take Him into my own hands!'"

"A' I don't believe I'll ever play you at the cards, my dear Clavers. You are too passing canny."

"But I hear you are a bit of a canny one yourself, Tam. You've lined your own nest since you came to Castle Deane, aye, to the tune of fifty thousand merks."

"One has to obey the law and impose fines. Then of course there is the quartering of the troopers. I can't very well allow them to keep the goods they seize. It might spoil them. But these damned Highlanders who have arrived this month are a different matter. They are under the command of Mar and Perth, who have brought down 6000 of these caterans. They are confined to Renfrewshire, thank the devil, and have quartered thirty of their barbarians along the road in the parish of the Mearns. They've got hold of that bonnie wee Castle of Mearns. You know, in that old keep I could hold of an army. They used to remove the wooden staircase which reaches up to a doorway eleven feet up the wall. Their soldiers knew their military strategy in Jamie the Second's time all right. I hear that lawless bunch have vandalised the place. It would be a disaster if the same happened to Bridgehouse in Linlithgow, Cardross House, Newhouse in Kinross, and Airdrie House in Lanark county."

"And you are such a paragon of virtues, General, that you never maltreat people and places."

A sudden, despairing cry echoed up from below, penetrating even the massive stone floor.

"Ah, what was that?"

"The Thieves Hole," grinned Dalzell. "An obstinate rebel from Lanark who was there when the insurgents passed through but says he didn't join them and what is more to the point can't give me the names of the rich fat Lanark burghers who were involved. If he perhaps can, a pretty penny in fines can be made. So he is having his tongue loosened down there among the toads and rats, fit company for such spawn. But how is Galloways these days?"

Don't provoke me, General!" Claverhouse's calm deserted him momentarily. "The shire of Lanark is bad enough. We were at the head of Douglas the other day and went round and over Cairntable. Then we were at Greenock-head, Cummer head, and through all the mosses, moors, hills, glens and woods, spread in small parties, ranged as if we had been hunting partridges. Our party even went as far as Blackwood but could learn nothing of those rogues, curse their traitorous hides. It had been rumoured that a large body of armed Whigs had been driven southward from about Hamilton. A long haul was made for nothing and a tiring return over the moor by Coalburn and through the hills more easterly, leaving Douglas and Lesmahagow a mile or so on our right."

"Galloway is much quieter now but it has been difficult and exacting. The churches have been deserted and no honest man or minister is safe from these marauding hillpeople. The first thing I had to do was provide magazines of corn and straw in every part of the country, that I might go with convenience wherever the King's service required. If I moved from one part to another, nobody knew where to surprise me. We quartered on the rebels and tried to destroy their sustenance by eating up their provisions. But the clever fanatics quickly perceived our designs and sowed their corn on untilled ground. So I determined to hunt them down systematically and took several. While many fled the country, yet at least we managed to ding them all from their hidden haunts. A good policy has been to bring to prison their servants and bring their wives and children to starving. This has made them accept the safe conduct and glad to renounce their principles. The collectors of every parish have been ordered to bring in exact rolls upon oath, attested by the Minister. They have been read every Sunday after the first sermon, and the absentees marked. If they remain obstinate they are severely punished. If I ever hear of a parish that is considerably behind, I go there on Saturday, and tell them that Claverhouse will be present at sermon. Whoever is absent on Sunday, is punished on Monday. There have been cases where they would not appear at church or court. On these occasions I have had their goods arrested and then offered them a safe conduct. This was a sharp measure, and many responded smartly, including two outed Ministers whose reputation was really disorderly."

John Graham was a man of his own profession merely, an exact, technical soldier and strategist, but no great politician and diplomatist. He had the talent to form military combinations and see how physical force could best be brought to bear upon any object. At the beginning, in an age of venality and sordidness, he had contrasted favourably with most public men of his day, being more sober and decorous, more diligent and industrious in the execution of his trusts. Occasionally he felt some little spark of chivalry for the service of his masters. Essentially Claverhouse was proud and ambitious for a wider sphere and higher position, and isolated from all sympathy with the masses. The Scottish Episcopalians saw in him the champion who would fix their ascendancy beyond all reach of attack. He was inflamed with the passion of a Grand Inquisitor. In his bosom seemed to be hoarded the whole accumulated rage of his party against the Presbyterians, certainly those who stood obstinately by the National Covenant.

As the years had passed in which he marched, planned his controls, and perpetrated killings, from the rank of a true and legitimate officer, he had dropped down and down to the lowest thing a man wearing a sword could be. As Captain John Paton described him after the nickname the Parson's Drudge, which Gustavus Adolphus gave to General Graf von Tilly, his enemy of the Catholic Holy Roman Emperor's forces, the Parson's Drudge. This ideal Jacobite knight understood well, however, the realism of pounds, shillings, and pence lands and estates. The world, in particular, south west Scotland, was an oyster, which with his sword he opened. By strange accident, the more the west country lairds were harried, the more he enriched himself with fresh estates, the more the blood of the fanatics there was shed, the more the gifts of money flowed from the Treasury into his pocket. The right or wrong of a thing was to him a thing indifferent. Enough that there were disturbances, and that he was ordered to quell them. Enough that people were disaffected, and that he was ordered to strike an exterminating blow.

As he continued his conversation with Dalzell, he attempted to justify his code of conduct. "In the letter I wrote to our Commander-in-Chief, I told him that in any service I have been in, I never inquired further in the laws than the orders of my superior officers, and, as I said to the Chancellor, I am as sorry to see a man die, even a Whig, as any of themselves. But when one dies justly for his own faults, and may save a hundred from falling in the same way, I have no scruple."

During the mutual encouragement in their evil designs of these two arch villains, a drama was being enacted on the edge of Kilmarnock, which added a tailpiece to their afternoon. A Covenanter, whose sympathies had been told to the town garrison, was being hunted. Passing through a vennel, he turned swiftly in through a doorway shaded by the arched pend entrance. The stabled cattle bellowed in alarm but the good woman received him immediately into her kitchen and offered sustenance, but passing through to the back he ran through the door left ajar. Leather riding boots sclathed on the cobbles outside and with sweat beading on his brow, he half fell into a ditch, six feet deep in a stagnant water used as a natural sewer. A clump of thorn bushes covered the bank. Acting on instinct, he stood up to his nostrils in the muddy bed with his head concealed in the bush. The angry and frustrated hunters returned to the woman's biggin. Baulked of their prey, her answers were never going to satisfy them. Seizing her she was led to the Castle of Deane. Claverhouse was enjoying a sumptious meal of roast venison, duck, pheasant and lamb abundantly washed down by a vintage claret, from his host Dalzell, whose lack of gentility of eating habit was only equalled by his lack of restraint in the amount. The classical habit of deliberate sickness after a great meal needed no inculcation in General Tam who regularly spewed in his cups. His rage knew no bounds when the distraught woman was brought before him to interrupt his gluttony.

"What is the cursed reason for interrutping my cups with this pious viraga?" His own crude attempt at humour eased his temper, looking over at Claverhouse for approval. A disdainful gleam was in the latter's eye, and the haughty lip set off the almost effeminate delicacy of his olive features. Even in such features however there was a clearly querulous and dissatisfied expression.

"What say you, Sir John?" Dalzell asked when he heard her guilt through suspicion. "Shall we afford her the delights of the Thieves Hole, our pleasant bottle dungeon? Tis enough that she's suspected. We have some delightful creatures for company there. What with the fallow deer, squirrels and foxes in the grounds of the Deane Castle, we really care for our guests!" He guffawed, the ale running down his unkempt beard, as the poor woman paled.

At that moment an officer entered to announce that the two men had arrived who were bail for the prisoner who had become dangerously ill in the bottle dungeon. Dalzell had granted their petition but bound them to bring back the prisoner at the appointed time, living or dead. The officer said they brought a body. "Aha, they have kept their word. Allow it to lie outside the prison door till his carcase has rotted out the Covenanting disease enough for a decent Christian burial!" The commander snarled savagely. "Take this witch out and throw her into the Thieves Hole. I'm sure my Lord Boyd will be glad that it's in constant use. My Lord is unavoidably absent just now." Lord Boyd had preferred to leave for one of the hunting lodges on the three hundred and fifty acre Deane Estate rather than share his home with such a vicious ruffian.

The small palace portion of Deane Castle where the banqueting hall was, had been built by Lord Boyd's ancestor in the mid fifteenth century with the attached tower and wall surrounding the courtyard. There were a large number of windows in the Palace and the projecting battlements of the tower allowed the defenders to fire down more easily. But the high Keep was built about a hundred years earlier for defence, the walls being two and a half metres thick, with few windows and none of them below where the bottle dungeon extended for twenty feet. The terrified woman was led out along the battlemented rampart to the Keep, and as they went she attempted to wrest herself from the guard and throw herself down into the courtyard. Two soldiers managed to grasp her wrist as she teetered on the edge. Roughly they hurried her below into the Keep. There in the floor of the prison was the circular hole down which unfortunates were lowered twenty feet into the gloomy dark of the bottle dungeon, its greasy walls extending out below. The distraught woman, barely conscious, was let down roped round the waist, by the jailer who shouted to the man already there, "Here's company for you, apart from the creatures whose home you've invaded. Let out the rope, and then you can do one another a favour by holding the other upright. You known how we like you to stand upright and stay awake." The screams of the woman before she fainted in the depths of the Thieves Hole echoed hollowly, strangled in its bottle shape. The Devil's pride was riding high on the Covenanters' backs, spurred by the Mad Beast of Muscovy and Bloody Clavers.

16
An Unexpected Help

Three men lay sunning themselves under a rocky crag on Clinchfoot Hill on the outskirts of Sanquhar, known to the worthies of that small town, on the borders of southern Ayrshire and the northern limits of Dumfriesshire, as the old fort, as its name signified, indicating Norman settlement in the dim past. A Covenanting stronghold, Captain Paton and his two friends, Joseph Whiellens and Tam Stirling, knew that they would have sanctuary if but once they reached its marches. Even Paton's great body was visibly in a condition of exhaustion while the others were totally drained of physical resources. Their's had been the life of animals for weeks.

"Aye, it's been a lang wheen time, lads, these last four weeks o' hiding in these soaking moors and flooded streams. I'm sure water has got into my bloodstream. Noah must have felt like this."

Joseph Whiellens, a long string of a man, retorted with a deep sigh, "Ah, but it's grand at last to bask out in this beaming life giving sun. The blessed warmth is creeping into my bones and drying these clothes that seem to have been constantly soaked with moisture all through this weary month that Claverhouse's dragoons have hunted us like the fox and hounds. Only this fox has been too wily by far. Master Reynard has himself been a help to the Covenanting cause on occasion. Daniel McMichael of St. John's town of Dalry said that his life was near to the gate when hunted close by two soldiers on the hills, with their bloodhound hot on his scent. McMichael had hidden deep in the heather but the hound was in an unerring mood. When discovery and death were inevitable, our Reynard did jump up and led the foolish dog and his masters a merry chase after his red coat."

"It's true, Captain, that I've been so tired and hopeless with these weeks of cold and misery so that capture, yea even death itself, might have come as a relief. But ye-e-es," Tam Stirling yawned and stretched his short wiry frame, a younger man than Joseph. "Today the sun is shining, fine and warm. It's Sunday and everything seems peaceful and quiet. Even Clavers must have given up by now though methinks his pursuit of the faithful does extend beyond duty or even his misplaced loyalty to King Charles. Surely Sanquhar must be safe by now and we can return to a dry bed and regular meals? It's a toon that disnae spread bitterness amang its folk, dividing them into hares and hunters."

"Curate Kirkwood is truly a Christian man, even though a King's man. He believes in letting a man's conscience govern his actions, not to poke and pry and haul men away to prison and death. He is not a partridge hunter."

Suddenly there came round the rocky crag a Captain and troop of dragoons. The Captain's face mirrored his astonishment and pulling on the reins caused the horse to shy with a great high kicking. His broad brimmed plumed hat fell off but with a curse he dragged the large horse pistol out from the holster on the saddle. A sense of satisfaction suffused his voice and a crowning triumph.

"Hands up and surrender, else you are all dead men." Tam Stirling was the first to come out of the numbing paralysis which had frozen his limbs. Bitterness filled his heart. "Caught like rats in a trap! So it has come to this!" He made to put up his hands in kind of dazed fashion. "I'm so tired and hopeless after these nights of cold and misery, that even this is a relief."

Joseph Whiellens couldn't believe what he heard. His friend had taken leave of his senses. "Not for me it wouldn't, Tam. I hae a wife and bairns to live for." He jumped up and struck the Captain's horse on the nose with his hazel stick. The animal reared and the pistol's shot flew off target.

"Good man, Joseph Whiellens! Grab Stirling. He's paralysed. But now is our chance. Down this gully!" They all rolled down a rock strewn gully a few yards from their one time haven of rest. It was steep and covered with bushes. "Now, run for your life. It's me they're really after but if they catch you too, we all go to the same place, the Tolbooth, and then the Grassmarket, or if they're merciful, the Iron Maiden. We've got the start o' them, for they'll have to ride round the hillside if they dinna want to break their necks. Here, this way down the burn; if we lout low, they will scarce see us for the trees. It's as dark as hell in this copse."

"Brethren, I beg your pardon for my cowardly, spiritless surrender back there." Tam's normally reedy tone was thinner than usual as he ran. "It was not the true spirit of the Covenanter, nor the true spirit of the Stirlings!"

"Dinna fecht yoursel' man. We're all just a little bit of pity in the Master's hand and made of nocht but flesh and blood in our earthly temple. But what is immediately necessitous is that we show these dragoons what a Covenanting fox can do to outwit them and their clodhopping ways."

"It winna tak' muckle to trick these thick-headed soldiers. In these bog lands they will never catch us. I don't know which has the greater clumsiness, their own great boots or the hooves of their large steeds."

"But as you can hear, my lads, they be firing in every direction when they chance to see anything which might possibly be a human being moving. Nae, Tam, dinna look back, in case your courage forsakes ye. Ah, here we are at the spot where this burn reaches the River Nith, close to the Kirk and Manse of Sanquhar. Perhaps the goodwill of your Curate Kirkwood might be called to be tested sooner than expected. For we must cross the Nith to seek cover, for the banks on this side are smooth and green. Nae sae much as wid hide a flea here, far less a hedge or a wall to hide a fugitive."

With a cry of almost amusement, Whiellens pointed across the fast flowing Nith. "Here, hide yourselves under this wide spreading elm. Look over there for yourselves!"

Stirling laughed bitterly, "How can ye believe it? There's as peaceful a scene, full of harmony and innocent fun, as one could imagine. There's the Curate Kirkwood, playing a peaceful game of bowls on the sunny village green wi' a half dozen of his special cronies. Some I recognise as King's men like himself, and, see for yourself, there are some of our companions who favour the Covenant. How does life provide such irony? What are we to do?"

The great bulk of Captain John descended on him, forcing Tam towards the flooded Nith, still not subsided since the week's rains. "In ye go!"

"But our way is blocked! Had it been night we might have hid till day in an outhouse and gotten our breath. But here in broad daylight . . .?" Stirling's sentence was unfinished but needed none. Escape seemed hopeless.

Paton growled, "I'd rather fall into the hands of Curate Kirkwood than the gentle clutches of these cursed troopers behind. In ye go." He brooked no refusal. So half swimming, half staggering through the swift flowing Nith waters, the three desperate figures made for the opposite bank and the scene of peaceful bowls.

It was an animated game of bowls which was in progress on the riverside green. One of the players was jocularly giving to Curate Kirkwood some good humoured banter.

"Well, Curate James Kirkwood, you'll need to pull out some rare shots if you're to avoid defeat of overwhelming importance! A body kens whit weight we in Sanquhar place on the bowls! Its a wheen better way of settling the differences between Whigs and Royalist King's men."

The Curate, a distinguished man of silver hair and gentle manner, smiled with his light grey eyes crinkling at the corners. "Aye, indeed. Many a true word's spoken in jest! It's much less injurious to life and limb if hurtful to the pride for a' ken fine you Covenanting worthies lay a lot of store by your handling of the bowls, aye and the curling for that matter, when the crack of the stones splits the sharp winter air. But, again, man" Kirkwood chuckled, "we all have our bias and that doesnae just go for the stones. The Covenanter thinks his spiritual freedom is at stake while the King's men are of the opinion that they are disloyal to their lawful King. There are always two sides to the guinea."

"I'm siccar you are going to put a bias on the next bowl that you are about to play because if you don't weight it towards the tee then we are like to be the winning side." The Curate played his ball towards the tee with great care and deliberation. His eyes were quite naturally fixed on the final ball when, suddenly, he became aware of three dishevelled figures, dripping and wretched. Astonished, he started back, but summing the situation in a minute before Tam Stirling gasped out, "The dragoons are on us! Where can we run?" As he spoke Whiellens staggered and grasped the Curate's arm. "Steady, my man, Ye are indeed desperate figures, with your sodden clothes, drawn faces and hunted look in your eyes." He looked up across the river. "Ah, there are your pursuers unless I am much mistaken." The sound of trampling hooves and shouts are heard across the surging waters. In a trice Curate Kirkwood was transformed into a man of urgency.

"Quick, throw off your coats! And you, Captain Paton, yes I recognise you even as a Royalist to His Majesty and clergyman in the God appointed Episcopacy, I must say you present a heroic figure. You are suffering for your beliefs. I abhor this cruel hounding, the antithesis of the example of a loving Christ. So, take a bowl in your hand and play the next round. Your loof is muckle enou' its evident.

And, you two, walk across the tee and make as though you were calculating how the bowls lie. And for God's sake, turn your faces the other way, for they are as white as my surplice on a Sunday." By this time the angry and frustrated dragoons were splashing across the river, but with their attention too fixed on the precarious task of taking their steeds over the rock strewn bed and swirling waters. The players were only an innocent group. The three they caught were by now in position and engrossed in the deadly serious game of bowls. The Dragoon Captain forced his streaming beast up the bank and doffing his broad feathered hat with an ill concealed grace accosted the Curate. His tone was surly and one casual observer could see that his loyalty to the Episcopal Kirk was a matter of convenience and hunting and killing were his real business.

"Saw your Reverence anything of three of these traitorous Covenanters who will continually do anything but fight. They ran down the hillside across the river. Do ye ken what direction they took?"

"Kirkwood's countenance changed not a whit but retained a bland suavity, masking any emotion other than indifference.

"I neither saw them cross the burn nor turn up or down the river. I say this most truthfully much as it may seem unlikely. Perchance these rebels took their way through yonder wood, then doubled back to the hills. As you can see, gentlemen, my friends and I are engrossed in a fascinating game of bowls. You should join us. It would give you a welcome relief from the tedious business of hunting these hill preachers and their blind, slow-witted followers. You must be tired of catching them like the tod does the rabbits that wander so foolishly out of their warren into the trap of its deadly maw."

The soldier's visage was embarrassed. He hastily mumbled. "E-er, no your Reverence, we er — must hasten. Bowls is not exactly my game and as far as these others, they would prefer much more to lift their arm to a good stoup of brewed malt ale at 'The Spreading Eagle' in Dumfries town! As for these three Whig-maleeries, methinks they'll soon be 'glorifying God in the Grassmarket'. We don't usually have any trouble bringing them to earth sir. God damn 'em! Ee-er excuse me, your Reverence, I mean we'll have to be on our way." He wheeled round with a muttered curse and galloped away towards a wood along the river a half-mile distant. No doubt was in his mind that his quarry were skulking in its depths. The troop trailed out behind like a line of bedraggled washing.

When sufficient distance had been made, Kirkwood shouted, "Right, gentlemen, like Drake, let us finish our game of bowls before further business. First things first, you know." So the game was set in motion again. The last bowl was the Curate's and with accuracy he despatched the granite stone, but his luck was out as an obstructing bowl caused his to collide and spin off hopelessly out of the running. To a shout of triumph the pro-Covenanter faction claimed a victory. The atmosphere was cordial, in strong contrast to the tension of moments before.

"Well, men, I seem to meet with frustrations and obstructions in all my dealings with you hillfolk, whether in religion or in play. I can't beat you in either!" However, he said it with a wry grin, "we now have to see you dried out and fed satisfactorily. There's only one place for that! That place, gentlemen, is the Manse Byre!"

Paton stiffened offendedly. "We have been hunted like animals but we do not live like them! I'd rather remain on the moorlands, damp though they be."

Kirkwood applied something like a balm to the wound. "Dinna be offended, man; it's for your own safety. I daren't take any chances, though its twenty five years since I was made priest by Archbishop Spittiswoode, and by Gods grace I have done my best to keep true to my ordination vows. It is my duty to seek for Christ's sheep, including you hillmen, and not to poke, and pry, and haul men to prison because, despite much provocation, they follow their own consciences, as I follow mine. I am a shepherd of souls, and neither a dragoon nor a hangman. Do you believe me?"

"Forgive me. Your sincere heart is plain to see."

"Come along then before there is a change of mind from your true enemies. The barn is piled high with straw in the corner, ideal for a long restful sleep. There is also an ample supply of bannocks, bread, and cheese at the Manse and my housekeeper will serve the victuals. Some good malt ale is not lacking. In your own time you can make your way to the hills in a direction other than that taken by the troopers. The Glendyne Burn offers a hidden retreat, inaccessible to all but the most sure footed steed and intrepid rider. Its sides are so steep that even the sheep can hardly keep their stance and the lambkins are never endangered. A more entire seclusion than this is rarely to be found.

The Glendyne solitude stretches for almost three miles, about three miles east of here and its width at the bottom is only five or six times that of the brawling stream that rushes through it. That faithful but eccentric preacher Peden has resorted to it on occasion. Though I don't agree with his politics and have often found Covenanting preachers to be a crack-brained lot, yet Peden did appeal to me as a godly man and gentleman of culture. I once caught him preaching in a Sanquhar household on my visiting rounds. Bold as a peacock, he up and tells me I am welcome to hear some words from the Lord that will nourish my soul. He indicated a seat as if one of his parishioners. But to my amazement, the words were laden with power and authority and his face shone like Moses. His dark eye fixed on mine with a magnetism. Sometimes he stopped and looked up, listening to an unseen voice. I cannot but think it was God's. After he did accept my hospitality and together we did relish a good bottle of Burgundy as a gift from God's grapevine. Rev. Peden did wax eloquent on the merits relatively of Rhenish wines and sherries, and those of Burgundy and Bordeaux, like an expert. The man's knowledge of the smuggling routes in Fife and most particularly the tunnel through the cliffs at Dysart, astonished me. The government gaugers would give a heap of guineas to gain such knowledge, and I only do through a nameless captain who keeps my cellar full. Mr. Peden, it seems, flits round this land like a ghost, now in Fife among the smugglers, now in the bleaklands of Glenmuir between Muirkirk and Sanquhar."

Captain John retorted jokingly, "You are mair a friend to the Covenanters than to your own party, James Kirkwood. You take every opportunity of screening us and it is weel kent that you allow Covenanters the key o' the Kirk to meet there in the night season, in the cauld winter weather. Doesn't it appear wonderful that such meetings can be permitted so frequently in a place so near the town of Sanquhar with soldiers quartered in Drumlanrig Castle nearby?"

The curate smiled cheerily, "Eerie sounds are heard at the dead o' night in the Kirkyard. The folk never imagine that they proceed frae a company o' puir, praying people, but think that ghosts and bogles are haunting the dreary place o' the dead in the mirk night, and this prevents discovery."

"But what about the Castle? That does not explain about it?"

"I am often with the family of the Marquis of Queensberry and am never absent when Airly and his troopers come. I am therefore cognizant of their plans afoot. Queensberry thinks I'm a great wag and is mightily entertained by my humour. But none of you need be afraid of the Curate of Sanquhar."

17
Strange Soliloquys

The prophet's mantle had fallen on the kindly curate Kirkwood, for that day when Paton and his friends experienced their ingenious escape, Sandy was esconced in the deep folding fastness of Glendyne only some three miles away. The width of the glen at the bottom was in many places little more than five or six times the breadth of the brawling torrent that rushed through it. Dark, precipitous mountains, frowning on either side, rose from the valley level to a great height on the eastern extremity which was furthest from Sanquhar, a cluster of hills gathered to a point and from here a glorious view was afforded through Ayrshire, Lanarkshire to the north, and Galloway and its Mull southwards. The defile below was matted with woodland, thick brambles and hawthorns, snaking their way between willows, beeches and the occasional oak. The air was balmy with bright May weather. Music was all around. The larks were rising, and the laverock piped to the co-oing of the wood-dove while the wild bees hummed among the hawthorn and heather.

Sandy was intent on making his way in Monaive direction, for he had a preaching to conduct in the hills to the west on the Sunday two days away. He had need of food and lodgings and a place dry and sheltered to prepare his message. But a priority was to discover the intents and whereabouts of the enemy, otherwise his conscience would be for ever sickened that he had led innocent folk to their death. To gain such inside information a bizarre method had been adopted by the Covenanters in the area of Sanquhar. The key to this secret lay in a giant oak tree which stood on the banks of the Garple Burn, which itself rose on the dark moorlands and gurgled its way till it finished in the Nith. In its journey the Garple passes through the beautiful lands of Eliock, two miles south of Sanquhar. Eliock House itself stood in a pleasant wood, and was in the possession of the Dalziels of Carnwath and the Earl of Carnwath sided with the oppressors. Eliock House therefore was a station for a troop of dragoons who used it as a base for marauding far over the surrounding lands. Sanquhar lay on the main intercourse between northern Galloway and the Upper Ward of Lanarkshire and, as such, was the scene of a flow of activity. Eliock House also commanded an excellent view of the river Nith, but the key which occupied Sandy's mind was not Eliock House, but the great oak which stood in the grounds. It was to there that he started to lope up the slope in a way learnt through long practice to save his strength. His brogue shoes needed saving as he avoided sharp rocks and bog patches.

Coming on an outcrop, he peered down to the confines of Sanquhar, and saw that all was clear. The ribbon of road seemed safe. Sighing with relief, Sandy turned to find the easiest way down. Suddenly his heart stood still, frozen with an unexpected sight. Soldiers were within a few hundred yards. He stumbled drunkenly from the edge. This time there would be no reprieve from the hangman's noose and the option of the plantations. Tripping on a heather root which flung him into a bog pool, he made for a patch of woodland, conscious instinctively that he had a slim chance of gaining it. His own spirit was low, run down by hunger and exposure. The contrast with the earlier promise of the morning was very traumatic. But, dragging his weary limbs, he reached the sheltering darkness. The open moor was an enemy. But the wood was allied against him as the branches caught and tore at his cloak. Fear was cold on his brow. It wasn't just the gallows but the torture of the thumbscrews and Boot that caused doubts of his faithfulness under extreme pressure. He knew his own flesh and blood and how the metal would mercilessly twist the finger bones till unrecognisable. The Boot, Le Brodequin, was straight from hell in its devilish simplicity, as the iron frame encased the shin bone and staves were driven in between until the crushing was unbearable. The glint of water sparkled through the wildly waving trees and he plunged towards its bank. Somehow he had ended at the Glendyne Burn again. The earth crumbled beneath his feet where the stream had eroded. In an instant he had slithered down and below to discover a deep cavity hollowed out by the ceaseless water. Sandy had barely hidden beneath the overhang when the thunder of hooves thudded on the banks. Lying flat, his blue bonnet covered the crown of his head as his face sunk into the mud. In a moment a crushing force grazed his cheek and drove the bonnet off his head and into the clay. A horse's hoof had sunk right through the smooth turf on the edge of the brook. Unsuspecting, his pursuers had driven on over the Glendyne after their quarry. Astonished at the nearness of his escape, Peden slipped back in the direction of Sanquhar and Eliock. He was certain that was the last direction the enemy would expect, entering the lion's den at Eliock House.

Keeping to the dips and hollows, he reached the environs of Eliock and was able to admire from a little way distant the elaborate gardens and herbs. He had heard that the Earl of Carnwath was an enthusiast for the new herbal Physic Garden established in St. Anne's Yards, lying to the south of the Abbey of Holyrood, by Andrew Balfour and Robert Sibbald, two Edinburgh physicians. Sandy was interested in all natural creation and recalled his conversation in the Tolbooth Tower with the young man Gregory. Medicine in Edinburgh had been in an appalling state. What surprised him was that a cruel persecutor like Dalziel of Carnwath should have any gentle pursuit of the botanical kingdom. Human nature was always perverse and contrary. Tearing his attention away, he scrutinised the special oak tree. Sure enough it was there, the horizontal stick placed across between two spreading branches. It appeared inconspicuous to the casual observer, but to the hill folk it held special significance. It meant that there was information to pass on, vital to the Covenanters' safety and that that evening at sun down was the time appointed. Alexander Peden settled down to wait.

A very strange scene had been enacted inside the kitchen of Wilson, Laird of Croglin in the parish of Tynron, the previous night. Wilson of Croglin was, like Ferguson of Craigdarroch, another Laird in the Moniaive district, of that ilk who never openly avowed their attachment to the Covenanting cause but cherished a strong sympathy with the sufferers, and endeavoured, within the uttermost of their power, to serve them, without risk to themselves. The example had been set by Ferguson to his fellow Laird. James Brotherstones, Minister of the parish of Glencairn, where Monaive was situated, had been ejected at the Restoration. He was of those who remained firm to his principles, both doctrinally and ecclesiastically, and not a few of his parishioners followed suit, some winning the crown of martyrdom. Rebels were not lacking, and when the troopers left Monaive one day, they seized at the hamlet of

Caitloch a number of suspected Covenanters, including Alexander Ferguson, the son of the farmer of Threerigs, the cousin to Craigdarroch. Being conducted to Monaive to be examined by the authorities, it happened that Ferguson of Craigdarroch was among the examinators when the prisoners were introduced. Alexander Ferguson had had a number of musket balls in his pocket which he scattered unnoticed among the thick grass by the wayside, to divest himself of everything which in the view of his enemies, might be deemed suspicious. Now, when Craigdarroch saw his cousin's son among the rebels, he was deeply distressed. He was fully aware that the slightest evidence of his being a Covenanter would ensure the ruin of this fine young man before him, and perhaps the ruin of the whole family. Craigdarroch deliberately did not seem to recognise his kinsman and Alexander, catching on his ploy vaguely, took no notice of the Laird. Anything like mutual recognition would be unfavourable, possibly disastrous. Meanwhile Craigdarroch, keeping a blind on his eyes, frantically searched for a devise for rescue.

He was therefore sitting apparently at ease and casting a careless look at the prisoners, when, all of a sudden, as if addressing Ferguson of Threerigs as his shepherd, exclaimed, "Sandy, what business have you here? How have you come to leave my sheep on the hill without permission? What right have you to go strolling from house to house, exposing yourself to danger in gratifying your taste for silly gossiping? Begone, sir, begone immediately, and attend more carefully to your flock, else you may expect a quick dismissal from my service."

On his being accosted in this authoritative manner by his kinsman, Ferguson took his hint and stole away as if ashamed, under the weight of the reproach which had been sharply administered. In this way, the young Ferguson of Threerigs escaped, retiring without interruption and without a question being asked of him. Sometime after, Craigdarroch had met him and congratulated him on his seasonable deliverance, at the same time as warning him to exercise great caution in the future.

"I am," he said, "as warmly attached to the cause as you are; for it is the cause of liberty and religion. I have been successful on this occasion in effecting your rescue by simple means. But it will not be in my power to deliver you a second time. Information has been lodged against you as a suspected person, and by no means will I avail again. Therefore, my young friend, look to yourself."

So it was that Wilson of Croglin took a leaf from Craigdarroch's book by a most extraordinary way. He was a Justice of the Peace, and so was well acquainted with the designs of the party in power. The nonconformists in the parish of Tynron were kept in a condition of comparative safety under his sheltering patronage. Several of the tenants of Tynron parish had been denounced as rebels but none were hauled before the authorities. Both Claverhouse and Sir Robert Grierson of Lag, who was as savage in his cruelty, were enraged. Lagg, when in Galloway, resided at Garryhorn in the parish of Carsphairn which was not far off, but even he was puzzled how they escaped his net.

Wilson of Croglin used an ingenious means of communicating with the Covenanters. It was his custom when returning from the meetings held in the district, to walk into the kitchen at a prearranged hour of the night when the domestics had retired to rest, and in the kitchen took place a soliloquy like that in the wood of Eliock. In fact it was through the co-ordination of these two scenes that Sandy would find out the coast ahead. The event at Tynron had taken place the night before he reached Eliock.

If one had been a silent observer at Croglin House in Tynron parish and gazing sleepless out over the darkened lawn, a figure could have been seen shortly after midnight, flitting between the laurels and rose bushes. He took stock for some seconds behind the trunks of the horse-chestnuts and weeping willows which cast their leafy dress over the little stream in the grounds. Then he crept across the lawn and slid along the wall to a tiny postern gate, seldom used even by the domestics. Davie Coulter, man of the Covenant, had reason to be thankful to Wilson of Croglin, who in fact had cleared his name of a trumped up charge of theft when accused by Captain Douglas of the garrison in Dumfries. In reality he was suspected of Covenanting leanings, and some gardening rakes, mattocks and hoes had been planted in his cottage's thatched roof by a well known local ne'er do weel hired by the dragoon leader. But Croglin got wind of the plan and privately sent two of his burliest manservants to the howff that the rogue frequented. The message was passed on that if that worthy did not admit to seeing some shadowy figures, strangers all, stuffing the agricultural implements under the thatch, his future would be strictly limited. Davie Coulter was grateful, as his elderly mother was dependent on his wages from his labour on Auchinairn Farm.

Even now he tapped softly on the door. After a pause, pregnant with meaning, the bolts were drawn and a hand drew him in as if there was an audience who might not approve. The young farm labourer was led through a maze of corridors to a small closet with three doors running off it to the kitchen, the hall, and to the stairs up to one of the wings. His guide stopped and indicated some mutton and ale on a shelf. He then left Davie to set to and the quietness descended again. It was not for long, because a calm and deliberate voice could be heard in the kitchen. Davie Coulter applied his ear to the door and peeped through the keyhole to see an unusual sight. The master of Croglin was standing in the middle of the floor clad in nightgown and red pirnie with his feet clad in old bauchles, a ridiculous figure but made completely so by his seemingly talking to the iron chain on which the pots were hanging in the spacious hearth. He occasionally struck it with his cane as if to emphasise a point. The strange speech was clear to the listener.

"Though we must not tell the secrets of our counsel to any mortal creature, yet, as thou art neither flesh nor blood, I may tell thee, Hog ma Drog. Thou art my trusted friend, Hog ma Drog, and very useful to me at present. For though I may not tell the discussions of His Majesty's Council to any mortal creature, having taken a sworn and solemn oath to that effect, I may, with an easy conscience, tell them to thee; for thou art but cold iron and sooty at that. Janet will have to tell the kitchen lass to be more eident and diligent wi' her brushes." His tone was low and even. "Well, to business. The chief decision was that my Lord of Rothes is intent on bringing a flight of his hawks down from Dumfries to Thornhill on Wednesday morn. They plan to swoop on the hills round about to pick up a blackbird and thrush or two for the sport. Also it would be useful to Prophet Peden to ken that an inkling is abroad that he is to preach in the area of Eliock and Sanquhar. If that is so, it wid be better if he and the others ettling to attend were to tak' tent and disappear for the time being."

"One last thing before you go to sleep and fall off that pendent chain, Hog Ma Drog. Willie Crombie is suspected of having a pile of firearms hidden under the hearthstone. He would be advised to move them or even destroy them. I'll say a goodnight to you, Hog Ma Drog. Thanks for your patient attention. Such onerous things are a heavy businsss. I'll let you return to Tir Nan Og, the Land of the Ever Young, as the Celtic people call it. I'll off tae my warm sheets. The kitchen's cold without the fire and I'm loath to chance burning you." It almost seemed that the chain swey shook in agreement but maybe it was the wind gusting down the chimney. The Laird's step echoed in the empty corridor and silence reigned for some minutes before Davie Coulter, face pursed in a concentration of mind at the critical news, moved quickly out of the postern door. In no time he was back in Tynron village and even old mother Coulter slept soundly, unconscious of her loving son's nightly activities.

Next morning would do to spread the word, and early with the laverock he was abroad. Dayspring, the young colt on Auchinairn Farm, was saddled and he also harnessed the wind as the keen breezes swept across the Galloway hills, following him down to Willie Crombie's. A moment and he was off to the highway and Thornhill. A certain elder of the outed Church of Scotland was grateful that day. The real difficulty lay ahead of ascertaining if Sandy Peden was already in the vicinity of Sanquhar. If he was, the customary rendezvous was at the Eliock oak by prearranged sign of the stick laid across the branches that would bring down that will o' the wisp from the hills and only then for vital reasons. The great oak suited them ideally as no one would suspect rebellious ongoings so close to a Royalist stronghold. The plan was that, if there was a message to pass on, a broad stick would be placed across the branches and the messenger retire to wait, well hidden. If, when he returned by sunset, the stick was removed, then a Covenanting refugee was esconced among the spreading roots.

Peden had his own special sign known to the brotherhood, oak leaves intertwined in a little crown chaplet with an acorn in the centre. This was, for Sandy, his prophetic way of showing that their faith though small like an acorn, would produce at the end a crown of glory, the stephanos of the athlete. Aye he was a weird gangrel body, thought Davie, as he urged Dayspring along the dusty track, avoiding the ruts formed by the great coaches during the heavy fall of a sodden earth arch. Two months of relative dryness had hardened it like another runrig. James Nisbet, an Ayrshire ploughman from Mauchline way, whom he foregathered with at cattle marts in Ayr, had recounted to him how once he had been walking behind the harrows when a troop of horsemen made him take to his heels. The dragoons baulked at the Mosshags but fired; but James Nisbet, having knots in his hair on each side of his head, a bullet took away one of his knots. Terrified, he ran on and came upon Peden who had darned himself into a Mosshag the night before.

"Oh Jamie," he said with a laugh. "I am glad your head's safe, for I knew it would be in danger." And with that he calmly took out his knife and cut off the other knot of hair! God's gangrel, Nisbet had called him that day.

It was late afternoon when a lathered Dayspring approached Eliock estate and, cantering into a small copse of hazels, Davie Coulter tethered his beloved mount and laid the small sack of oats tied to his saddle bow, down on the sward. Vigilant for the enemy, he chose a broad hazel stick and carefully approached the wood of Eliock. A haze still hung over the atmosphere from that warm May day and seemed to contribute to the silence. Without delay he laid the stick across two massive boughs, clear but sufficiently hidden by foliage to all casual observers. Patience was now the watchword as he sat in the copse and thought of all the work of harvesting in two months time. It certainly was hard because most of the young Galloway farmhands had taken off to the hills, thinking the Covenanting life was a great adventure, rampaging the country, defying the soldiery, a few with sword and musket but many with hoes and pitchforks. Inspired by the prophetic sermons of such as Peden, John Welsh of Irongray and Gabriel Semple of Corsock, sometimes a little wild to Davie's way of thinking, these young men had been filled with zeal for the Covenant. But now the nub came when, after the pristine fervour had been dampened by the cold moorland smirr, they couldn't return to their cosy bourocks in the Farms. No longer was it a game of high fun.

In 1678 the Highland Host under Claverhouse's command had arrived in the south west. The Privy Council had ordered all the heritors and life renters to sign a bond, not only for themselves but also on behalf of all who lived on their lands, not to attend Conventicles or to have any dealings with the rebels. Most of the Galloway landowners, led by Cassilis, Ravenstoke, the Gordons, the McDowells of Freugh and even Sheriff Agnew, protested vehemently against the injustice of such a bond and refused to sign. In reply the Privy Council in 1677 ordered 6,000 Highlanders to be sent to teach the rebels a lesson. For the first four months of that year they lived in free quarters, plundered, pillaged, killed cattle they didn't need, stole, and drove off all horses they could lay their hands on, and tortured and outraged the people indiscriminately, never stopping to enquire whether they be friend or foe. They had ransacked Lochnaw and other country mansions of heirlooms, pictures and family treasures that had been accumulated over generations. Auchinairn Farm had undergone its share and quartered six Highlanders for a month. Their matted red locks, seemingly rusted by their drookings, had terrified the farmer's bairns. The kitchen would have been a reekin midden with their uncouth eating habits, unless the worthy spouse had kept a clean house without risking offending the northern invaders. Davie had ground his teeth in frustration but it would have been suicide to get in their way. A skene dhu in his gullet would have been his end. But in late spring the Highland Host were sent north as it was always their custom to return home at seed time and harvest. Their departure was like that of an army at the sacking of a besieged town, with baggage and luggage. They were loaded with spoil, a great deal of horses, and no small quantity of goods, whole webs of linen and woollens, silver plate, bearing the names and arms of gentlemen. Davie Coulter had fumed inwardly, as he had watched them marching off with loads of bedclothes, carpets, men's and women's garments, pots, pans, gridirons, shoes and various furniture. Good riddance, he had proclaimed to an impartial sky and uttered a curse on these celtic curs and their seed.

The sun had set and he began to creep back to Eliock, before the night disappeared. It was in the gloaming that he inspected the oak and its base. Sure enough, there lay the chaplet of oak leaves with the acorn, enclosed in a niche of the great roots. Sandy, the great prophet himself was here. Taking a deep breath and making sure he was not observed, he leant against the trunk and casually addressed the silent sentinel.

"O fair and stately tree, many's the time that I have stationed myself in meditative mood under your wide-spreading boughs and mantling foliage, to listen to the murmuring of the gentle stream, and to hear the delicious music poured from the throats of the songsters that fill your leafy branches. I have come this evening to taste again these enjoyments. Tomorrow I shall be back at Tynron and labouring up at Auchinairn Farm at the threshing and avoid all the troopers who will be pursuing some of these unhappy Covenanters, who are understood to be lurking in some place not far from here. Especially that Minister they are always after, Peden, the Prophet of the Covenanters, should ken that it is abroad that he is to preach to the hillfolk around Eliock and Sanquhar and the hawks will seek him out to tear him like a helpless blackbird. God protect him and the other innocent folks round Thornhill who will be surprised when Lord Rothes descends on them from Dumfries. Perhaps the winds will take my prayer through the night air. And so adieu, my favourite tree; and may you stand unscathed by the winds of Heaven, and untouched by the woodsman's axe, till I visit you again."

In such a cautious and strange manner did the trusty lad convey the information intended for him who occupied the cavity underneath the roots which stretched up into the hollow trunk; and equally he cautiously withdrew without taking the slightest chance of communicating personally with Sandy. For even in addressing a deaf tree, there was danger if his speech should be heard by a listening ear. The thickets themselves had ears that were wide open to every suspicious whisper. Fully a quarter of an hour had passed since young Davie Coulter had departed, before Sandy Peden emerged from his hiding place and stole away unperceived. Informed of the designs of the enemy, he resolved on an immediate action before dawn. Thornhill must be appraised of the danger imminent. It was a good ten miles by way of Enterkinfoot which presented no difficulty to his long, hill hardened legs. The problem was where to gain secure refuge before the loom of the light touched the skies and Thornhill itself would be no haven. No alternative lay but to return again Sanquhar way and seek his friends at Glenglas cottage. This meant double the journey but the bolt hole in the false gable end at Glenglas was as discovery proof as he knew, and by now Sandy was acquainted with some outlandish refuges.

So he loped off silently, keeping to the shadows, with prayer constant on his lips to the Lord for the means of spreading the alarm in time at Thornhill. It was a village exposed to ruin if Rothes could pin his long harboured suspicions on the population. The whispers of the darkness closed around him as he slipped from copse to copse, avoiding unnecessary hillocks. His mask was scarce needed in the inky black and the miles passed uneventfully, his heart only jumping once when a white blur rose suddenly to bolt off like any mountain hare startled from its form in the long cotton grass. At last the dim light of Thornhill was faint below as the glow of the few peat fires, still gleaming from dying embers, could be seen through the windows of late night dreamers and tellers of fabled stories.

Uttering the often used signal of three whaup cries, in the hope that the people were still sufficiently alert from the drowsy peat flames, Peden flitted down to the cottage on the outskirts of Thornhill, nearest the path. There was no point in arousing the whole village. The empty echo of his call had scarce died out when a shadow passed in front of the peat fire and a hand silently appeared from the door to pull him inside. Mrs. Smith, whose husband William often spent whole nights in the inaccessible linn at the head of Ballachin Burn when it was known the dragoons were out, was on other occasions like this, a guardian angel, who watched by his couch. Sometimes she performed her housework by the cheerful light of the blazing fire and sometimes she stood attentive to listen for aught of a suspicious nature. As the night wore on she would estimate that every passing hour lessened the chances of unwelcome visitors, and that her husband, refreshed and invigorated, would hie away in safety before the break of day to his cold refuge in the Ballachin Burn Linn. So it is not hard to imagine that Mrs. Smith heard the plaintive whaup call with welcome ears, schooled in the signs of the Covenanting brotherhood. Almost before she had opened the door William Smith was rubbing the sleep from his tired face and Sandy felt the close affectionate embrace of two loving Christians.

"It's been a long time, Rev. Peden. You were always the one to appear at unexpected times and in unexpected ways."

"Tis even so, Smith, strange are the turnings of my life in this earthly pilgrimage. No longer is the sunny Glen of New Luce my parish, but the whole of Covenanted Scotland, and over the Border besides, in the ancient land of Northumbria by Otterburn where I have preached. It is however as a harbinger of danger that I come. Through the Eliock Oak it has been passed on that the hawks are out tomorrow under my Lord Rothes from Dumfries. Your man must spread the word and absent himself."

"Asking your good sense, reverence, would it no be mair advisable that I and the ladies of the parish pass on the alarm. Ere now we have done it by notes in our food baskets in the very presence of troops. William and the other hunted men can retreat to the Linn up the Ballachin."

"Aye, I don't relish having to run with half my clothing as on the last time. That Linn is a cold cleuch in inclement weather. One could get the mortal shivers. Forby, I love to spite the enemy, and winna forget when that rogue Bloody Clavers came on me in the moonlight reading my Bible. He was so surprised that I almost escaped. He has probably never read the Word during the light of day and certainly never practises it. When taken and commanded to guide them to the Conventicle to be held that night at the Clauchrie, the great red stone above Closeburn, a most opportune heavy black cloud veiled the moon and in the darkness I hid in a tall broom bush. Enraged, they thrashed about and Clavers ordered them to fire at random amongst the bushes; but God kept me safe and gave warning to the assembled conventicle. It was rare and canty I felt that night, Mr. Peden."

"Good for you, William. You have been an elusive prey aye for Claverhouse. Let's hope you have caused him a good bout of indigestion." They all three laughed quietly before Mrs Smith noticing Peden's sudden silence, speired the matter.

"I must be on, since your talk of Closeburn only too clearly shows that it must be threatened too and my friend Luke Fraser of Glenmead in Nithsdale is not far away. Ejected preachers and wanderers have found many a shelter and unbounded hospitality at Glenmead. It is but three miles more and I can still be back Sanquhar way before sunrise."

"Never, Rev it's midway through the nicht already. That's sixteen miles in all back to here! Remember the garrison at Drumlanrig Castle will be on alert early and the price is high for your head. A thousand merks would make any dragoon risk his life." Smith was concerned.

"I must go. Strength is to the bold and the faithful. I feel sure it will turn out right. Goodbye, faithful ones." With a raised hand of benediction and a swish of his black cloak, Sandy was gone.

His legs were strong again and he steeled his mind to concentrate on the distance back. A runner must always live ahead, as if the miles being covered had been already run. His body was able but fear gnawed at his thoughts as the moor seemed endless. The very animals seemed against him. Red grouse, roused up, heckled him from the heather with a strident "Go back, go back". At last Glenmead was ahead in the mountainous interior of Nithsdale. No delay could be brooked, though Luke Fraser was a real joy to him. Appraising Luke of the danger, he accepted his grateful thanks, refused food, and headed north with the wind in his face, rising with the coming of dawn. The loom of the light hadn't quite appeared. The sweat had begun to glisten on his forehead and he wrenched the wretched mask off, realising how much he hated wearing it. His personality was somehow clouded by it and now he felt himself again. The cloak was hampering and his heavy breeches clung to his thighs with sweat. Cracks in the sky had begun when he reached the Enterkin foot, where the Pass begun to Wanlockhead between the overhanging Lowthers in which the famous ambush had taken place. Only bold Black James McMichael, a man of bold and hasty temper, as well as great energy, could have achieved it. Sadly he had shot the commanding officer taking the minister and five prisoners to Edinburgh for trial and certain death. The latter were freed but the triumph was clouded by the unnecessary death.

He thought back to the time nostalgically when he had planted an ash tree by the grave of young Daniel McMichael, his brother, buried in nearby Durisdeer. A brave martyr, Daniel had been shot on the snow white fields of the dark Dalveen through the Lowthers.

He remembered how young McMichael had helped distribute the Communion tokens before that famous gathering at Auchengilloch and wondered if the ash had burst into greenery again.

Rousing himself from the lethargy weighing down his mind and body, Sandy was just in time to make a wide circuit beyond the Castle of Drumlanrig. Dawn had truly broken when he made Sanquhar. The deep ravine of Glendyne cut drastically into the hills over to his right. As a refuge its appeal was not inviting in his present state. Tiredness clogged his limbs and sleep dimmed his eyes, as it penetrated his senses that he had covered twenty six miles, the marathon which the ancient Greek runners had initiated. In his way Sandy Peden has brought good news equal to that of the Spartan athlete.

With hope he looked up the valley of the Yochen and knew then he would succeed. His exhaustion vanished magically. The dwelling-house of Glenglas near the source of the Yochen had been partly constructed for the purpose of affording a hiding-place to the destitute Covenanters. At one end it had a double gable, the one wall at a distance of a few feet from the other, leaving a considerable space between, extending the whole breadth of the building. This narrow apartment was without windows unless it might be a small sky-light from the roof. Vigorously ascending the hill skirting Sanquhar, Sandy headed up the bank of the Yochen, which is a beautiful stream discharging itself into the nearby Nith on its south side, exactly opposite Sanquhar town. Its banks were clothed with wood, close to the river's edge; a specimen, on a small scale, of the extensive forests which, in remote ages, covered the greater part of the country. He splashed across the shallow stream and saw that its bed was composed of a blue whinstone for the most part, and that it had been worn smooth and deep by the constant action of the current, so that his muddy brogues slipped and slithered. The sun was up and his figure, bedraggled, with hair lank and wild, stared back from the clear waters. Shaking his shaggy locks, he pressed on through scenery charmingly picturesque, beauties savoured usually by fishers, shepherds and the persecuted hillfolk. At its source the Yochen formed a kind of meeting-place for the refugees of Ayrshire, Nithsdale and Galloway where, from the green and sheltered spots on the high ridges of the mountains, they could easily and comfortably spot if anything hostile was taking place.

All of a sudden Glenglas rose up, aptly named the Grey Glen, as the hinterland of mountains cast a grey shadow over it. The cottage loomed ahead and he wondered why the road kept to the other side of the Yochen stream. With boldness hiding his relief he hurried with the last vestiges of his strength to Ralph Williamson's home. This man's wife had died and he had been somewhat of a recluse three years since, as in fact his wife had been a dominant influence over his rather simple style of thought. She had been a highly talented artist, educated at Edinburgh University, whom he had met on a rare excursion to the famous Aulk Reekie to shop among the labyrinthine Luckenbooths. This highly sophisticated woman had been taken with the uncomplicated country man and his blunt but gentle manner. Sadness had enveloped Ralph after the early death of his comely wife, leaving him a young daughter. She had died from a pneumonia bout, contracted when out looking for him one bitter night, searching for sheep among the bleak hills that stretched to Carsphairn. Her delicate frame designed for the studio and drawing rooms, had wasted away.

The sparkling early morning sun shone on the gloomy face of the shepherd as he responded to Sandy's knock. Compassion soon displaced sorrow as the story unfolded. Transformed from introspection to an active force to help another in need, he seized the hunted prophet of the Covenant, almost a dead weight, and gathering the latter's arms round his shoulders, he half dragged Sandy to the kitchen. Fainting and seeing as through a red mist, Sandy still had the consciousness to notice the carved figures of a weasel, fox and what resembled a raven, on the shelves, and scenic oil paintings. Williamson the shepherd allowed him to slump to the floor to prepare his place of asylum. The entrance to this asylum was not by a door, but by a small, square aperture in the inner wall, called by the country folk a bole. This opening was generally filled with the "big Ha' Bible", and other books commonly perused by the household. The fine Edinburgh lady had been an avid reader. The books in the bole were now removed and the kind cottager forced a brandy in a pottery beaker down his lips. Revival was followed by sustenance as a leather flask of fresh milk and cold roast capon from the previous night's meal brought new life. So, pulling himself and pushed by his friend, the minister crept into the interior through the small hole and found his feet in the prophet's chamber behind the wall. Like the room provided for Elisha by the Shunnamite woman, this place contained a bed, table, stool, and candlestick. The residue of heat from the night's fire still afforded a sufficiency of heat since that large fire was situated close by the inner wall.

In this situation the prophet of the Covenant was secreted for four days, while his food was stealthily conveyed through the hole by

Ralph Williamson. Total exhaustion had drained his being, and for three days he lay as a dead man; when danger threatened his host blocked the bole hole. Once soldiers had entered searching but departed immediately, unsuspecting. On the fourth day Sandy's naturally tough constitution had reasserted itself and the Covenanting minister was able to continue on his pilgrim way. But before his grateful farewell Peden asked his host, "Where do you go to worship with friends?"

Williamson pointed over the wild ranges of the hinterland. "Yonder is Carsphairn, where I carried my bairn once the twelve miles to be baptised and there I go when my heart grows weary for company."

"Aye, Ralph, there are nae Christians like the Christians o' Carsphairn and nane that hae mair moyen at the throne of Heaven," sighed Sandy Peden.

"Be that as it may, there is naebody I like better to see dit the door of our house than you, Saunders Peden. For you always bring the Master wi' you."

"You will be richly repaid for admitting wandering friends into your home for Christ's sake. We can never get aforehand wi' Him. Gie as we like, He gies far ayont us."

18
Muckle John Gibb

In an age of high religious feelings and extremes, it was not surprising that it should give rise to some fanatics, subject to mad extravagances; and no more so than Muckle John Gibb and his Sweet Singers of Borrowstounness. Between the blatant cruelty and paganism of the persecutors and the pure religion of the sincerest Covenanter, there were madcaps with curious religious practices. This was the dire result of living in an age when everything tended to exasperate human nature and to unsettle nerves, which were tender, and intellects, which were weak. Inexplicable comets and portents filled the northern Scottish sky. Curses were reiterated everywhere. People's ears were excitable and ready to pick up the most appealing message for the moment, especially if it appealed to their martyr complex and no true Covenanter, like Sandy Peden and Donald Cargill, sought martyrdom for the sake of it. So it was that one of the rare occasions on which the paths of these two men, whom many others saw as so similar in their prophetic visions, came together, was in the Darmead area, the bleakest imaginable moorland between Shotts and Harthill; and the reason was to confer on the answer to a strange zealot who had arisen.

The evils and cruelties of the times broke the hearts of some and unsettled the minds of others, so that amongst the Covenanters some ran into serious extremes. Some flaunted the blood of two martyrs, Potter and Stewart, on a handkerchief. Peden and Cargill were concerned about these extremes and had arranged a meeting. Normally Donald Cargill, who had assumed a leadership in the Covenanting movement after being driven from his ministry in the Barony Church of Glasgow, frequented the Lothians and east coast area, leaving the west to such as Alexander Peden and Richard Cameron, whom the two old prophets admired as a young valiant for truth. But the Shotts wind-blown heights were a half way spot where both had preached. Sandy was grateful for his steed from his brother Hugh on Ten Shillingside Farm, for it was a long trail from the low pasture lands of Ayrshire. When he arrived at the cottage in the isolated parish of Eastfield, he applied the head of his stick to his mouth which was a whistle giving a bird sound in a prearranged signal. Alexander Peden was looking forward to meeting again this man whom he knew to be affable, affectionate and generous. The story was well known in Covenanting circles now of how in his native Rattray district of Perthshire beyond the Tay, when chased by the enemy, in a desperate situation he ran for a rocky chasm where the river Ericht narrows. Mounting a huge rock, Donald took a flying leap across the river, where a slip on the treacherous rocks would have meant death in the torrent below. It was too much for the hunters to give an encore, and the place came to be known as "Cargill's Loup". But Cargill's open humorous nature came out in an answer to a Covenanting brother who congratulated him on his great leap. Laughing, he said he had had to take a fifteen miles run, all the way from Perth, before he could do it!

As Sandy, Donald Cargill was essentially a lonely man, with his wife Margaret Brown dying after a year and a day. However, he was of a more timorous nature, and obviously shy at meeting Peden in such a personal circumstance, though indeed a few years older than Sandy. His quaint, chubby, but reticent features, surrounded by a mass of curly fair locks, broke into a quiet smile as he came out from the porch of Eastfield cottage to wave his greeting. He had just returned from a happy respite of three months in England. There were brave English hearts among those who took the Covenant. In the time of his absence the delusion of the Gibbites had arisen.

"Aye, I'm fair glad ye gave the whistled signal for the place is alive with Government 'Flies', Sandy," Cargill spoke half humorously for his life had been filled with remarkable escapes. He held out his hand, seized by Sandy's muckle sized loof, just as he was dwarfed by the Ayrshire man. Peden had more respect for this man than most and the aura of discipline and self denial was easily recognisable.

"Since Airdsmoss, troopers, informers, cess-collectors, excisemen, donators, and sequestraters, and all sorts of Government 'fly' spies, have roved about this country incessantly, making life intolerable, Donald." Donald let him into the warm cottage and they chatted while the porridge was heated again on the hearth.

"The character of these 'flies' is worthless. We only have to look at that praying Irishman, James Gibb, whom we now know Claverhouse employs to betray the Coventiclers; and I have heard it said that Bloody Clavers once stated, if he had raked all hell, he could not have found his match in mimiking the Covenanters. The prayers of that praying Irishman are those of a damnable hypocrite!" It was unusual to hear of harsh words from his gentle lips, explained by the pressure of the times. "One thing is certain, he will never win the 5000 merks offered by the King and Government for my capture. I'd tell his false tongue anywhere. Ha, they call me one of the most seditious preachers, a villainous and fanatical conspirator!"

"Things have come to a pretty pass when the legal procedure for detecting a Whig or Cameronian has been brought to such a pitch of perfection that a suspicious sneeze, a diffident reply, or a misunderstood reference, is enough to imperil a person's liberty. Have you heard of John Scarlet, Donald?"

"The name has some vague reference. Tell me more."

"This Scarlet is a tinker, confessedly illiterate, a soldier dismissed from the service, an unabashed polygamist, who wanders about the country with his harem. Here's the rub. On occasions he breaks into piety, probably in the guise of a Whig. John Scarlet is undoubtedly a Government fly who has sworn that he has been one of Welsh's bodyguards, and even joined the bodyguard of Richard Cameron. Now two years ago near Loudon Hill, early on an April Sabbath day, two infantry soldiers quartered upon a farmer who had not paid his cess, were roused from sleep. One of them, going to the door, heard an angry shout strangely unlike a Covenanter's, "Come out, you damned rogues!" A shot laid him low. A second shot and a sword assault also wounded his comrade mortally but before he expired, the dragoon was able to identify John Scarlet as his assailant. Yet the odium of the murder has been cast upon the Cameronian party."

"Yes, they are perverted times, Rev. Peden. Worshippers returning from Conventicles have been stripped of their clothes as far as decency has permitted, and the clothing has been retained as evidence. Is it not ludicrous to picture 'Bonnie Dundee' and his slashing dragoons returning from a Sunday raid, with their saddles hung with the coats and breeches of the men and the petticoats and shawls of the women, and the horses' nosebags full of Bibles and other oddments of the chase? Such is the work of heroes today!"

"Even boys entering College or beginning trades have to produce Certificates of Church attendance, Donald."

"Well, shall we turn to discuss the reason I have called our conference, the wild preacher sailor from Borrowstouness, and the Gibbites or Sweet Singers, the three men and twenty six women who have foolishly given up all to follow this self-styled prophet. They have been running up and down the streets in a furious manner, uttering prayers which have consisted chiefly of curses invoked against everyone, including the Covenants and Covenanters, and singing plaintively the sad psalms, the 74th, 79th, 80th, 83rd and 137th. This giant sailor whom I would that he had kept to the seafaring trade, has appeared on the scene as a great deliverer filled with the Holy Ghost, and deluded these people into thinking that he would right wrongs by the destruction of all human inventions. They even call him King Solomon. The married women have deserted their homes and husbands, contrary to all natural affection and commands of the Lord about homes, and if the husband, in his endeavours to win his wife back to rationality, took hold of any part of her dress, she indignantly washed the place, as to remove an impurity. They have left their soft warm beds and covered tables for the discomforts of the cold moorlands."

"Is it true that they have destroyed Bibles with human additions, as chapters, verses, pictures, prefaces, printers-marks, and even the Psalms in 8 metre?"

"O, yes, not only that but all contrivances to make life comfortable, ale, tobacco, not that we have many of these comforts, eh Sandy? And then they burn the Covenants and relative documents, repudiate the King and his officials, educated clergy, the calendar and its terminology, and everything human, apart it seems, from bread, water, and air. I think they put my fasting and meagre diet to shame. Muckle John Gibb has said that he will refashion humanity into a perfect temple, worthy of himself, and that he is the second Solomon. But we know that he is a diabolist, and Satan, that dark dog, has filled him and can use him to cause much trouble to the Covenant throughout our land."

"We must try to rescue the men, Walter Ker, David James and John Young, and the Borowstounness women, who include the Stewart sisters, probably deranged at the death of their martyred brother Archibald, and an Elspeth Granger, whom Gibb has led out into the Pentland Hills to a remote deep slough morass called the Deer-slunk. They are expecting to see the sinful and bloody city of Edinburgh go up in smoke and ruin."

"People's minds have become feverish and excited enough with inexplicable portents and strange sights. Did you see the great shooting star which they call a comet, in the skies last December? What a strange phenomenon! I shall never forget that clear, frosty night when between five and seven at night, I was walking up the Edinburgh Cowgate, keeping alert for any danger, for sooner or later, Sandy, my narrow deliverances will run out. Suddenly the night was lit up as a magnificent star blazed across the sky with a great tail trailing from the foot of it, pointed as it came from the star, and then spreading itself. It made a broad ascent into the heavens and the stream was seen throughout the night. It continued for over a month till half way through January, receding from the west by degrees every evening. Also, as the days passed, its beginning would be from a more elevated position by degrees, with its stream then mounting to our zenith. No mention has been made in our history of a like comet which grew smaller and smaller till it disappeared. Some think it portends great judgements on these lands for our sins. For never has the Lord been more provoked by people. Rev. Robert McWard, him that was close wi' Cameron abroad in Gronigen, was dying and asked friends to carry him out to see the comet, and then blessed God that he was not to see the terrible days that were coming on Britain and Ireland, especially upon sinful Scotland."

"Maybe, maybe, Donald, but the public mind is in a highly excited state owing to the terrific appearance of this comet overhead, which I myself saw in the fields of Ayrshire and thought for a fleeting moment was, as the star in the East announced the Birth, the Dayspring from on high to announce the Second Coming; and the excitement is also engendered by the presence of the Duke of York in Edinburgh and the news of the struggles in Parliament for his exclusion from the throne. A merchant in Edinburgh has said that, looking at the comet, he saw a fire descend from the Castle down the city to the Abbey where the Duke was staying, and heard a voice saying, 'This is the sword of the Lord.' A man in a soldier's apparel came up to Sir George Munro of the Edinburgh garrison in the street, and bade him go down and tell the Duke of York, if he did not extirpate the Papists, both he and the King were dead men. Munro turned to get witnesses to what the man had said, and when he looked again the man had mysteriously vanished. To crown all, a hypochondriac fellow came out to the street and proclaimed that the Day of Judgement was to take place next day. He offered himself to be hanged if it should prove otherwise. He did not quite get his wish, for he was clapped up in the Canongate Tolbooth, not quite the fate of a prophet!"

"Unusual creatures have been seen recently in Edinburgh. Just last

November I witnessed the strangest animal, not long brought to England for exhibition. It was a great beast, with a great body, and huge head, small and dull eyes, lugs like two skats lying close to its head, with a large trunk coming down from the nether end of the forehead, of length a yard and a half, in the undermost part small, with a nostril at the end. By this trunk it breathed and drank, casting up its meat and drink into its mouth below it, having two large and long bones or teeth, of a yard length, coming from the upper jaw of it, and at the far end of it inclining one to another, by which it digs the earth for roots. It was backed like a sow, the tail of it like a cow's. The legs were big, like pillars or great posts, and broad feet with toes like round lumps of flesh. When it sucked up the water with its trunk, which holds a great deal, it put the lower end in its mouth by winding it in, and then it jaws the water into its mouth as if from a great spout. The owners even taught the creature to flourish the colours of our country with its trunk, to shoot a gun, and bow its knee to make reverence with its big head. People were persuaded to ride upon it though they were very fearful. But great merriment was had by folk when some people farmed this creature, which they call an elephant and cost £2000 sterling, for £4000 for several months to show through the country. They refused to pay in full on the ground of failures in the contract, that the owners had not shown all it might do, especially drinking. The reply was that it could not drink every time it was shown! Nature will have her way. It has gone to litigation!"

"Yes, weird times, occasionally touched with humour. However these ascetic Gibbites are a serious threat to the land. They lay far more stress upon the duties of prayer, fasting and mourning than upon Christ's satisfaction, obedience and intercession. They pay no attention to the word of any man, and say they read nothing but the pure text of the Bible. Davie Jamie is a good scholar lost and a minister spoilt. How funny that Borrowstounness should produce both such fanatics as the Sweet Singers, and a sweet Christian as Marion Harvie, the unconquerable serving-maid from that town, who with Isabel Allison of Perth, a gentlewoman, went to the scaffold, singing the twenty third psalm. I feel you are the man to go to Muckle Gib out on the Pentlands and give him one last chance of repenting of his wicked ways. We both have the gift, Donald, and you are to go." Their faces radiated a close smiling brotherhood as they hugged one another affectionately, their love beyond words. The parting was brief and Sandy saw Donald Cargill's small rotund figure leave Darmead Moor going east to the capital whose streets and alleys he knew so much better than the Ayrshire Covenanter.

Cargill's time in Edinburgh was necessarily short as he well knew the danger, remembering his many narrow escapes around the city of Glasgow both before and after Bothwell. It was still a miracle to him that he had preached to thousands publicly for eighteen Sabbath days little more than a quarter of a mile from the city, around Langside; and, though the Psalms were sung loudly, they were uninterrupted by the militia. On another occasion, when the house of his lodgings in Glasgow was searched by musketeers, he walked through them and escaped, they thinking he was the goodman of the house. He would not always be so fortunate, so that, going up the High Street below the Castle, he kept to the shadows. Looking down on the Nor Loch, he saw some tiny figures on the frozen water, and thought to himself how foolhardy they were. Three men had been drowned that February, by falling through the ice of the Nor Loch. They had a proverb that a fox would not set his foot on the ice after Candlemas on the second of the month, especially in the heat of the sun, and it was now two o'clock; at any time the fox was so sagacious as to lay his ear to the ice, to see if it be frozen to the bottom, or if he heard the murmuring and current of the water below. Donald hoped those below would learn the wisdom of the fox not too late, as one of the funmakers slipped. He himself would need all the wisdom available to combat the Satanic-inspired cunning of the gigantic Borrowstounness seaman, turned self-styled prophet. As always, Peden the Prophet was right in his advice that John Gibb should be given an opportunity to repent.

Walking through the city in the direction of the green beckoning Pentlands, he passed the Heriot's Hospital, a charitable children's institution, and pulled up sharply in surprise. Some of its children, clearly recovered from their sickness, were offering a piece of paper to a dog in sham action. At this time many things were done in mockery of the Test of spiritual and political allegiance to the King. Smiling, Cargill leant unobserved against the corner of a tall Land. A youngster could be heard petting the poor mutt. "Come along, you tyke, sign the Test Act, and show you are a loyal subject of King Charles! Since you have become an important personage, keeping guard on the yards of Heriot's Hospital, you therefore have a public charge and office, and so must take the Test." But the dog, naturally preferring a bone, absolutely refused the paper, barking in antagonism.

Another lad shouted, "Let's butter it up and it'll swallow the Test whole. I'll get some in the kitchen." In a moment he had reappeared with the paper totally greased. This time the dog eagerly grabbed at the missive and set at licking off the butter. However when done, it immediately spat out the document.

"Right," cried one. "He has condemned himself. This jury finds him guilty of disloyalty, just like the honest Marquis of Argyll, Let's hang him." Alarmed, Donald Cargill saw that the joke had ended, and they had seized the poor tyke and in a trice tightened a noose round its neck. Sickened, he hurried off on his serious work, from the sight of the dog still struggling as it hung from a door lintel.

The green folds of the Pentlands soon swallowed him up. But now the sun had gone down and the hills became greyer as he headed for the remote recess of the morass called the "Deer Slunk". Here he knew were some of the wettest flow mosses of the region. He began to feel a shivering as if the eyes of "Solomon" Gibb and his unholy crew were on him. At last he came to the morass. A cold easterly wet fog had come down in this Godforsaken spot between Clydesdale and Lothian.

Suddenly there emerged from the haar two men, one huge and dark. Muckle Gibb lived up to his name, his massive head surrounded by a flowing black beard. His wild eye gleamed like some animal and Cargill prayed for the Holy Spirit.

"I am the Rev. Donald Cargill of the Covenanted Church of God and I have come to you, John Gibb, to interpret the will of the Holy Spirit and give you a true exposition of Psalm 37. Do not fret because of evil men."

The appearance of Gibb was like that of Balfour of Burleigh, murderer of Archbishop Sharpe, fanatical; but there was something different here, a possession and air of abstraction about Gibb's wildness, an alien spirit.

"You are an imperfect, conventicling apostate. I have heard of you and disdain compliance with such men." There was open contempt in his looks.

"I beg of you to hear me at least before you dismiss the truth and continue with your strange delusions."

"They are no strange delusions, for the fog that surrounds the wicked city of Edinburgh, scene of martyrdom, will be turned into a conflagration like to that which destroyed Sodom. But there is no reason why we cannot discuss things, is there, Davie James?" A cunning had crept into his tone, Cargill discerned, as Gibb turned to the quiet figure behind him.

"A Christian will always listen, Solomon." There was a sincerity about Davie James.

So they led Cargill to their camp where the small group of men were armed like buccaneers, Cargill noticed, especially the wicked knife "Solomon" Gibb carried in his belt, relic of his sea-faring days. The women were sitting singing like sirens. Cargill thought they might be some holy harem to Gibb, these Sweet Singers. Gibb was now all hospitality, rough as it was. A Sweet Singer arranged a bed for the two leaders together, and the Covenanter settled down for a sound rest, for it had been a long trek from Edinburgh. The ex-buccaneer seemed to slip into a ponderous snore immediately.

During the night Cargill was disturbed in his sleep by a vision of a cut throat and a voice with urgent authority telling him to leave and pray the night through. Quietly he rose, careful not to awake the fearful giant. Retiring to the edge of the Deer Slunk, he sought God in prayer. The morning light was streaking the sky with bands of red when he rose from his knees, having concluded that this man Gibb was an incarnate devil.

Cargill was shocked by the state of mind he had found these people in; especially their leader. Only a divine intervention could save such a man and he was sure he would soon be arrested. He returned at once to Edinburgh and within the week, at his backstreet lodgings, he heard that the whole sect had been seized by a troop of dragoons at Woolhill Crags, another very desert place, and carried to Edinburgh; there the men were put into the Canongate Tolbooth and the women into the Correction-House, where they were soundly scourged. After a short while most of the poor people who had suffered this temporary derangement, cooled down, and were one by one set at liberty. The women returned to their deserted husbands, and ultimately to their right minds. Cargill had written to them in the Tolbooth, warning them that the devil was sowing tares among their thin wheat. It did not change Gibb, who was subject to bouts of diabolepsy and paroxysms of madness, which some said were caused by the visible visits of the black dog, Satan. Muckle Gibb roared and blasphemed while his fellow prisoners prayed.

In May the Duke of York was visiting Edinburgh despite the rising tide of hostility to him and his oppressive policies, and as his carriage was passing the prison, five of the women not yet released threw offensive rubbish at the carriage. Rigorous treatment was meted out to them. However, the Duke of York, wishing to give an appearance of leniency, took an interest in these mad folk and in August he arranged for them all to be liberated on condition they renounced their disloyal principles and give bail. It was in vain in regard to John

Gibb, as he, along with James, who remained inexplicably loyal to the wild heretic, and two women, returned to their extravagant practices, singing only the psalms of lament in the streets and burning Bibles publicly. So they were immured a second time, where "Solomon" Gibb began his roaring and hollering again.

How Gibb got his deserts there amused Rev. Donald Cargill no end and he was certain Peden would enjoy it greatly. In the Tolbooth was a lithe young Christian lad of eighteen, George Jackson. He was so sick of the roaring of Muckle Gibb that he sat on him, thrust a napkin into his mouth, and battered his head against the floor into a dead silence, not even a growl. Sadly young George Jackson was to go to an early martyrdom; while others said they preferred the gibbet to continuing in the company of Gibb and his Sweet Singers, with their profanity and vulgarity. Muckle John Gibb's destiny was strange, as the Council ultimately sent him, Davie James, and two women to the American Plantations, where Gibb's exhibitions of diablery brought him fame among the Red Indian tribes of the interior where he escaped to. His madness to them was a manifestation of the spirit of the Great Manitou and, becoming a mighty chief, Gibb was evil to the end, threatening the coastal settlements with an Indian uprising. But God's spirit spoke to David James and rescued him from his obsession with Gibb, so that he became a respectable clerk in New York and associated himself with some new world sect who built a church there.

19
Faithful Unto Death

The lonely crofting farmhouse stood neat and whitewashed among the hills some five miles from Muirkirk in the county of Kyle, called by official bodies, Ayrshire. Such was the situation of Priesthill Farm that a traveller journeying to Cumnock from Strathaven or a burgh of Lanarkshire would only know of its existence if he were to deliberately depart from the roadway and follow the muddy track which climbed into the endless folds of the hills. A small, cheerful stream chuckled its way over a pebbly bed as brown, speckled trout darted their adventurous journey to some unknown destination. Sheep munched away their life on the spartan slopes, unconcerned about the momentous events being worked out in the breadth and length of Lowland Scotland, at the price of many a Scotsman's blood, man of the Covenant or man of the King.

But human presence was evidenced by voices coming from the neat cottage and they were decidedly concerned with the state of things in the Kingdom. Simple peasant stock they might be, but John Brown and his good wife were of that class of educated peasantry which shamed many an ignorant Lord and took its origins and pride in the spiritual Revolution that had taken place in Scotland and England a hundred years before. The Reformation had given the Bible, that great educator, into the hands of the commonality. Other books thought for you, while the Bible taught one to think. In the cottage a homely scene could be witnessed as John and his wife Isabel had their two bairns gathered round their knees and were enjoying the spiritual food that their guest, the Rev. Alexander Peden had afforded. Sandy had lodged with his good friends often and the bond was deep between the family and this prince of wandering preachers. To some he might be God's gangrel, but to them he was just Sandy. Since his father was a bonnet laird at Auchincloich in the parish of Sorn, he knew that he could claim the company of gentlemen, and many were for the Covenanting cause, whether openly or not. Many Sandy admired like the brave Earl of Cassilis who had suffered a loss of £32,000 when the fifteen hundred wild soldiers of the Highland Host were quartered on his estate in Carrick. When they finally began to fight among themselves and were withdrawn they took all they could, including the very blankets and cooking pans. Peden was honoured to bring comfort to this noble and valued his friendship along with that of the Boswells of Auchinleck. But always did he look forward with an unequalled pleasure to fellowship and homely banter with the Brown family. Priesthill was a couthy place and the Browns a canty folk. Life was bare but sincere, and the bare legs and feet of the youngsters, below their threadbare though clean breeks, were a healthy brown, from playing by the burn on the long summer nights. One boy was the son of John's first marriage till fever had claimed her at her prime. His emptiness had been solaced when the love of Isabel Weir became his. The little one a bairn no more, was hers, but the wisdom of Solomon wasn't necessary to have seen her as not the mother of both. She always liked to chaff Sandy Peden and his dark eyes twinkled when she chided him as rejecting the beauties of womanhood.

"Och no, woman, I havenae time to be dallying and courting. Now, I ask you, how could any woman trail with me over the wildnernesses and trackless moors that I follow. Anyway I have my pipe to console me".

Sandy chuckled as he brought out from his black cloak an old oaken pipe hidden in its voluminous folds. The thick knitted woollen pouch of tobacco was full. Wines were not the only things smuggled into the caves and quiet inlets at Lendalfoot on the Ballantrae coast.

"Well, Rev., if you were to ask me, I think you are not just a little afraid of the fair sex."

"Aye, it could be, Isabel". Peden smiled wryly as he sucked the worn stem. Never would he tell these dear ones of the trauma at Tarbolton these many years ago. It had scarred his soul, but he had prayed for a spiritual oil to heal any bitterness and women had often hung on his words and been enchanted by his mystery. Somehow the mystery which so many times hung around the feminine sex was reversed in his case.

Sandy turned to John Brown and looked earnestly into the serious brown eyes of the carrier. The prominent nose and high bridge spoke of a deeply sensitive nature. Everything was neat about him. His thick auburn hair was well combed and the beard of a lighter hue seemed to cover all of his chin and complement his hair without ever dominating his features. A high necked tunic and neckerchief were augmented by a tartan plaid wrapped obliquely across almost all his body.

"Well, John, do you regret that God gave ye a stammer in your tongue and caused an impediment in your speech. Did it not prevent you becoming a Covenanted Minister?"

No annoyance showed in the open face. Peden saw in him the nature of a Nathaniel, with no guile. Such people had no pride that was evident.

"It was hard richt enough at the time, Rev. Peden, to accept this defect that was the undoing of my ambition to preach. I tried to persuade myself that God speaks through a people of stammering lips. Did not Moses protest that he was a man of mean speech and God gave him an Aaron to be his mouthpiece? Jeremiah proclaimed that he was too young and said, 'Ah, Lord God, behold, I cannot speak for I am a child.' But the Lord told him 'Say not, I am a child; for you shall go to all that I shall send you and whatsoever I command you, that you shall speak. Be not afraid of their faces, for I am with you to deliver you.' Then the Lord touched Jeremiah's mouth and told him 'I have put my words in your mouth. See, this day I have set you over the nations and over kingdoms, to root out, and to pull down, to destroy and throw down, and to build and plant.' The weeping prophet they call Jeremiah. Dinna we need ane sic as he? For this year of grace, 1685, is the worst year in a terrible time."

The hill preacher sighed with pain. "Indeed we do. This year has reeked reddest, John. Our persecutors, Claverhouse, that godless man and his evil henchman, Grierson of Lag, equal the Emperors of ancient Rome and the Spanish Inquisition in their atrocities. Our ain Richie Cameron, the Lion of the Covenant, a Richard the Lion Heart, more worthy of the title than any godless Crusader, has fallen at Airdsmoss, and my heart bleeds for I know he was your beloved brother".

"Richie has his reward now. To know him was like heaven before its time. Though there were those who said he was muckle warlike for a man of God, yet his hand was forced and I think that he only took the pistol and sword when no other way was present. But yet, I rejoice in my stammer which has prevented me from entering the pulpit. For here I have my little crofting cottage of Priesthill, though of mean acreage and only a cow and twenty sheep, still this moorland home is my palace. I hold my own Bible School of theology, attended by youths from all the upland parish. In summer we hold our classes in the sheepfold and in the winter they sit around the peat fire here in the kitchen. We go over Walter Smith's 'Twenty two Steps of Defection' and rules for society meetings. I have expounded the whole Bible and Confession of Faith. For this I often have to flee like a hare to the mosses, while the troopers search the house. You'll have some more bannocks? Isabel, provide for our guest". Isabel bustled off to the corner where the large stone grate was set in the wall. Some of her special heather mead was popular with all her guests.

"Na, na, it is time for me to go. Mine is a pilgrim way, not for the likes of yourself. I have been ower lang at your home and put you in danger. I must make for John Muirhead's Farm and as the Lord leads, make for my ain Auchinleck. Isabel, dear lassie, you have a guid man. Prize him well".

Peden moved to the door and cocked his head out. "My, it's a rare haar for May!"

Isabel had come close and was looking searchingly at him, as if some unspoken word had caused her unrest. There was about Sandy for all his smiling expressions something gey unco and of the gangrel about him.

"You'll no be needin' that weird mask and that scary black wig of yours then. They fair give the bairns a frecht. We dinna need to tell them stories at bedtime of ghosts and broonies. A' I do is tell them you are coming. Where you get them I couldna thocht and I'm no speirin".

Sandy chuckled, "I hae sore need of it, strange though it be. But people, especially in the countryside, stay well away from the haunts of broonies and that suits me fine. James Gavin, a tailor in Douglas village, made the mask out of good tough cowhide and the bonnie wig from real horse hair. Poor Gavin, he had his ears cut off with his own scissors no long ago, and is to be transported to Barbados. I pray he escapes that life of slavery, as I did. But you must agree that it makes an improvement on my features, particularly the feather eyelashes. And one must never be too watchful with informers abounding. There are times when I write in code to my friends, lest discovery come. There comes a time when a man's enemies shall be those of his own household. But I confess a strong affection at times for this mask and wig."

He reached into his long cloak again, like a magician, to bring them out from the folds. The skin mask was as flesh coloured as tanned hide could be, and, though the eyes were rather crudely cut, they served the purpose, as did the slightly incongruous feathers which acted as eyelashes. The short beard of a different colour and material, looking like tough straw bristle appeared less realistic, resembling that of a scarecrow. It had a patch on its side of cloth as if someone had tried to grasp it violently to reveal his identity and partially succeeded. Sandy fingered it meditatively and did not volunteer an explanation and so Isabel did not ask. There were some things one didnae speir about. The long flowing locks were stitched onto a cloth net which fitted over the head tightly. Many a human would be jealous of such a tonsure.

"Rev. Peden, you are always an honoured guest here at our humble home to have a bed and simple fare. Ye did give me my dear man in holy wedlock these three years syne. Weel do I recall every detail of that ceremony. As for every woman of grace, marriage is special and particularly being in the Puritan fashion, here in the open air with God's creation around and the joys of God's presence."

"Goodbye, and God be with you both! My, its a dark and misty May morning". Peden strode away into the hills and as he went muttered to himself, "Poor woman! Poor woman! A dark and misty morning indeed!"

The words were meant for himself alone, but somehow the spirit of them communicated itself to her unmistakably. She felt a shiver run through her body. There was no perceptible wind.

As she waved goodbye, Isabel half whispered to herself, "What was that he said? Aye, Prophet Peden you are. When you did pronounce us man and wife and one flesh how can I forget your words, your terrible words, 'Isabel, you have got a good man but you will not enjoy him long. Prize his company, and keep linen by ye to be his winding sheet; for you will need it when you are not looking for it and it will be a bloody one.' Ach, maybe puir auld Sandy was affected by the terrible sufferings he has seen these many years. Even he is human."

John Brown joined his wife and together they shouted, "Farewell, Sandy, till the next time! Dinna drop that food parcel. Get that grouse skinned and in the pot before the maggots are at it, and quench your drouth on the buttermilk before it turns."

The black garbed figure had almost merged into the mist when he turned to wave from the edge of a nearby hillock before descending into the rocky gill beyond. An atmosphere of darkness seemed to have fallen over the household. The very air was charged with threat.

"Well, Isabel Weir, are ye glad ye changed your name to Brown?"

"Sometimes I wonder, John Brown. Ye havenae muckle o' this world's goods, a cow that milks only when she pleases and twenty sheep that stray a' ower the place. I'm no sure I struck a rich bargain at a'. Were ye lonely when your first wife died?"

"Aye, it was a severe time, Isabel. She was an understanding spouse as ye are and so appreciated what a man goes through when one half of him is taken away. I loo'ed her well. Rheumatism and consumption are a terrible scourge on these moors when the damp rains come and the sun is not seen enough to dry out the bones. But Annie died with a smile of joy on her lips, The Lord's time had come. Then three years ago He sent me a really good thing. Aren't we told that whoever finds a wife finds a good thing?"

"So that's all I am, a good thing?" Isabel laughed affectionately.

"Awa wi' ye, lassie." His arm slipped round her slim waist and he gave her a loving squeeze.

"Oh, look, its John Browning, your nephew. Whit's fashin' you, son?" A tired teenager had arrived at the farmhouse. He was a young replica of John Brown. But there was more than a breathlessness about his distress. "You haven't walked all the way from Chapelhope Farm? Is this just a visit to be friendly or have you come to help us with the work on the croft, for we could do with it."

John Browning stammered and gasped, "I don't mind giving you a hand, but its mair urgent work that we maun be about, for the dragoons are likely to be up to their devils work. I and some of my freens had a set to with a party of soldiers in Newmilns this day by. We cracked a few pates and Clavers is no gonnae take kindly to that."

Brown's plaided arm went round his shoulder assuringly. "Dinna fech yourself. There's no chance o' a rencounter this day. It's too dark and misty. Even the hillfolk will be staying snug at home this morning, tight in their cottages, and the heather folds and gorges, not to mention the many caves and dens that our dear brother and pastor Sandy Peden has snuffed out like some friendly old badger." He laughed good naturedly. "I opin maybe he uses his prophetic gifts to discover these caves. The one in the cliff face on the Auchinleck estate is a rare refuge indeed and I believe the Rev. Peden has anither under his cloak around Kilbryde near Sanquhar but the one I jaloose is best o' a' is at Crickhope Linn beside Closeburn, doon by Thornhill way. Its a real nature's closet up a rare narrow gorge and in ahint the waterfall itself. Even a snuffling old badger couldnae find that wan oot. Bloody Claverhouse and a' his thievin' dragoons would hae no chance o' finding old Sandy therefore. It is like a needle in a haystack for them. What a man he is. Those who accuse him, even among the Covenanting party, of cowardice and leniency towards the indulged are so wrong. He is a man of peace and more guid quick than dead." Anger for the rare occasion had entered his tone but shrugging it aside, Brown reached for the mattock by the hearth. "Onyway, let's you and I go and cut peats. There's no danger of the hawks being out today in this haar. Forby Isabel is fare needin' peats. The signs are the summer's gonnae be a dreich one." His nephew grasped a spade and trudged behind the uncle he loved so well.

But evil has a way of trapping the innocent. The commendation to be wise as a serpent and harmless as a dove is not empty advice. John Graham at this time was in a relentless mood. Since Drumclog and his ignominious retreat to Glasgow, his pursuance of duty had been fanatical and most successful. From having a commission with his company of dragoons in Dumfriesshire and Annandale, alone to deal rigorously with those who were dogged or stupid enough to continue attending conventicles, John Graham of Claverhouse was appointed as Sheriff-Depute of there and Kirkcudbright and Wigtown as well. In his own words, this country of the south west of Scotland had been very loose and, in his own peculiar irony, there were as many elephants and alligators in Galloway as loyal citizens.

He had imposed the Cess tax as rigorously as he could. In September, 1678, three regiments of horse had been added to the King's army, north of the Solway and Cheviots, with the Earl of Airlie in charge of one, the Earl of Home of another, and John Graham of the third. Charles, ever attracted to an attractive face whether male or female, and some hinted furtively at Court that the former he held the more dear, insisted that his handsome, gallant Captain, but lately returned from the Netherlands, be in command of that regiment. Now the Cess tax was expressly designed to upkeep this military force, whose work was breaking up Conventicles and Field Meetings. The people hated it and Claverhouse found that the stronger resisted. It particularly annoyed him, as the fines of all who are not landowners he was allowed to keep for himself and his troop.

Two things above all motivated John Graham of Claverhouse. One was an unquenchable loyalty to the Stuart king, faithful despite his multiplicity of failings and inconsistencies. The other was a consuming ambition and personal greed which saw him pocket fines wholesale. The very year before he had acquired the great estate of Dudhope near Dundee, an extraordinary pleasant and sweet place, with a good house, excellent yards, fine parks and forests. He had greatly coveted Dudhope for a long time. Being so near his family estate and Claypotts Castle made it all the more desirable. But his obtaining of it was such in its method as Niccolo Machiavelli would have considered of the highest worth. His machinations were quite ingenious and even now as he grimly rode out at such an early hour over the moors, John Graham permitted himself a smile of self satisfaction, scornful of those he used. Dudhope had belonged to Charles Maitland, Lord Hatton, and brother and heir of John Maitland, Lauderdale, the Secretary of State for Scotland. So he was swimming in deep waters. But for twenty years Charles Maitland had been the Master of the Mint in Scotland and at last after many years he had been found guilty of corruption. By currying favour with the Marquis of Queensberry and the Earl of Aberdeen, President of the Court of Session, he won their support for his claim. Charles Maitland had been tried and found guilty. He was fined originally £72,000 but this was reduced to £20,000 in addition to losing many of his possessions. Now John Graham knew that the Marquis of Queensberry was hankering after a Dukedom and though there was no love normally lost between them, he used his influence at Court on his behalf, both with Charles and James Duke of York, his patron, to plead his cause and eventually the position was granted. As for the Earl of Aberdeen, who, Graham knew, also was in need of money, he arranged it that, of the fine of £20,000 on the former Master of the Mint, the Earl of Aberdeen should receive four-fifths and the remaining fifth to Claverhouse himself. So it was that after the intricate endeavours of a year and a half in April, 1684, Colonel John Graham of Claverhouse was granted the Charter of Dudhope Castle.

 Less successful had been his courtship of Helen Graham, heiress to the Earldom of Menteith, her cousin, who was childless. It was a marriage of convenience that he proposed, as it was to advance his military and state position. He wrote with a very diplomatic zeal to the Earl of Menteith whom he won over, assuring him that Caesar had more satisfaction in the succession of Augustus than if he had a son of his own who would probably not have turned out as wise. Claverhouse never did lack confidence in his star. He assured my Lord that no one toiled as much for honour as he did but did not attain much. However all was in vain, and the bitter taste of defeat was his, as at Drumclog, when in 1682 Helen was betrothed to the

Earl of Conway. Though he had never gained a closeness to the girl he became ardent at the close and would have taken her in her smoak perhaps without her dowry. Her mother, a very cunning woman, was probably the chief obstacle. His marriage when it did come showed a strange quirk in Graham's nature. The girl he married came of Covenanting stock. The strange anomaly of human beings was revealed here again, as so often in history. Jean Cochrane was the daughter of the well known Ayrshire House of Dundonald and of the widowed Catherine, daughter of the Earl of Cassilis, as staunch a supporter of the Covenant possible. Claverhouse enjoyed to confound even his royalist friends, totally perplexed at their hero's choice. They were still perplexed, Claverhouse smiled quietly to himself. It was just as well that the girl Graham's mother upset his suite. Jean Cochrane was a much more faithful lassie despite her Whiggish connections and that doctrinaire mother. She must have preached to her husband on his wedding night, Claverhouse thought to himself. But Jean was different stock. A dark eyed buxom wench and, as he had said ironically to his friends by way of some explanation, if she had been right principled she would never, in spite of her mother and relations, have chosen a persecutor, as they called him. But even now his sonsy Jean took second place in his heart and when the nuptials were scarcely over, the best man, Master of Ross, son of the Lord of Hawkhead, quietly whispered to him over the carousings and banquet, that General Tam Dalzell had told him of a new conventicle to be held at Black Loch near Slamannan. Claverhouse had stormed across the hall of Dudhope Castle and in a short time was booted and spurred to lead his troop to chase for the dogs across the moors. It was in vain, for the Covenanting scouting system was well informed and developed by now.

Two days later, after a brief interlude of love with Jean, he was out again this time to Douglas where they had caught the tailor James Gavin, hiding under an overhang of a riverbank but betrayed by the yelping of this dog. They had cut off the ears of his dog of a master with his own shears. Now this early morning as he came across through the Earl of Home's land where, apart from Gavin, he had had such a notable lack of success that his suspicions of that gentleman were aroused, Graham made for Crossflat Farm near Cairntable Hill where it frowned above Muirkirk. He had hoped to find Peden there. But the bird had flown, like the whaup that he imitated. Confirmation of his deep rooted suspicion of my Lord of Home could not have been stronger. He hated that bland, soft faced, gentle-toned nobleman, who presented such an innocent exterior. It was known as an uncomfortable fact that there were some who stood between the Royalist and the Covenanting parties, and, while they ostensibly belonged to the one party, in heart and principle they belonged to the other. Providence used this medium party to restrain the persecution. These persons were held in high esteem by the Noncomformists, even though they did not take the fearless stand they had themselves done. But fiercesome would be their end if discovered by the authorities. Claverhouse had long suspected the smooth Earl of Home and the Lairds, Ferguson of Craigdarroch and Wilson of Croglin of secretly passing on vital information to these stuipd country bumkins. They weren't clever enough, he solaced his chagrin with, as they swung their steeds away from Crossflat.

"Head for Priesthill Farm. That prating carrier John Brown, I'm sure, is a friend of Peden's and affords him reset and shelter. Hurry before this cursed mist gathers again and hides our quarry. Forby its damned cold this morn, is it no, Sergeant Drummond?"

A thickset grizzled looking man with a deep red beard and shaggy locks hanging over a tartan plaid of predominant red with blue and green banding, seeming to cover all of him, was muttering to himself but recovered sufficiently to assure his agreement.

"It is indeed, Sir John. Its colder than Kinlochrannoch in midwinter when the earth's like iron, and the water's just as hard, and even the mountain hares, which aren't wise enough to stay at home, have their eyes freeze in their head."

"I can do without your Highland stories, and stop your cursing in Gaelic, Sergeant Drummond. You think I don't know what you Highland rabble are saying in your outlandish gibberish! Well, I'm thankful that I am not able to discourse in your heathen language but to understand you simpletons is not so difficult. You behave like spoilt children, so when you get hold of an ordinary piece of furniture amongst the plunder and spoil what we rightly relieve these Covenanting Whigs of, you treat it like some priceless gem that you had never seen the like of before, and squabble over it like children. In these primitive Highland castles of yours you must live like pigs!" Here he laughed at his own wit. "Whereas these field preachers and their sheep-like camp followers have no need of these material things since they live so much in the open air with their God, they should thank us for relieving them of these burdens!" His laugh sounded hollowly in the enshrouding mist.

Sergeant Roderick Drummond was in his inmost heart most

dissatisfied with this hunting and harrying of fellow Scots in these faraway Lowlands. His soul was sick for the rugged and glorious Bens of Lawers, Schiehallion and Farragon. The shielings in the glens belonged to Gaeldom and differed from these Lowland villages. Roderick had always sought to follow the clan motto to gang warily. He remembered with pride how his honoured ancestor, Sir Malcolm de Drymen, had at the Battle of Bannockburn put down caltrons, these spiked stakes, into the ground that were the undoing of so many of the English knights, who were impaled on them. He was proud of his ancestral credentials. He was a second cousin, far removed, from the fourth Lord Drummond, James, who became the Earl of Perth. But it was rumoured among some that they came originally from the Drennans of the Stranraer district which would make Roderick of common blood with those of the Covenanting faction. It was no surprise then that conflicting emotions chased one another across his breast as an officer in the Highland Host brought in from the north to subdue these rebels. His integrity was sore tested and he much preferred to chase the red deer in the Perthshire glens. At least the deer offered a sporting chase and needed a cunning, born of the life in the wild, to catch one. So often the Covenanters were helpless and passive. Some of his Highland soldiery were hard to contain in their rough ways, and had not been brought up to respect womenfolk as he had. But, aye, this Peden was different, a will o' the wisp, who faded into the misty hills.

"Ochone, Sir John, I would not demean our loyalty to yourself and the cause. I fight as a solider of His Majesty. Anyhow gey little baggage hae we catched in this wilderness, beggin' your pardon."

"To the job in hand, Captain Drummond. It's that madman, Peden we must get in chains. He fades through our fingers as this mist. There are times when I don't think he's real, and I never thought I'd say that of any man. We almost had him on Auchencrouch Farm and a damned haar like this today fell like a cursed blanket round us. He has the weather at his beck and call. But this quarry is going to be run to ground in his lare. A true bloodhound never leaves the scent."

"An' lets no forget, sir, the upstarts that attacked oor troopers the ither day in Newmilns at the hostelry of the Bears Head. Johnny Anderson had his pate cracked by one of them Whigamores. Noo they'll no be expecting us to be abroad marauding in this weather, little jalousing that it hides us as it hides them. To be out this time o' morn, wi' three troops, bonnie and well set up for a dinging down, is a joy to my blood, to be sure! To think they expect us to be abed, an insult to His Majesty's dragoons!"

"Some of you are a pack of shiftless layabouts with not an ounce of smeddum between you. Private Anderson and his fellow fools will have more than a broken pate among them before I've dealt with them! They're a disgrace to the regiment. I've a mind to post you all to General Dalzell's command. You ken he shot two troopers who stole. Hold, Drummond! Do you see two figures there working at the peat?"

"Aye, they're digging at the peats, I expect, sir. Hold there!" Their steeds slithered in the damp hillside. The two men, John Brown and his nephew, saw them and involuntarily started to flee. The youngster, having bare feet, did not make much speed and his uncle refused to abandon him. The soldiers gleefully bound them and then hogtied them behind their saddles.

"Ride to Priesthill. Perhaps the real prize is skulking there. You're the one they call the Christian carrier, John Brown aren't you? I hear you hold illegal meetings in different houses round here, corrupting the youth and teaching them things they're better not to know. The peasantry of this country are too damned well educated for my liking."

Brown fixed his calm brown eyes on the handsome boyish smooth features of the famous gallant of King Charles. The stammer had disappeared as if magically. "Socrates was accused and condemned to drink hemlock for corrupting the youth, when all he wished to do was exhort them to question all preconceived ideas and be honest to their own spirit."

"None of your damned moralising and philosophising. We Royalists may have the peacock's feathers but you rebels have the peacock's pride underneath. Its time to break that pride." They had arrived at the farmsteading and Isabel, hearing the harness jingling afar, had come out to the yard. Despair had frozen her face and paralysed her tongue. The nightmare of Peden's prophesy was being enacted.

"Ransack the house, Drummond. See if there be any treasonable papers and materials."

"I'm no traitor, sir, but an honest carrier, barely solvent with twenty sheep, a stirk and an old mare, together with debts to pay, two years rents to my Lord Loudon, a loan to a relative, a debt to the minister, one fee to a lass and one other to the herd laddie here, John Browning."

"But you don't deny that you've been holding your own school of heretical theology, attended by youths from miles around, and there they imbibe all the poison of their rebellious ideas." Claverhouse was working himself into a frenzy of hate in which was mixed the chagrin of frustration. Peden was not there. His good looks were almost ugly in their diabolical spite. No longer was he really in command of his emotions and master of the court intrigues. Here was a man he did not understand. The chance of the man's character being true and sincere in the stand he took, Claverhouse pushed to the back of his mind.

"I do hold Bible Classes for the young of the district. In the summer they meet me in the sheepfold here, and in the winter sat round the peat fire in our kitchen. I did teach them to strive against sin and to resist false doctrines. We realised it could mean martyrdom. But they were not rebellious principles. We did go over Walter Smith's 'Twenty two Steps of Defection' and 'Rules for Society Meetings'. But the principles were always loyal to a righteous sovereign."

"You wily equivocator. You are worse than the Jesuits whom you say you abhor. You say righteous. Do you question the righteousness of His Majesty King Charles? Can you say 'God save the King!'"

"I'm not in a position to save anyone. But I pray for all within the election of grace."

"Do you doubt the King's election?"

"Sometimes I doubt my own, Sir."

"You are an eloquent smooth tongued rogue."

Claverhouse turned to one of the peasantry who had guided them across the hills. "You villain, did you ever hear this John Brown preach?"

"No, no. He never was a preacher. In fact, my Lord, he always had a terrible stammer up tae the noo. But it seems to have disappeared miraculously."

"Well, if he has never preached in his time, meikle has he prayed. Go to your prayers! For you shall immediately die!" Brown fell to his knees. Grateful for the last opportunity for praise and supplication, he turned his face to the grey heavens, and, in the Covenanting manner, never short of words to address the Deity, he poured forth a flood of Scriptural words and thanked God for all his mercies. His general supplication for Scotland and the evils that dragged her down took an equal time, as he prayed for a remnant to be kept in the unhappy land. Claverhouse sat enraged on Satan, his stallion, and three times interrupted, only just containing his impatience.

"I gave you leave to pray. You have begun to preach". He smiled and sniggered mockingly at his own wit.

"Sir, you neither know the nature of preaching nor of praying, that calls this preaching." He had turned on his knees to challenge his persecutor and then, just as deliberately, turned away to his God to finish his devotions. Singlemindedness always marked out the Covenanter, as their enemies had found.

"Take leave of your wife and children." For a fleeting moment John Graham thought of his Jean at home in Dudhope, so soon deserted on her nuptial bed. She must be aware that he King's business came first. He anticipated her warm embraces when he returned. Absence always made the feminine heart more appreciative he found and had made a point of observing it with women. No high principled dame held him in affection. But again he could not abide the trollops that Dalzell often frequented with. No surprise was it that that coarse soldier had never married.

John Brown had embraced his Isabel tenderly, as she held his child cradled in her shawl, and the six year old boy from his first marriage grasped her skirts. "Now, Isabel, the time has come that I told you would come someday when we first spoke of marriage."

Tears welled over her lashes and her bosom heaved. "John, I can willingly part wi' you."

"That is all I desire. I have no more to do but die. I have been in happy case to meet with death for so many years." He kissed her and the children. The bairn had begun to whimper as the fear of her mother passed through her body to the innocent infant.

"God multiply your purchased and promised blessings. Goodbye, dear ones!"

Claverhouse had drawn up a line of six soldiers with Drummond in command. They levelled their muskets but an observer could see a sluggish reluctance about their movements. Drummond was distinctly uncomfortable and shifted his gun from shoulder to shoulder.

"Sir John, sir, could we not just be taking him back to the Tolbooth in that bonnie Edinburgh, where he will get his deserts after the judge gives him a trial. Well now aren't we hurrying it a wee bit? He doesnae look very harmful to me. There would be no fault in making sure he's guilty."

"You yellow livered dogs! Cowards. I'll have you all horse whipped and court martialled, yea hung at the Gallowgreen."

In a rage, so that his smooth olive skin was become a dark reddish blue shade, he pulled his great horse pistol and shot John Brown through the head at close range. His blood and brains were scattered by the blast.

"What do you think of your fine husband now, woman?"

Isabel had thrown back her shoulders and a light glowed from her being.

The mist had departed, and a golden ray penetrated slanting onto the scene of tyranny and bravery enacted in that moorland place. Heaven was watching, the mystic would say.

"I thought ever much of him before, and more than ever now."

"It were but justice to lay you beside him."

"If ye were permitted, I doubt not but your cruelty would go that length but how will you answer for this morning's work?"

Contemptuous to the last, Claverhouse responded. "To man I can be answerable, but as for God, I shall take Him into my own hands!"

But the bravado was given the lie by the slight quiver of his handsome olive cheeks. John Brown's dying words had left an impression on his conscience that time could not erase. Mounting his stallion with a hurried curse, John Graham rode off down the river-bank at a gallop, with his men strung out behind.

For hours after Isabel Brown sat frozen with grief, despite her words, with no friend to comfort her, so remote was the Priesthill cottage. Finally she set the bairn down, gathered up her beloved husband's smashed brains and tied them with his head in a sheet. Then tremblingly straightened his body and covered him with her plaid. At last the flood of tears broke as the weeping racked her frame. It was some hours more before word reached Jean Brown, a neighbour in Cummerhead, who had lost her husband at Pentland, and this old Christian woman arrived at Priesthill to share Isabel's grief and help bury the body at the end of the house.

The murder had been committed between six and seven o'clock that morning and Alexander Peden was eleven miles away. An hour later he reached John Muirhead's farm. Without warning he lifted the latch, and entered the kitchen, scaring the family who were continually on alert and nervous about the soldiers presence, Relief eased their minds though something was clearly wrong with Sandy. He asked permsssion to pray with the Muirhead family. During his prayers, he cried for vengeance against the murderers of John Brown. When they lifted their heads, Muirhead asked with trepidation, "What do you mean by John Brown's blood?"

"What do I mean? Claverhouse has been at Priesthill this morning and has murdered him." Sandy then recounted the strange portent he had seen in the skies crossing the moor. Just after sun rise he had een a bright clear star fall from heaven to earth. It had been a sign from the Lord. A clear shining light had indeed fallen that day, the greatest Christian that he had ever talked with.

20
The Glens Of Antrim

Prospect-glass in hand, Alexander Peden stood like a classical seer on the Antrim coast, longingly scanning the shoreline of Scotland, that bloody land. But he had only exchanged one bloody land for another when he crossed to Ireland during these dismal days. Ill at ease, and wishful to return, he had often prayed and even confessed to a few, that the Devil and he rode time about upon each other.

He perked up as his nostrils smelled the fresh scents of water, moor, and rich farmland mingled with the smell of the sea, and the landbirds' song with the mewing of the gulls. The sea had taken on a green luminosity in the sunshine. Purple appeared in it, mixed with layers of brown, so that the tints of the wet seaweed strewn about the seashore were repeated in the sea itself. But more beautiful than the colours of the sea was the seashore sculpture, littered prodigally for miles along the whole shore. Some of the rocks were rounded, black, and shiny as seals. Others were white, and sharp-edged and still more of a yellow, ochrous stone, wrought into weird shapes by the erosive tides of a thousand years. At some places the yellow and white rocks were piled up in a suggestion of a gigantic castle ruin which had fallen from great heights. Occasionally, on the landward side of the road, woods reached down to the sea. The eagle eyrie of a road ran precariously along the north Antrim coast. Sandy found it refreshing and different from the moorlands of Ayrshire.

The outline of southern Scotland was extremely dim, and he couldn't make out detail apart from a grey blob which could be Portpatrick, he guessed. The Scottish haar didn't help. How funny it was that the sun was shining brilliantly in Ulster, while Scotland was deep in mist, the mist of his deliverance often. Having satisfied his longing with one last nostalgic look, Peden closed the tin and copper alloy speculum of the telescope. He was grateful that prospect glasses had been invented not long ago by their Dutch friends. Hans Lippershey and Zacharias Jansen, spectacle makers in Middleburg, had made them in considerable numbers. Holland had been a second home for the Scots. His dear friend, Richie Cameron and Robert MacWard, had been given rare gifts in Rotterdam, as honoured guests and brothers, in no way foreigners. His heart became cold as he remembered Airdsmoss and Richard Cameron's terrible death. One night he had crept up to the Edinburgh Netherbow to see the stark face staring from the gate's spike. Like Richie's father, he had recognised the strong pious features immediately. The same feeling had almost overcome him with a longing and loneliness to be with Richie. Sandy experienced the heart tearing desire when he visited the scene at Airdsmoss by Muirkirk, when his soul was in its deepest depression.

Visibly shaking his angular head as he closed the prospect glass to be hidden in his voluminous cloak, he was grateful for this precious gift from Cameron. It was said that Lippershey was given 900 florins for his invention, though Galileo, the Italian, had really developed it with the concave lens at one extremity and convex at the other. When he was rescued from transportation partly by the intervention of Lord Shaftesbury and his "Brisk Boys of Wapping", the Whig Lord had told him of a man Isaac Newton in London who had produced a telescope which was so successful that he saw the satellites of Jupiter and the horns of Venus, magnifying them thirty eight times. Newton had discovered that different colours refracted light in a different way. Sandy at any rate was satisfied that his own prospect glass magnified thirty three times.

But this was the third time that Peden had crossed to Ireland for refuge like a hunted stag. These times were still uneasy for him. There was always fear of traitors, even in this voluntary exile. On previous occasions he had hired himself to farmers in Antrim, not just to get sustenance but also a shelter for the night. Having landed at Larne, such was again his destination among the famous Glens. Of the nine Glens, he had found the most beautiful of them all, Glenariffe, the arable glen. Some of the others had names which recalled battles of long ago: Glenarm, glen of the weapons, Glencoy, glen of the sword, Glencorb, glen of the slaughtered and Glendun, glen of the fort. Of the rest, Glentaise had been named after Taise, the beautiful daughter of an ancient King of Rathlin, an island off the adjacent coast. Sandy's Scottish patriotism burned fiercely when he recalled that it was in a cave on Rathlin island that King Robert Bruce had watched a spider spinning its web with a patience that inspired him to try and try again for the victory which he achieved at Bannockburn.

Yes, he liked this land of Ireland, with its magnificent, lonely beaches and lakes, rivers and coastal waters overpopulated with fish. He had penetrated to the great inland sea, Lough Neagh to find its waters rich in salmon, eels, and freshwater herring, known to the locals as pollan. God had done a fair to middling job on the construction of Ireland, but maybe because he was so busy with the rest of the world, he left her a bit short in seasons. All four blended into each other so gently that there was not a lot of difference between them. Sandy had found that the Irish accepted that state of affairs with mild philosophy. When the rain was pouring down as if to batter holes in their head, the Irish thanked God for a fine soft day, assuring Peden that he shouldn't mind the rain in Ireland, because for one thing, it was gentle, and for another, no one else was complaining. They were a hospitable people who liked to make others happy.

Yet, though he had always received a warm bed at the friendly farms where he worked, Alexander Peden often had to assume a labourer's disguise. The Irish army of King Charles was large and expensive for the country: 16,000 horses and 5,000 foot, who acted as a police force, distributed over the country in small garrisons. They were constantly engaged in suppressing Tories, the Irish bandits. Sandy wryly smiled as he thought what strange bed fellows the Whigs and Tories made, as enemies of the State. Fortunately for the Tories and Peden, the army was ill paid, often inefficient, and even mutinous, also short on equipment. There had been an increase in customs and revenue to pay for it, making the Royal annual revenue £200,000 and certainly the army had been prepared to cross to Scotland in 1679 to help suppress the Covenanters. The Irish Army had also provided part of the garrison of Tangiers during England's short ill fated possession of that pirate's nest, where Middleton's bone had penetrated his heart from the fall down the castle stairs. This move was of double advantage to King Charles, as it both saved English money and enabled him to keep English troops at home where there was danger. Protestant and Roman Catholic loyalties still simmered below the surface and there had been the threat of a Popish Plot in 1678. Archbishop Oliver Plunkett of Armagh had been executed, a peaceful man of genuine loyalty. King Charles had wanted so much to get rid of Ormond, the Lord

Lieutenant of Ireland, a strong Protestant, but was finding it difficult. Ormond was a man of ancient family and possessed great estates. He had been the Lord High Steward of England, Chancellor of the University of Oxford, and one of the leaders of the old Cavalier party. But Ormond's greatness lay in his character, solid rather than brilliant, shrewd but honest of purpose, based on a strong piety. He was a good judge of men and events. He was important for Peden as he maintained the Protestant ascendancy in Ireland, even though Episcopal. The Papists would have given Peden short shrift, and there would have been even fewer homesteadings to afford refuge.

Sandy now turned with a sigh and made his way up the twisting coast road, intending to cut inland to the Glens of Antrim at the first opportunity. Bushes were bejewelled with fuschia, and gold plated with honeysuckle. He passed an arch of rock with a gaping hole, called Madman's Hole since a suicide some years before. Climbing landward through a gap in the hills, he tramped up the valley of Glenariff, one of the greenest, now spreading like a peacock's tail to meet the blue and jade, radiant in the early evening sky. It would have needed a strong heart not to be moved by the sight of the valley's waterfalls and pools lying below the wooded flanks and the flat topped Lurigidan Mountain which, in the Covenanter's minds eye, was like a pagan altar raised up to a pagan sky on black cliffs, no less awesome than those frowning over the north coast of Antrim. There he had climbed the strange columnar structure of black rock which went to make up the Giant's Causeway. The eleven mile walk, he was told, was the stepping stones of the famed Irish giant, Fionn McCool, who also with one mighty sweep scooped out the hole which became Lough Neagh and threw it into the Irish Sea to make the Isle of Man. It was a good story he thought.

Cows were waiting in the fields to be milked, while the air tinkled and hummed with the sound of falling waters of the cascades from the Fall of the Mares and Fall of the Hoof. He had come on a prosperous appearing farm in a niche of the Glenwherry into which he had made his way. Its fields were yellow with ripening corn and some prepared in bales. A buxom woman was tending lettuces, cabbages, and what looked like a herb patch, with dill and fennel. She raised her head wearily as his shadow fell across the garden.

"Would you be wanting a servant for threshing?"

"Aye, we do indeed as its harvest time and what would your wages be a day and a week?"

"The common rate is a common rule."

"Tis true, but here's my man, Willie Steel. This stranger is wanting labour, Willie."

"You're real welcome for we don't get many visitors here in our remote valley. This is Mistyburn Farm and yonder's the Misty Burn. Farming is hard labour and the poverty in the land before the Commonwealth has continued even the same since the Restoration."

Sandy betrayed no great emotion other than normal. "I'm fair pleased sir. As you will gather from my brogue, Scotland's my home, and we hear many stories from over the water about poor harvests."

"Your lilt betrays you. Its softer than the harsh accents of Belfast. The export of cattle, sheep and wool to England has been most important and because of their cheapness suited to the graziers of the west of England. But now, unfortunately, it has alarmed the cattle breeders of the London market who have induced the English Parliament to pass Acts to prohibit cattle from Ireland."

"Aye, power and money are never far apart."

The farmer scanned the travellor suspiciously. "You don't talk as a country workman. Have you done this before?"

"Oh, many a time and it makes one philosophical, this continual vagrancy. Our Scottish gaberlunzie men, professional beggers, become professional philosophers as well as jesters and singers of folk tales."

"There's ower mony vagrants here, I'm thinking. Every second man you meet in Ireland is a tinker. Whatever, come away in tae the farmhouse though you will have to bide in the barn with the servant lad for sleeping quarters. Its rare and cosy in the straw, and forby, you have nature's company, little white furry ones, with privileged visits from Yoohoo, our snowy barn owl." He laughed good humouredly.

That night, bedden down with the shy country lad in another stall, Sandy could not sleep and felt an overwhelming burden for Scotland as if her suffering was a black cloud threatening to suffocate him. Ignoring the hay, he knelt in a dark corner and felt as if his shoulders could not rise from the position of supplication. A deep groaning was wrung from his heart and he scarcely recognised the sound as his as it echoed to the high bare rafters. So it was that the long night was spent and the light, filtering through the timbers, brought relief. There had been a lessening of the weight when he was convinced that his prayer had physically turned the evil aside and saved some innocent Covenanters. The servant laddie did not say a deal but glanced sidelong a glance at the stranger, as they threshed together in the fields of gold. He worked hard, this Scot, as sweat poured freely from his dark face and the lank hair hung in heavy locks.

But his curiosity was too much when the same happened the next night, and the lad burst out to his mistress, "This man sleeps none, but groans and prays all night. I can get no sleep with him. I'm fair scared of him, to be sure. He threshes well, not sparing himself, though I think he's no used to it. When I go and put the barn in order, the stranger goes to a corner, and prays for the afflicted Church of Scotland. He says they are all in a furnace." There was a mixture of respect and fear in the voice of the boy, an honest but simple lad, brought up as the farmer laird in the strict Ulster Presbyterian tradition, imported but two generations before from Scotland with the Ulster Plantation of Queen Elizabeth and designed to implant a deeply loyal population in Catholic Ireland. Mrs. Steel was equally fervent in her faith.

"Don't you worry, Danny boy. I'll listen tonight from my bedrooms and if there is undue noise I'll overhear it. We'll fathom this mystery soon, even though the outcome is bad." The identity of the newcomer was revealed sooner than expected as the farmer's wife was prepared to carry some bread and cheese to the men gleaning and accidentally came across Peden kneeling in the long grass beside the corn field. Unobserved, she eavesdropped. What she found out hurried her posthaste to her husband, harnessing the huge work horses.

"Ask him if he is a Minister."

"Ask who, madam? This old horse is a faithful servant and preaches many a sermon by his straight furrow. He is never put off by rocks and distracting birds. But I jalouse you mean our polite gentleman labourer?"

That evening the farmer took the opportunity to enquire of his guest as they delved into the great bowl of potatoes in the middle of the table.

"Sir, I would be keen that you be free with us as to who you are. I will be no enemy to you but a sure friend."

"I am not ashamed of my office." Sandy's look was frank and straight. It was a relief to give the revelation to his Irish friends and immediately they refused to allow him to sleep in the barn and insisted on giving a fireside bed to their honoured guest. More difficult was the attempt to persuade Sandy to give up the threshing and minister in Bible teaching. Many from neighbouring steadings gathered for these services.

There was a servant lass in the Steel household, with a certain something of slyness to Sandy's mind in her demeanour. A shiftiness was shown in the manner in which she served the kitchen and Sandy stared at her to divine her trouble. An air of catastrophe was about the girl and he frowned darkly as the feeling was transmitted. It was as he did so once that Mrs. Steel noticed it and was perplexed as the girl had always been dutiful. On mentioning it, the Covenanter gave a swift reply.

"Put her away immediately, for she will be a stain to your family. She is with child and will murder it, but will be punished for her cruelty and selfishness in taking the child's life. Eye for eye, tooth for tooth and hand for hand. Sadly the law is still as cruel as the crime." A prophetic silence reigned in the kitchen, broken by the arrival of the servant girl, and an obvious embarrassment was exhibited by the Steels. Mrs. Steel made an ill disguised attempt to see how pregnant the lass was under her loose smock and blouse. The girl sensed the surveillance and bridled angrily without saying a word.

"Jenny, you've broken God's law and man's. You're to leave this farm and never be back unless you are converted to Christ our Lord. When we took pity on you as a waif wandering the wastelands of Belfast's slums we had great hopes that God's grace would enter your heart but you have stubbornly resisted all our ministrations. I often wondered where you slipped off to, Jenny, during the times of worship. I fear that jackanapes, Tom Crozier, has been led astray by your licentious immorality. What a waste when you had all the fine lads of Knockbreda Presbyterian to choose frae." The girl's eye slits were spitting venom and ripping her apron and waving a razored mutton carving knife at the Steels, she screamed at them as hypocrites and Peden as a black visaged devil, to storm out from Glenwherry Farm.

Sure to his prophetic word, the girl progressed downwards, had the baby aborted, and finally, after becoming infamous in a Belfast brothel, was reported by a fellow prostitute for her abortion to the authorities in Carrickfergus where she had fled to. A cruel age condemned the girl to be burned under the shadow of Carrickfergus Castle, the usual punishment for malefactors in that land, once the home of saints and singers.

Sandy had long since left his dear friends, and continued to travel through the parish of Connor. It was a dark misty night after an afternoon when his mind saw the poor farming lass in a waking dream screaming her last gasps and he shivered at the horror. Sometimes the gift of faraway second sight was a heavy burden. His surroundings did not encourage his spirit, a bleak, soggy ground under a grey soggy sky, which stretched endlessly. His body cried out for a dry shelter and rest. The only habitation visible was a large gloomy looking house a mile ahead. As he approached he experienced an unusual silence, despite there being considerable light from the many windows. An unnaturally pale faced man answered his knock.

"I would be deeply obligated for a shelter for the night. It's dreich weather for a vagrant labourer."

The white faced man had a mechanical tone which seemed to come from an alien source, inhuman and dead.

"This is a Quaker house and we believe in the worship of silence. Our God is so great that we dare not speak in His presence. You are a stranger but very welcome and will be kindly entertained; but I cannot wait upon you, for I am going to the Meeting."

"May I attend along with you?"

"You may if you please but you must not trouble us. For reverence is everything."

"I shall be civil, I promise you, sir'"

Sandy was led into a wide room with many gathered in absolute silence, a cringing silence. Some had their faces turned to the wall, while others had their cloaks over their heads. Sandy slipped quietly in at the wall pew, not wishing to disturb the service. As time passed, they continued to sit in silence as was the Quaker custom. Peden was cold and felt there was a fear and emptiness there. The Quakers had always been classed in Scotland along with the Independents of Cromwell as heretics, though Sandy was convinced it was in ignorance, and recalled how the Rev. Zachary Boyd of Glasgow Cathedral had his attitude changed by Cromwell after long dialogue at his headquarters. The reason they were called Quakers, it was claimed, was because they trembled at the Word of God, but probably it was originally derisive as, like many other religious enthusiasts, the Quakers trembled in their religious meetings and showed other physical manifestations of religious emotion. The Society of Friends had adopted the name without embarrasment.

Men often preferred prejudice. Even as he mused, he raised his head towards the rafters, as inspiration was lacking around him. A strong apprehension seized him, as from a hole in the loft came a black raven to alight on a man's head. The man stood up violently and shouted with such vehemence that foam flew from his mouth. Madness was in his actions. It flew to a second man, and a third, perching on their heads, with the same terrible results. For a moment Alexander Peden was paralysed with fear, his spirit enclosed in ice. With a superhuman effort, he prayed aloud to pierce the darkness all around. A shaft of light shone down from the same hole in the rafters, and he experienced the Holy Spirit's power. By now his host, in a state of confusion, was dismissing the company, an assembly of shambling, cowed people. Turning to him, Peden spoke the word of the Lord like a John the Baptist.

"Did you not see that evil? You will not deny yon afterwards? Wickedness has come to roost among you."

The leader's response was a suppressed anger. "You promised to be silent." Biting his lip, the Prophet of the Covenant waited till all had departed, before denouncing the scene he had witnessed.

"Twas always thought there was devilry among some of you, but never thought he had appeared visibly, till now that I have seen it. Oh for the Lord's sake, quit this way, and flee to the Lord Jesus in Whom there is redemption through His blood for the forgiveness of all your iniquities.

The poor man broke down under the exposure of his sin and such was the emotion tearing his being that he began weeping.

"I perceive God has sent you to my house, and put it in your heart to attend the Meeting, and permitted the Devil to appear visibly among us tonight. I have never seen the like of this before; let me have the help of your prayers, for I resolve never, through the Lord's grace, to follow this way any longer." His voice was shaking and he fell on Sandy's shoulders as a baby. If truth be told, the Covenanter was himself scarce in calm possession of his nerves. His feet had been unsteady and he was glad to quit the house of evil. That night he slept out in the bracken.

At this time the parish of Glenwherry was sparsely inhabited and the Presbyterians were not sufficiently numerous to support a settled pastor of their own, but were attended by the ministers of Ballyclare and others of the surrounding districts. So it was that in the summer of sixteen eighty four Alexander Peden travelled much in the mountainous pasture and bogland, visiting the parish in freedom, a liberty his heart rejoiced in. Striding the principal road from Ballymena and Keels to Larne, he felt his youth again, and often he would branch off into the moist mountainous tracts where numerous small rivers ran down into the Glenwherry river. There he loved to watch the cataract of shining water shooting down into the whirlpool or cauldron, which gave the name to the area, Glenn a'Choire, glen of the cauldren. Standing on a rocky hill nearby, Sceir a'Choire, rock of the cauldren, his view was magnificent. Often he dropped in at the two corn mills, at Clattery-knowes and

Mistyburn, with his old friends, the Steels, to watch the great fifteen feet breast wheels grind slowly on their work. The seemingly effortless movement of the mighty stones gave him a sense of peace.

But the wheels of destiny were grinding on and one day early that August, when visiting Margaret Lumberner, a Scotswoman, an extraordinary shower of great hail came on, such as he had never seen the like. The lady was rather afraid.

"What can be the meaning of this extraordinary hail?" The thunder on the stone roof was like huge boulders.

"Within a few years there will be an extraordinary storm and shower of judgement poured out upon Ireland; but, don't be frightened, Meg, you won't live to see it. You'll be in a better place and go peacefully."

"I'm ready, Mr. Peden," she answered quietly. Sandy never ceased to marvel at the faith of others.

The winter of that year came and he felt it a harbinger of severe things and climactic events. In the February of sixteen eighty five he was sharing in the home of Mr. Vernon, an elder in the parish of Connor, and was listening to the wise words of Mr. Vernon's father in law, John Kilpatrick, a very old and worthy Christian. It was good to have a father in the Lord. There were so few he could turn to for the deep things.

"John, the world may well be without you and me," said Sandy touchingly. The old man turned his grizzled face, mapped like Glenwherry by its rivers, and answered with fixed eye, "Sir, I have been very fruitless and useless all my days, and the world may well do without me, but your death would be a great loss."

Just then the spirit overshadowed the man from Sorn whose life had been so much of the hunted. "Well, John, you and I will be both in heaven, but your body will have the advantage of mine, for you will get rest in your grave till the resurrection. But for me, I must go home to the bloody land of Scotland, and die there. Then the enemy will lift my corpse to another place." The faces of his listeners filled with sympathy and he added quickly, "But I am very indifferent, for I ken that my body will lie among the dust of the martyrs, and though they make whistles out o' my bones, they'll all be gathered together again and I'll have a glorious resurrection."

The hearts of the household were saddened by his prophecy and in vain he tried to cheer their spirits, for he was everywhere loved. After dinner he determined to uplift them by a joyful word from the Bible at family worship. Yet that fateful night of prophecy was not over and at eleven o'clock Sandy suddenly halted in the old familiar way, fey with the Spirit.

"What's this I hear?" he cried three times. Rising to his feet almost unconsciously and listening intently, he leapt and clapped his hands. "I hear a dead shot at the throne of Britain; let him go yonder, he has been a black sight to these lands, especially poor Scotland. We're well quit of him. There has been many a wasted prayer waired on him'"

"Who has died, Mr. Peden?" The household was agog.

"None other than King Charles himself. That unhappy monarch, Charles II, I cannot but say, both treacherous and lecherous, who has made the Lord's people tremble in Scotland these many years gone by, has got his last glut in a lordly dish from his brother. He's lying with cold in his mouth. He said a week ago that he would be so happy to have his house covered with lead and the following Saturday he was put in his coffin". The uncanniness of Peden's knowledge was shown since the King had moved into a new palace in Winchester. The thick licentious lips, a fountain of wit from a humorist, who laughed uproariously at all Puritanism and seriousness, were silenced forever. Seized with an apoplectic stroke, the King had no hope of recovery, with his body sapped by his own vices. A Jesuit priest, Father Huddleston, brought into his death chamber, had witnessed his tearful confession, and he received the last rites of the Roman Church of which he had always been a secret member. So died the merry monarch, the gay court idler, hunter of moths, and friend of little dogs, but it is doubtful if a single citizen north of the Tweed sincerely mourned his departure, and the hunted hill folk drew a deep breath of relief.

There was an awed silence after the utterance of Peden, for no news had come to Ireland of Charles' death and did not come till twenty four hours later. The overwhelming power of the spirit was still present the next day when Sandy addressed a gathering in a beech wood near to Vernon's house. After reading Psalm 59, he charged none to sing it who could not sing it believingly. For the first few lines there was almost silence as few dared to open their mouth. Then John Muirhead and John Waddel, who came from the parish of Cambusnethan in Scotland, could not certain themselves, and broke out singing with their full strength. The rest of the Psalm was sung with loudest vehemence.

After finishing, Peden was about to preface his sermon, when with great finality and conviction, he cried, "Pack, and let us go to Scotland. Our honest lads in Scotland are running upon the hills and have little either of meat or drink, but cold and hunger. The enemy are pursuing and murdering them. Their blood is running like water upon the scaffolds and fields. Rise and let us go and take part with them, in case they bar us out of Heaven. Secure Ireland, a dreadful day is coming upon you in a few years. Folk shall ride many miles and shall not see a reeking house. I see hunger in Derry. Many a black and pale face shall be in Derry, and fire, fire shall be upon a town, whose name I have forgot, which shall be completely burnt to ashes. And for the profanity of England, the formality and security of Ireland, for the loathing and contempt of the Gospel, covenant-breaking, burning, and shedding of innocent blood in Scotland, none of these lands shall escape ere all be done. But despite all this, I'll tell you good news; keep in mind this year, month, and day, and remember that I told you that the enemy have got a shot beneath the right wing, and they may rise and fly like a shot bird, but ere this day seven years the strongest of them all shall fall."

Shortly after they left the beech wood, and with each deep in meditation over the portent of the Prophet's fearful message, he himself made off quietly for the coast and Carrickfergus. That night he slept under a hedge, though it was a sharp February, but he was on the run again, anyway the constellations stood out like diamonds on black velvet. Drinking his fill, he contentedly rolled over in his old dark cloak under the hedge, darning himself among the prickly thorns like a happy hedgehog.

Next morning the still cold enveloped him, though it was a human presence that woke Alexander Peden, his instincts now tuned after many years as one of God's wild creatures. John Muirhead ducked down beside the hedge. A Covenanter knew where to find a Covenanter.

"Have you any news, John?" Sandy was at once alert.

"There is great fears of the Irish rising."

"No, no, the time of their rising's not yet. But they will rise, and it will be dreadful when at last they do."

"Alexander Gordon of Kinstuir is over from Galloway and has agreed to hire out his barque. He kens you don't dare to enter the public ports but has agreed to land you and any others at some remote creek near Lendalfoot." Muirhead was happy to pass on the good news.

"I will not sail the seas with Gordon of Kinstuir. When the news came to Ireland of the release of the prisoners last August in the Enterkin Pass ambush, as they were being taken from Dumfries for trial in Edinburgh, many Scots were glad of the news, especially that Kinstuir had escaped! What I say is, what's all this Kinstuiring, Kinstuiring? There are some of those released there who are worth many of him. You will all be ashamed of him before all is done.

Never go by outward appearance. Let's make for as near Carrickfergus as possible without being observed by the garrison of the castle."

"Aye, there's a parcel of over twenty of us Scots exiles waiting there hidden outside the town, yearning to return home, among them Robert Wark of Glasgow."

"That's good."

They made good speed for all that Muirhead could not keep up auld Sandy's full pace. Still being in a difficult strait for a boat, Sandy spoke seriously to Robert Wark.

"Go and take that man with you and the first man you find with a vessel, compel him to bring it. For they will be like the dogs of Egypt whom God restrained. Not one of them will move their tongues against you."

Barely an hour later they returned and Wark waved gleefully from the ship, the Red Hand, as the fifty foot brigantine sailed with difficulty round the horn of the hidden bay, there being but a whisp of wind. It had been as Sandy said and Wark was jubilant. Strangely the Prophet was under a cloud.

"I have lost my prospect glass, lads, with which I was accustomed to look over to the bloody land and tell you what our enemies and friends were doing. If I can get the uppermost of the Devil again, I'll ride hard. I've been praying for some time for a swift passage over, and now Alexander Gordon is away with my prayer wind." Even as he spoke, Gordon of Kinstuir's ship was disappearing slowly over the horizon, as the light zephyr almost died down. "It would have been better if he never saw any wind. He will wound the Covenanting interest, as I say, before he goes off the stage."

By now there was a complete calm and depression settled on the whole party. Not a breath encouraged the twenty six and Peden on board the brigantine. Anxiety was great as any moment some of the garrison of Carrickfergus Castle might sight them just outside the bay and within easy range of the canon. Standing high on the fo'c' castle, the Minister of the Covenant prayed fervently. Waving his hand to the west, from where he desired the wind to come, he cried out, "Lord, give us a loof-full of wind. Fill the sails, Lord, and give us a fresh gale, and let's have a swift, safe passage over to the bloody land of Scotland, whatever happens to us there." When he began to pray, the sails were all hanging straight down, but before he ended they were all blown full like bladders. Suddenly the wind seemed to come from nowhere with a rush, a miracle in a cloudless sky. At once they disembarked those seeing them off, and gaily the Red

Hand skimmed across the Irish Sea with a full sail.

During the voyage, it came home to Peden that the twenty six Covenanters were hot spirited lads who evidently wished to fight. He noticed that they were armed to the teeth with guns and steel. The din of the Killing Times had penetrated across the sea and he knew it was the rebellion under the Earl of Argyll in which they contemplated fighting. The Earl of Argyll, son of the great Marquis had striven to reconcile his Presbyterian religion with his loyalty to his King. But he could not take the Test Act recognising the King as head of the Church and was imprisoned in Edinburgh Castle. He would have suffered death but his stepdaughter's visit had enabled him to change clothes and slip by the sentinels. Chaperoned by William Veitch, one of his Covenanting friends, under the assumed name of "Mr. Hope" he travelled to London by roads which were comparatively unfrequented. Soon he crossed to Holland, the kind haven for the persecuted, and from there was organising an expedition with the Duke of Monmouth against the Popish King James, who had succeeded on the death of his father Charles from a stroke.

But the enthusiasm of the Scots Earl was much greater than Monmouth as the expedition was extremely hazardous. The Duke was so much in love with the retired life that he was not keen on the bustle of life, far less politics. However, with three good ships, the Anna, the Sophia, and the David, loaded with arms, ammunition and all the necessities of war, the Earl and three hundred men sailed for Scotland. As well as two of Argyll's sons and fine men of sincere moderation, he had two fanatics, Major Richard Rumbold, one of Cromwell's soldiers who had hatched the Rye House plot to kill both Charles and James, and Balfour of Kinloch, the squint eyed murderer of Archbishop Sharpe on the Magus Moor. With two such it was ill fated from the start, and after landing in Argyllshire at the end of April to raise the standard of insurrection at Campbeltown, and many marchings and counter marchings with crossings of Loch Long and the Gareloch, it all ended sadly with the capture of Argyll, dressed in a peasant's clothing, at Inchinnan, near Paisley. The death of the great feudal lord came at the hands of the Maiden, the guillotine, which Argyll, gentleman to the last, embraced and said it was the winsomest maiden he had ever kissed.

All this Peden foresaw through a darkly glass more than ten weeks before, as the Red Hand was surging across the waves towards Ayrshire. So he counselled them to spare their powder as that rising had already completely failed. The hot blooded Covenanters were initially morose in their reaction but respected Sandy's words of prophesy highly. They agreed to keep themselves from any rash actions and with a high spirit of patriotism, the windswept shore of southern Ayrshire was reached.

21
Death Not The End

When the brigantine, "The Red Hand," landed on the Ballantrae coast in a lonely cove, Alexander Peden sensed a heaviness in his spirit, and yet there was a gladness that he was back in Scotland, and a welcoming door was opening again. But things were coming to an end and time was short, he was sure. The persecution had been stepped up, as the Killing Times of the last few years had witnessed. Before parting from his twenty fellow travellers on the gravel beach near Lendalfoot, he addressed them in a strained voice.

"I tremble to think what will become of the indulged, backslidden Ministers of Scotland, traitors to their oath, their ordinations and their souls. As the Lord lives, none of them shall be honoured to put a right pin in the Lord's Tabernacle. They do not stand for our Lord's Kingly prerogative as Head of the Church. The time is coming when you and I may travel forty miles in Galloway and Nithsdale, Ayr and Clydesdale, and not see a reeking house, nor hear a cock crow. But be encouraged, lads, for good days are coming. Leave the sins you have commited in Ireland buried there. We don't need them spread around here."

When the greater part had taken their farewell, thanking him again for his part in their miraculous deliverance at Carrickfergus, and he had waved them a goodbye with his blue bonnet from the edge of the shore, he asked the remainder what house they would go to. Most had some destination of safety planned, and Hugh Kennedy of Cassilis answered promptly, "I'm set for Cambuscarron where there are friendly folks."

"Hughie, Hughie, you will not get even your nose in there, for the Devil and his bairns are there."

"Na, na, you're wrong there," said young Kennedy and took his farewell.

Sandy sat down under the lee of a large rock to await his return. He knew that the remainder of his life would have few companions and be lived mostly in the wilderness where only the cry of the whaup was heard. His massive boned frame was beginning to be bowed down by the constant pursuit, grief and mental turmoil of the past twenty years. He felt his sixty years keenly now and had not slept often recently, burdened by the unhappy state of Scotland. Yet somehow in the midst of it all, as he sat there, staring out over the gentle breakers lapping the cove, he felt there was a rosebud in the East, promising to break through with the dawning of a new age of freedom, when the Stuarts would be banished forever.

Time had passed quickly and he was in a half-sleep, an ability he had perfected through his hunted life style, helped here by the quiet waves, when a scrambling of small stones roused him. Hughie Kennedy had returned, suitably chastened.

"You were right again of course, Mr. Peden. The house was full of troopers. Thankfully I spied the enemy horses tethered behind, and, as I was escaping, heard the fearful cry of a defenceless woman attacked by these cursed soldiery. They are void of natural affection surely."

"Aye, I'm afraid it will mean her making away with herself," said Peden with deep compassion. "The Lord will surely forgive her, as she is not in her right mind. Come, let us hurry to another house where I certainly have an errand of mercy to perform for a good wife. You understand, Hughie, as we read in Deuteronomy, how we can know when a message has not been spoken by the Lord. If what a prophet proclaims in the name of the Lord, does not take place or come true, that is a message the Lord has not spoken. That prophet has spoken presumptuously. Do not be afraid of him. I challenge any to say that my words have not come true."

"I'll abide by that, Rev. Peden," Kennedy answered promptly. As if in confirmation of his words, they found a woman who was lying sick in great doubts and fears and Sandy was a great comfort to her. They then went eastwards, though contrary to the prophet's inclination, and came to the top of a hill, two miles distant from their destination. Sandy halted suddenly as if meeting an invisible barrier, Kennedy stumbled against Peden's great bent back, and the only thing that prevented him falling headlong down the screed slope was his strong blackthorn stick.

"You can jalouse how weak I am and can see how broken and

bowed I am! Not since that black day of Bothwell Brig have I slept in a proper bed! I have been like a Nazarite because of the vow that was upon me. Did you ever see me in Glen Luce in New Luce pulpit? Not even Ritchie Cameron could have overcrowed me then for strength and stature. I stood as a young tree by the rivers of waters. Look at me now, so crooked by the caves and moss hags that I couldn't even walk upright to the scaffold."

"Dinna be sorry for yourself, Rev. Peden. There are many who have paid the supreme sacrifice. As you have said yourself, you've been a hundred times caught like a partridge in the net, and always escaped. You are God's man. Forby, that blackthorn stick is for walking as well as cracking a few pates with, since you are a man of peace," quipped Kennedy grinning.

"True, and it's for imitating Nature's sounds to communicate with our friends," answered Peden, pursing his lips against the whistle on the end of his stick. "And I have nae lost my sixth sense, like our friend here, the whaup. Observe that one." The plaintive cry of the moorland bird echoed across the valley below with its koor-lee. "Its cry can often be heard when mating time has come, but it is a different call when they are alarmed — a startled scream. From the guardian of the nest, standing sentinel on the skyline, it is a warning to its sitting mate, who slips silently from the nest and makes her presence known as long as the intruder is about. She keeps up a whoo-wee, much different from her other cries. When the young are hatched from its bit apology of stick and wisp of grass on the ground, I have oft seen them run towards a man to draw him off. That useful book Deuteronomy even tells us what to do if we come across a bird's nest beside the road, either in a tree or on the ground, and the mother is sitting on the young or on the eggs. Do not take the mother with the young. You may take the young, but be sure to let the mother go, so that it may go well with you and you may have a long life. So all these stories about our Covenanting brethren killing off the peesweep and others as dangerous to their safety are damnable lies. See, there she goes." The dark brown and buff coloured bird with barred wing and tail, rose heavily, gull-like in flight, tucking in its green legs, and took off with slow measured beats. "Though it does not suggest speed, our whaup is quick on the wing and I love nothing better than to see them fly chevron shaped in a flock. But, seriously, my friend, I will not go one foot further this way, as I scent danger. Yonder herd laddie below. Cry him up here."

Kennedy fetched the boy, a bold fresh faced youngster. Sandy addressed him gently, "Here's a groat, laddie. Gang doon tae that house and fetch us meat and news."

"I'll dae that, Rev. Peden, without any payment, an you want," replied the boy, smiling at the astonished minister, who, however, insisted that a Dutch groat might grow into a a guid Scots pound.

When the lad arrived at the house the wife gave him meat immediately and then whispered urgently in his ear, "Run, laddie, and tell them that the enemies are spread, and we are looking for them here every minute." As she said this, a platoon of eighteen dragoons came riding up the track, and the captain shouted, "Stand, you dog!"

The boy responded appropriately to this form of address and scurried off throught the yellow gorse spiking from the hillside, yet more as a rabbit. Six pursued him for half a mile and fired hard upon him. The ball went close by his head. All this Peden saw from the hilltop, and was praying desperately, "Lord, shall the poor lad, who was going our errand, begging bread to support our lives, go and lose his? Direct the bullets away from his head, however near, and don't let them touch him. Good Lord, spare the lap of your cloak, and cover him, I beseech you for his deliverance." As if in answer immediately a dark cloud of mist rolled down from the hill, appearing in the clear blue sky behind, and hid the boy from his merciless pursuers. Later after the frustrated platoon had cursed and blundered till tired, the boy slipped quietly back to direct some comical mockery at their departing backs.

"The minister said it might grow into a Scots pound from a groat. This is for your bravery," said Hugh Kennedy, slipping the coin into his hand, while Peden was busy opening the food parcel.

Sandy and Hugh parted shortly after, as Kennedy made for the ancestral seat of the Cassilis family, the lonely keep set on a crag between Colmonell and Knockdow, the scene of Sandy's arrest. Hugh could have wished for peace between them and the Kennedy's of Culzean, and God knows, Mr. Peden had often enough tried to bring harmony but in vain. Sometimes he thought Scottish nature was intractable when involved in family feuds. Peden himself got the gift of a horse at Glenover Farm, where he heard that the red headed man had been found one morning in his little shop with his mouth and eyes agape. A goblet containing some sick smelling potion lay tumbled beside his corpse, and the people of Colmonell always told it that the red headed stranger had died accidentally trying one of his own weird herbal mixtures. The Glenover farmer put it that no one ever gets away with anything. Sooner or later in the end, a good God will see that the wicked perish and get their deserts, while the faithful who keep faithful will be rewarded.

Light hearted with the thrill of a horse after leg weary weeks,

Alexander Peden swung the bit kindly, pulling her nose for Sorn and Auchinleck, homesick for his childhood haunts. Somehow he knew with certainty it would end where it had all begun, those long sixty years ago. God's timetable was exact and in order, with not an item out of place. The mare was frisky as he cantered, but responding to a rider she knew was unaccustomed to the saddke of late. Keeping to the lesser tracks, he passed by Pinwherry, Barr, Crosshill, Kirkmichael, Dalrymple, and was making a detour round by Stair to cross the free flowing Ayr at an unlikely crossing, where the river was widest. The weather had deteriorated badly and storm clouds were threatening. The air had become bitter and the water would be even more so, he could be sure.

Just then he sighted a dragoon troop and before he could take cover in a nearby linn, they were hallooing furiously. His blood was flowing and the adrenalin pumped vigorously, as ancient primitive feelings surged through him of the delight of the quarry at leading the hunters a merry chase. He was in imminent danger when the Ayr loomed up, high, cold, and fast. Without hesitation, Sandy and his steed plunged into the icy current which closed around them, causing him to gasp with shock. The force was almost overwhelming, threatening to sweep them rapidly downstream, and him from the saddle. The frightened animal snorted with fear as the water surged over its head at times, and forced up its nostrils. Sandy gripped the flanks with his long thighs, and praying in the animal's ear, sensed the brave beast respond with a quiver of muscles which drove horse and rider against the current and, in minutes, with a bound, dripping onto the far bank. The dragoons meanwhile had halted, hesitant, steeling their courage, their leader afraid to go first. Their steeds pulled away with rearing hooves, eyes rolling, and control was difficult. Sandy, with gay abandon, swung to the ground, and doffing his blue bonnet and swirling his tattered cloak, gave a gallant bow to his furious enemy. Crying above the wind and sound of the waters, he called to the officer and troop, "Lads, do not follow me. For I assure you, you want my boat, and so will drown. And consider where your landing will be." This scared them visibly, understanding almost unconsciously that they lacked the miracle of God's assistance which they had just witnessed. It brought a definite decision, and laughing, Sandy cantered off over the moors.

That night he slept in his cave on the banks of the river Lugar, between Mauchline and Ochiltree. As usual it was a careful approach by working his way down the ledges of the cliff above the cave, and then swinging from the roots and finally the branches, into the broad entrance, hidden partially by the saugh or willow tree screening his hiding place. A good night was spent, confident of his secure refuge, near where the Lugar joined the Ayr, and not far from his brother's farm of Ten-shillingside on the Auchinleck Estate. It was a quiet spot on a quiet river, surrounded by woods and gentle pastureland. Auchincloich, the old family possession, had been sold by this time. A loneliness seized his bones as he dwelt on the infant time on the farm, playing with the Boswell children, hiding in the hollow of the dried up gravel bed of a former stream which snaked up from the rear of the Barn, and especially watching fascinated as the weavers shuttle flashed. He would need to slip back to Auchincloich before going to reside with his brother at Ten-shillingside.

Word had leaked that he was back and as the news filtered, he was asked to preach in a sheep fold that Sabbath evening in the parish of Mauchline. He determined to use a message from his old friend, Amos, that shepherd himself from Tekoa, who stood firm as an oak tree against national injustice by tyrants. Sandy was sure that the Stewart dynasty was fast coming to an end.

He was preaching a challenging message to the small group of the bravest who had dared to attend during this period of extreme cruelty by the persecuting party. "I will set a plumb-line in the middle of my people. That means a measuring line." He looked intently at each as they lay in the straw of the fold, emotionally and physically exhausted from being on constant alert. "Oh, how few of the Ministers of Scotland will measure up to this plumb-line! Lord, send us a Wellwood, a Cargill, and a Cameron, and such like as they, and let's be quit of the rest. Sadly they are almost all gone, departed from the stage of this life's grim drama. Only a remnant remain." His grey head drooped onto his chest, hollow from lack of proper nourishment. Suddenly he lifted it and hope had returned to the gaunt features. "I'll tell you good news! Our Lord will take a feather out of anti-Christ's wing which shall bring down the Duke of York and banish him out of these kingdoms; and will remove the bloody sword from above the heads of His people; and there shall never again a man of the name of Stewart sit on the throne of Britain after the Duke of York, whose reign is now short; for their leachery, treachery, tyranny, and spilling the precious blood of God's people. Aye, the Stewarts will be pit off the throne and all the moyen in the world winna pit them back, never!"

The small group were awestruck by the authority in his face and tone, and he looked hard at them individually, "But where is the

Church of God in Scotland these days? It is not among the great clergy. It is wherever a praying young man or young woman is ahint a dyke side in Scotland, and most of you here are these kind of people. A praying party will ruin our evil enemies yet, sirs. A praying people will go through the storm. But many in this countryside know nothing of these things. The loss of a cow, or two or three of their beasts, or an ill market day, goes nearer their hearts than all the troubles of the Church in Scotland. I'll tell you what our great folk and nobles in Scotland are like. They are like so many ladies going to sea in a boat on a calm day, for their pleasure; and as long as the sea is calm, and they see the land, and are in no fear of hazard, they bid the boatman row out. But when'er the wind begins to blow a little and the waves rise and swell, and sight of the land is lost, then they cry out, 'Make haste to the shore.' So it is with our great folk, nobles, gentlemen, ministers, professors, and all ranks in Scotland."

That night after the meeting in the Mauchline sheepfold had ended late in deep and anguished prayer, Sandy moved like a shadow across the fields towards Airdsmoss, drawn again by the longing for Richie Cameron's presence. Ever since six years before, Cameron's head had been cut off at Airdsmoss and played with at football by their heartless foe, Alexander Peden had yearned in his moments of deepest depression to step off the human stage and meet Richard Cameron, the young Lion of the Covenant, on the stage of the Heavenly Theatre. He sensed the dividing line was now thin and the time approaching.

His mind was still not so clouded that he could forget to drop into Wellwood when passing through Muirkirk. There was the residence of Captain John Campbell, always a warm friend to the Cause. When he knocked at the mansion on the outskirts of the town, Mrs. Campbell answered.

"How is your son, Captain Campbell? It's been a sore while sin' we had a blether."

Tears appeared in her faded blue eyes. "Dinna you ken, Rev. Peden? He had left for the Americas. He can find no peace in his ain Scotland. He has had to flee to a land of strangers. All his loved ones are so concerned about what his future will be and I dinna ken how to fend in his absence." Her voice trembled and the old lady broke down.

A vision swam before the eyes of the prophet of a ship tossing on mountainous seas and the face of Captain Campbell remonstrating with a man, clearly the vessel's Captain.

"No, no, Mrs. Campbell. There is no need to be distressed. Send for him, for he will never see America. His ship has been turned back by storms." He stayed sufficiently to try to comfort the scarce believing woman, and headed for Cameron's grave.

He sat down on the lonely gravestone as he had before. Night had fallen, but the velvet sky revealed a myriad of stars and he saw the Plough and Orion, mute witnesses of his grief. With a great groaning sigh he doffed his blue bonnet, and holding it aloft, cried to the Heavens, "Oh, to be with Richie!"

From standing statuesque for a considerable time, Richie fell face down and lay as one dead on the grave. So many hundreds had died. Why had he survived? Was it because he had not shown the courage to join the Societies, those little groups of not more than a dozen Covenanters which had sprung up in every shire of Central and Southern Scotland for prayer and spiritual growth? But he had always been an individualist, made that way. He had not taken up arms as Ritchie Cameron. Self recriminations rent his soul and body. Was he indeed a coward? He had never been an extremist and so his counsel had often been scorned by the more extreme section of the Covenanters.

How long he remained in this lonely despair he could not tell, but at last he drew out his family Bible, a copy of Theodore Beza's version, published in 1599. Inside he had written, "Alexander Peden, with my own hand, at 23 years, 1649." and clipped beside it a piece of white silk from a Covenanter's flag. The old Bible had been a very dear possession and its well thumbed and dog eared condition with textual markings was ample evidence that it had been present at many a Conventicle on the hillsides of Scotland. An outstanding French Protestant theologian, Theodore Beza had become the heir to Calvin in Geneva, as Rector of the Geneva Academy and leading educator. His Greek edition of the New Testament had become basic to Protestant students and lay behind the Authorised Version of King James in 1611. Peden was glad that Beza had believed God decreed man's salvation before man's sin. The scattered marginal jottings indicated that it had been well studied. Power surged through his tired body again. Be of good courage and be not afraid, said the Word.

He must see once more that young preacher, James Renwick, about whom there had been so many rumours and malicious gossip. The father of lies had begun to spout out a flood of reproaches. Some said he had excommunicated all the ministers in Scotland, including some after they had died. Others said he was not even a

Presbyterian and that his aim was only to propagate schism by being an Independent or Anabaptist. Some put out that James Renwick had no mission at all and that he maintained the murdering principles and delirious blasphemies of Muckle John Gibb, comparing Renwick to Jannes and Jambres who withstood Moses. All these accusations James Renwick opposed and abhorred. Though they agreed on opposition to the succession in February 1685 of James Duke of York, a professed Roman Catholic, Peden and Renwick had differed in their estimates of the Duke of Argyll's ill-fated expedition. Renwick saw the enterprise as too exclusively political and secular while Peden welcomed the purpose to drive out the Catholic Stewarts. But in May that year Renwick had ridden with two hundred men into Sanquhar and affixed to its Market Cross a Declaration couched in terms akin to those of the memorable document which Richard Cameron had set forth five years before disowning the King and his religion.

Now that the sands were running out and many dear friends were no longer with him, Alexander Peden felt that he must see the young man whom he had never met, but had heard such hard things about and believed with difficulty. Captain John Paton himself had been apprehended at the farm of Robert Howie in Mid Floack in the Mearns, as a notorious rebel for eighteen years. Cornet Lewis Lauder had been awarded £20 sterling by the Council for his capture. Peden felt a lump in his throat as he thought of the honest Captain and the action, so typical of him, that was told of how, when the soldiers came on Floack, he refused the proferred help of his friends because it would bring them further trouble. He was weary of life and continual hidings. Sandy understood too well his feelings at the life of wandering. The Captain had never been a great orator but he had it from an eye witness account that John Paton's end at the Grassmarket in Edinburgh had indeed been heroic that May day, as he said a loving goodbye to his young Eaglesham wife, Janet Millar, and the six little children she had borne him. Their handfasting at the Eaglesham Fair years ago had been fruitful. Even General Dalzell, for the sake of his old comrade from Worcester's field, had done his utmost to save John Paton and had written to His Majesty for the Captain's life, but, as John Paton had prophesied himself, it was not to be. To all but his most bigoted enemies he had lived a hero, with a life of prowess and hairbreadth escapes, and was to die a martyr. As he ascended the scaffold, he handed his Bible to Janet and the bairns and said goodbye to them, all friends and relations, wordly enjoyments, preaching, praying, reading, singing and committed his soul to His God. Thus had died a brave and loyal friend and Sandy had cried unashamedly at this loss. The remnant was growing smaller and the loneliness more overwhelming. He therefore felt the loneliness even more acute when he was not able to rest in his old home in Auchincloich.

Renwick and he had been in disharmony, leaders in the one spiritual army, and Sandy, as he experienced a mystical feeling that the veil between this world and the next was thinning and eventually to lift, knew he could not end his pilgrimage with a discord between them. He must have a personal confrontation with this young, silver tongued, blonde-haired preacher with whom there had been a bitterness based on hearsay. Making his careful way to the cave again, Alexander Peden was aware that he was in no fit condition in his physical appearance to meet anyone of respectability. He had for years, usually slept with his clothes on and rarely had a bed to enjoy, while the hair of his great grey beard and shaggy flowing locks were unkempt and it wasn't clear where each ended. Washing and baths were not his priority and there had been no loving woman to attend him regularly. It was just as well that he would in the next world have on Sunday braws every day of the week. Here he was not fit to meet even a ploughboy in his dirty dress. Sandy contented himself that if Renwick was half the man he hoped he really was, he would be compassionate to the old prophet's forlorn condition.

The cave he had passed on word through a reliable friend for James Renwick to meet him at, was not the one on the Lugar between Mauchline and Ochiltree, approached by the overhanging roots of the huge beech, since he thought it too exposed during daylight. The entrance was not concealed, and he did not wish to lead young Renwick into a trap. But this cave was near to his brother Hugh's house at Ten Shillingside Farm on the Auchinleck Estate where it had been dug with a willow bush covering the mouth. It was a small cave on the banks of the Lugar River, close to its junction with the Dipple Burn. Sandy's strength was low and the vital life force was ebbing. Yet he refused Hugh's entreaties to hide in the farm and waited patiently, his head wearily resting on the yellow yarn blanket his sister Agnes had kindly forced him into accepting. Never had he wanted to involve his family loved ones in his dangerous life.

At last a slight swishing of the willow bush at the cave entrance disturbed his reverie and before him stood a slim, fair young man with an engaging countenance, ruddy and handsome, as was another young David. There was a meekness, humility and courage about him as well as the highest intelligence. The old prophet raised himself from his rough bed, for his keen eyesight was failing. "Are you the James Renwick there is so much noise about?"

The young minister knelt humbly on the earth floor. "I am James Renwick, Father, but I have given the world no ground to make any noise about me, for I have espoused no new principles or practices, but what our Reformers and Covenanters maintained."

"Sit down, sir, and give me an account of your conversion and of your call to the ministry, and the grounds you had for withdrawing your friendship from all the other ministers."

James Renwick told Sandy the sacred story of how, from a little child in Monaive village, Nithsdale, he had heard the Lord's voice, and his ordination at Groningen. At last he was quiet, awaiting the dying man's response.

Raising himself further with an effort, Peden commanded him, "Well, sir, turn about your back." When he did so, the older man remarked with force, "I think your legs are too small and your shoulders too narrow to take on the whole Church of Scotland. Your physique is too spindly. But you have answered me to my soul's satisfaction, and I am very sorry, James, that I should have believed any ill reports of you. Before you go, you must pray for me, for I am old and going to leave this world."

Tears had appeared in the young man's eyes and, as he poured out his soul in that dank cave, these tears ran down his fair skinned cheeks. At the prayer's end, in a sudden emotion, Peden grasped him by the hand, drew Renwick towards him, and kissed him affectionately.

"Sir, I find you a faithful servant to your Master; go on in single dependence on the Lord and you will get honestly through, and clear off the stage when many others, who hold their heads high, will lie in the mire and foul their hands and garments. Now it's my turn to pray for you, young Renwick." Sandy Peden then pleaded that God might spirit, strengthen, support, and comfort young James Renwick in all his duties, and difficulties.

"I am so relieved, Father, because it hurt me deeply that you listened to the slanders against me."

"Go your way now, boy Renwick, and be busy about the work God has put you to; for neither you nor I will see the other side of it." Despite the solemn prophecy, nothing could mar their lovely peacemaking.

When the comely youth had taken his respectful leave from the old champion, Alexander Peden summoned up all his energy for a last journey. As he felt that the end was very near, he wished to creep back to his old home at Auchincloich. Avoiding Sorn Castle in case the garrison there were abroad, he kept to the far bank of the broad flowing Ayr and hid in the flourishing foliage there, the trees entwined with an abundant ivy. Lord Sorn had always hated him, a local rebel from Sorn parish. It had annoyed him supremely that he had never caught that will o' the wisp, Peden. Even when he crossed the Ayr a safe distance on, his caution did not desert him. He knew the farm was in other hands, yet he wished a last visit to the endearing place, and he knew every cranny, not least the dried up gravel-bed behing the barn. By this he approached, thankful that the weather had been abnormally dry as he crawled up the curve of the former stream. Sandy remembered the terrible frost of three years ago, lasting from November to mid March, when the earth was as iron and a great snowstorm caused houses, flocks and men to be buried indiscriminately below a white mass. Many of the upland farmers had been ruined. Now as he burrowed along the sandy earth, he was delighted to see the rich waving corn stalks, like a jungle from his mole's eye view. How often he had followed the plough with his father as a youngster, happy, innocent days, ignorant of men's tyranny over men.

Sandy approached as close as discreet, and lay looking nostalgically at the familiar three roomed farmhouse, the smell of the soil and hay from the barn, the scuttling of the hens. Just then an honest looking man strode out, clearly having eaten, and heading to feed the cartle. For a moment he looked up and his light blue eyes had the faraway stare of the farming man. It seemed to Sandy Peden that he looked right at him and smiled. Though he realised it was impossible, it imbued Sandy with a contentment that Auchincloich was in good hands. Turning, he started back and headed for a preaching at Collingwood, near the Water of Ayr, to be his last sermon.

There was compassion in the congregation for their preacher's weakened condition but the old fire was in his words as he warned them.

"God has given you many preachings but before long God's judgements will be as frequent as these precious meetings. God has sent a Wellwood, a King, a Cameron, a Cargill, and others to preach to you; ere long. He shall preach to you by fire and sword! For He will let none of these men's words fall to the ground. As for me, I have run the race. When I am dead I would wish that my body should be carried to Aird's Moss, by Muirkirk, and buried beside Ritchie, that I may get some rest in my grave, as I've had little in my life. However I know you will not do it, but bury me where you will, I will be lifted again. You will all be displeased at the place where I shall be buried at last, but I forbid you all to lift my corpse again. God will be avenged upon the great ones of the earth, and the inhabitants of the land for their wickedness; and then the Church will come forth in a state of great prosperity. If I am only once buried, then you may doubt; but if oftener than once, then be sure that all I have said will come to pass."

The hearers were awed, wondering what he meant.

He returned to the cave that night, but early next morning he came to his brother's door at Tenshillingside. His brother Hugh's wife, Marion, answered, and the alarm showed that he had indeed scented the recent presence of the enemy.

"Where are you going Sandy? The enemy will be here. They came yesterday and were frustrated that they missed you. Though we gave nothing away, I'm certain Lieutenant Murray will be back again."

"I know that, Marion. I smelt the taint of their evil."

"Alas, sir! What will become of you; you must go back to the cave again."

"I have done with that, for it is discovered; but there is no matter, for within forty eight hours I will be beyond the reach of all the devil's temptations, and his instruments in hell and on earth, and they shall trouble me no more."

"You must come in, Sandy, and hide in the recess bed. They never noticed its existance the last time." Leaning heavily on her shoulder, Sandy was led into the kitchen where Hugh was still asleep. Leather stamped and gilded, a Spanish fashion was a favourite cover for the walls of rooms in the better homes in Scotland and England, and this was so in the bedroom at Tenshillingside. Hitherto such ornamental leather was introduced from abroad; but now Alexander Brand, an Edinburgh merchant, by a considerable outlay, had brought workmen and materials into the Kingdom. Going to the fireplace, Marion pushed a groove in the leather and a section of the wall seemed to open up.

"Go and rest quietly, Sandy." Marion Peden closed up the recess bed, as if it wasn't there.

Just three hours afterwards, the enemy came. A strict search of the premises was made. They searched the cave and the barn, overturning the straw and tossing about the heaps of corn. The outhouses was examined and the stackyard visited. The dwelling house was examined by the troop, who stabbed the beds with their swords which were also thrust up so that the glittering points came through the boards of the garret. Finally unsuccessful, Lieutenant Murray rode off in a high rage, vowing retribution.

It was forty eight hours later that Hugh and Marion sensed an emptiness and loss about the steading on awakening. Quietness reigned in the recess bed and when they opened it up, the Rev. Alexander Peden lay dead, face so relaxed as if touched by a gentle wand.

"Sandy's gone at last," said Hugh sadly. "After a weary pilgrimage, he has become an inhabitant of that land where the weary are at rest. Remember that he said we are immortal till our task is done. We must send immediately for Laird Boswell of Auchinleck to whom Sandy was aye dear. His patronage is our protection from the desecration of his corpse. Lord Sorn and Graham of Claverhouse would give Murray full permission for any blasphemy."

Sure enough the Laird of Auchinleck, David Boswell, a faithful friend to the end, was anxious to guard from insult what remained of their friend. He had his corpse carried hidden in their carriage over to Auchinleck House, and then secretly interred Alexander Peden's bones in the family burial ground in the town. There, under the shadow of the far stretching plain trees he was buried simply with few friends but the Boswells and their retainers present.

The Laird looked up at the heraldic crest above their own family vault, and turning to Dame Boswell, he said wistfully, "I think 'True Faith' is a motto more worthy of old Sandy Peden than the Boswells, Dame." Underneath the coat of arms of a quartered shield with above a hooded falcon surmounting a helmet, and at each side a leaping greyhound, were the Old French words 'Vraye Foy', true faith. "Though I often enough played with him as a bairn, and he was aye rare at hide and seek, especially in the hills, yet he was always a mystery and faithful to God to the end, unlike some of us."

But Boswell was wrong, for it was not yet the end. Soldiers in the garrison at Sorn heard rumours of his burial and forty days after the internment, Lieutenant Murray and a party of horse rode to Auchinleck, and furiously digging up the grave, burst open the coffin, and tore off the shroud. Then something very strange took place. Though the day previously had been without a breath of air stirring, there came a sudden blast of wind as a whirlwind, which caught up the shroud, and twisted it round the large, projecting, branch of one of the great plain trees in the churchyard. It seemed like a black arm pointing to Heaven, nature's protest against the sacrilegious crime. The local peasants often related to their grandchildren, how, though that branch withered away, the shrivelled arm remained ever since, pointing mutely towards Heaven.

For a moment Lieutenant Murray was aghast, and his face was frozen in fear temporarily. Then, shrugging his shoulders to cast off the spell, he yelled at his cowed soldiers, "Stop gawking, and fetch some of the local peasantry, probably rebels all, to come and identify the body. We want the right traitor to hang on the gallows tree." Some acquaintances of Peden were summoned and identified the decaying corpse, unafraid to show their sadness. Murray dared not send for the Laird of Auchinleck, who still had a powerful influence.

Satisfied, Lieutenant Murray had the body removed and carried by his men two miles to the Hill above Cumnock, where the common gallows stood. Their intention was to hang the corpse by chains on the Gallows at the Barrhill there. But word had gone out faster than a falcon to the Boswells and immediately Dame Boswell contacted the Countess of Dumfries, an old friend of theirs and of Sandy Peden. Without delay, they arrived at Cumnock with their numerous retainers and angrily remonstrated with Murray.

"How dare you commit this blasphemy, sir, against a much loved and respected Minister of the Kirk? By whose authority do you do this accursed thing?" Dame Boswell's voice was filled with scorn as well as righteous indignation. Lieutenant Murray, bridled, aware that his own authority was questioned.

"The man was known as a traitor. Such is the normal retribution for his kind'"

William, the second Earl of Dumfries, and Baron of Cumnock, who was opportunely residing with his Countess at that time in their mansion in the neighbourhood, here firmly intervened, "Sir, you are trying to do to the Rev. Alexander Peden dead what you have not been able to do to him living, hang him on the gallows tree. The gibbet was erected for malefactors and murderers, and not for such men as Peden. The impious deed of violation is inexcusable and I will report you to the highest authority, Lieutenant." The Earl, who had been entreated by his Lady and Dame Boswell, was in an angry and threatening mood.

"Mayhaps that authority will be the King, and that authority turn out to be mine," snarled Murray, but he was afraid to call the Earl's bluff, and after a long hesitation, during which he mentally noted the number of the noblemen's retainers and the incensed Cumnock populace, he growled at his men, "Let us show our contempt for the damned Prophet Peden and bury him at the foot of the Gallows Tree, with the other criminals we shot last year." A year before, two Covenanters, Richard Dun and Simon Paterson had been shot on that very spot and buried there. "They are well and truly buried." So, despite the obvious hostility of the crowd Murray supervised the burial of Sandy Peden's mortal remains. "That is the end of him," he said loudly as the mattocks were laid aside.

"Aye," said a graceless bystander, "Let's see him rise now and preach." But he was silenced immediately by those surrounding who hissed, "Shame on you! Have ye no reverence?"

"Be not so sure he has gone," said an old carlin, staring out over the mist covered moors.

But God makes the wrath of man to praise him. The place where the gibbet stood on the Barrhill became holy ground and the tree of shame became a cross of glory. Up to the end of the seventeenth century the people of Cumnock had formerly buried their dead in the Churchyard round the Kirk in the hollow at the foot of the hill in the town below. Now they abandoned their ancient burial ground and formed a new one on the Gallows Hill round Peden's grave. Generation after generation were to come and lay their dust beside Peden, as near his sacred dust as they could. Therefore the Prophet lies in the middle of his own dear folk of the West, who deemed it an honour that their bones should lie where Prophet Peden's lay. And so honour had grown out of dishonour.

Sandy Peden the Prophet had once said, "There was but a weak wind in the former trials of us Covenanters, and much chaff was sheltered and hid amongst the corn; but now God has raised a strong wind, and yet Christ's own people cannot be driven away. He will not lose one hair of his brother's heads, as He knows them all by their headmark. Death and destruction shall be written in broad letters on our land. It is best for you to keep within the shadow of God, and to cast Christ's cloak over your head until you hear Him say that the brunt of the battle is over, and the shower is slacked. Christ deals tenderly with young plants and waters them often. Keep within doors till the violence of the storm is gone. Yet I tell you, lads and lassies of Scotland, that the lads and lassies who have followed Him in this stormy blast, and have laid down their lives for Him, you will see on thrones, with crowns on their heads, and robes of glory, with harps and palms in their hands. If it had not been for the sacrifices at Pentland, Bothwell and Drumclog and Aird's Moss, we would all have been bowing to stocks and stones the day, and black idolatry. The generations which are to come shall take part in the benefits of the suffering remnant in Scotland."

So it turned out, within two years of Alexander Peden walking off the stage with his head held high, with the coming of William and Mary to ascend the throne of England, a sorry chapter in Scotland's eventful history was closed and the beginning of new hope and peace came for our torn and tortured lands. Momentous tidings had come from England where James the Second's Roman Catholicising policy had united Anglican and Nonconformist, Tory and Whig against him. A Catholic Prince of Wales had been born, and a future destruction of the religious liberties of the Commonwealth Cromwell and the Civil War had obtained, threatened. The crisis brooked no delay and a letter was addressed to the Hague, to William Henry, Prince of Orange and Count of Nassau, married to James' daughter Mary, a Protestant. It implored William to cross the seas and deliver England and Scotland, let it be said. The Glorious Revolution was the result and we can picture a winter's day on November the fifth, 1688 in Devon, with sixty five ships of war and five hundred transports from Holland anchored off shore in Torbay. The dangerous doctrine of the Divine Right of Kings had given rise to cries of 'A Free Parliamen' and 'The Protestant Religion.' The Queen, disguised as an Italian lady, with the infant Prince, had already sailed in a yacht from Gravesend to Calais, when the King made one abortive attempt at flight, embarking at Faversham in a customs house hoy, but the vessel was driven back by the stresses of a strong wind to the Isle of Sheppey where he was mobbed as a hatchet faced Jesuit in disguise. Back at Whitehall, he found that William, who had sent a body of Dutch soldiers to do duty at the Palace, refused to treat with him. Finally, unhindered, James set sail on a fishing smack from Rochester to Ambleteuse on the French coast, having stolen furtively through a garden at between two and three in the morning on the banks of the Medway. Thus ended the unhappy Stewart line of Kings' reign in Britain on 24th December, 1688.

But much remained to do. Men do not become tolerant at the scrape of a pen. However the new King William was wise. On a May day in 1689, the Scots, after nine days hard riding by stage coach from Edinburgh, arrived in London to offer the Crown of Scotland to William and Mary. In the great banqueting hall at Whitehall, the royal pair raised their right hands and repeated the Coronation Oath, clause by clause, as it was read out to them by the Earl of Argyll. The last clause was that he promised to root out all heretics and enemies to the true worship of God. There was a significant silence and then King William said firmly but graciously, "I will not lay myself under any obligation to be a persecutor." A just as significant sigh went up from many of those surrounding him. At last a new and kindlier day had dawned.

A last chapter had still to be written in Ireland where the Stewarts made their final throw of the dice with the lives of subjects still loyal to them, in a country where his religion endeared him and he had the most hopes of success. With the aid of Louis XIV, James landed at Kinsale in March, gathered his army and marched north from Dublin to crush Protestant Ulster. Londonderry set the heroic example for the rest of the Province, by shutting the gates, raising the drawbridge against the imposed garrison of the Earl of Tyrconnel. By this time the catchy martial ditty 'Lilliburlero', loved so much by Titus Oates, satirised General Talbot, the Catholic made Earl of Tyrconnel and Lord Lieutenant of Ireland. Some had jokingly suggested that this simple popular ballad had alone driven out King James from England. If Sandy Peden, Prophet of the Covenant, had cared, he might have foretold that 'Lilliburlero' would become the favourite marching tune of the British commando units in a world wide war which made the Covenanting struggle look small, though no less important. Yet his dramatic prophesy that day in Ireland was to be fulfilled so exactly, that a dreadful day was coming on secure Ireland in a few years, when people would ride many miles and not see a reeking lum, and the words, "O there will be hunger, hunger in Derry . . . there shall be many a black and pale face in you." The loyal inhabitants had armed themselves from the magazine and guardhouse, primed the guns on Derry's walls, seen their traitor governor Colonel Lundy steal out of the city disguised as a porter, and with only 7000 Militia, heroically defended Londonderry for three and a half months against a regular army of 20,000 under James. The countryside was laid waste for ten miles around the town and the only reeking houses were burning ones! The ensuing suffering from starvation of the inhabitants was such that they had to sustain life by eating horse-flesh, tallow starch, salted hides, and impure vermin. There was probably not a cat or a rat left alive in Derry.

When finally tidings reached England of the brave defence of Londonderry, a force was sent to relieve the siege under Colonel Percy Kirk, who again was dilatory and delayed at Inch, an island six miles below the town, being an unprincipled man, unworthy of William's confidence. However eventually three victual frigates and a man o' war as cover were sent and the first broke the boom on the river Foyle, only to run aground on account of the shock. The shrill cry of despair by the townsfolk lining the walls was such that their faces seemed to have turned black in the eyes of one another. Peden's words come back to mind. But Sandy's rose-bud in the East was to shine through, as the victual ship, attacked by the enemy, replied at them with a heavy cannonade and through the force of the rebound of her own guns slipped clear into deep water. Londonderry, and Ireland itself, was saved but not without cost as, out of the original 7,500 garrison, only 4000 remained and those like ghosts rather than living men. They were not too weak to march in procession to church and thank God for their deliverance. The victory at the Boyne river by King William, who had come personally to lead his army of English, Scots, Dutch, Danes and Huguenots, was inevitable and, when William crossed on July the first, the sad degeneracy to which the Stewart Kings had been reduced, was revealed by the fact that, while William personally led his troops and was in the hottest of the fight, superintending every charge, James kept at a wary distance, thinking more of a safe retreat than of victory. He fled to Dublin and embarked for France with a few attendants. The Irish in his army were known to have said that, if they could only exchange Kings with the victors, they would be only too glad to fight the Battle of the Boyne all over again.

As for Scotland and military opposition to the Glorious Revolution as it came to be called, this concentrated itself almost inevitably under John Graham of Claverhouse, that inveterate enemy of Alexander Peden and all Covenanters. Now Viscount Dundee, fiery Clavers, loyal to the end, it must be admitted, led an army of 2,000 Highlanders and 500 Irishmen to an open plain beyond the wild and gloomy gorge of the Pass of Killiecrankie to meet the 3,000 army of the new Convention of Estates in Edinburgh under General Mackay, a distinguished officer from the French and Dutch wars. The admiration of the Highlanders for *Ian Dhu Cean* or Black John the Warrior, was no way diminished by the merciless exploits which had procured him in the Low Countries the name of Bloody Clavers. Dundee, savagely cunning as ever, had deliberately led them through the Killiecrankie gorge and turning, trapped Mackay's forces. In this celebrated defile the road runs for several miles along the banks of a furious river, the Garry, which rages below amongst cataracts and waterfalls, while a series of precipices and wooded mountains rise on the other hand. The road is the only mode of access. Claverhouse resolved to allow Mackay to march through the pass and then fight him in the open valley at the northern extremity. He wanted a decisive result before Mackay was joined by a considerable body of English horse whom the Highlanders dreaded. He waited all day till the setting sun was shining directly in the troops eyes before leading a mad, fiercesome charge by his Highlanders and Irish to send Mackay's troops panic stricken in flight. But divine fate and a just destiny intervened to snap the life of that dark angel of persecution in his moment of victory. When spurring his steed and pointing to the Pass his raised arm kept apart of his side unguarded, and a random bullet, entering the opening of his cuirass, struck him in the armpit. John Graham tried to ride on, but, being unable to keep the saddle, he fell mortally wounded, and died in the course of the night' For long the common people of the low country could not be persuaded that he died an ordinary death. The story spread abroad that a servant of his own, shocked at the severities which, if triumphant, his master was likely to commit against the Presbyterians, and believing the popular legend of Claverhouse having a charm against the effect of lead-balls, shot him, in the tumult of the battle, with a silver button taken from his livery coat. A more substantial story was that of the famous pun used by Lady Stair of Balniel in Wigonshire to Johm Graham when he was Sheriff of that county. He had been criticising John Knox, the reformer, and Lady Stair responded, "Why are you so severe on the character of John Knox? You are both reformers; he gained his point by clavers, or talk, while you gain yours by knocks." The gay Royalist had finally got his knocks and an inglorious end came when the Highlanders, to whom all plunder was welcome, stripped the body of their late commander and left it lying naked on the field. As Peden the Prophet had often said, we cannot escape our reward, sooner or later. Graham's death made Killiecrankie more indecisive. Only for the convinced Jacobites and the Episcopal party was he the last of the greats.

The "rabbling' or expulsion of the false curates took place all over, sometimes administered with an undue harshness which Peden would have condemned. These curates, now pitifully at the mercy of the populace, were rabbled in Edinburgh and the surrounding villages with great gusto. They were regarded with hatred and disgust by the Scottish Presbyterian people, as usurpers, tools of a tyrannical system, and in most cases, they were unworthy people, unlearned and godless. Three hundred were ejected from the churches and manses, in the same way as Sandy Peden and others had been twenty years before. But theirs was a ceremony of disgrace. The curate was led to the Town's Cross, or another convenient spot where the folk were accustomed to congregate. His indictment was solemnly recited. The people were careful not to do the slightest harm to them or their property. Only the fringed garment, the symbolic vestment of a clergy they hated, was torn from him and trampled under a hundred feet. This primitive ceremony over, he was marched to the boundaries of the parish, and cast off without a word, or look of pity, regret, or goodwill.

As many of Sandy's friends well knew, he had a curious and continuous notion that the French would invade and yet land on British soil. Charles II and James II were assisted by French gold, and the great power of the French King was at their back. Possibly French regiments would have assisted James II if he had not fled from the kingdom. Now when Sandy lay in his grave, some kindly reverential hand planted two old thorn bushes, one at the head, and one at the foot of his grave. Though it is a sweet, sight soothing, tranquillising spot, yet the legend arose among the people of Cumnock that their neighbours across the Channel would overrun Scotland, if the two thorns were allowed to intertwine. Accordingly, year after year, the women of the town were accustomed to go to the grave, and carefully cut off the branches that seem to interlace. For a long time the fear of a French invasion survived in the parish of Cumnock and small children would whisper under their breath about the local wood flooded with rivers of blood. But those who had the insight of the spirit recognised the exaggeration of the human imagination, unlike the prophecies of auld Sandy Peden whose words were always fulfilled. His memory remains fresh and alive wherever tales of Scotland's heroes are told by the fireside. Of those who marched and lived and died under the Blue Banner of the Covenant, Sandy Peden the Prophet had a special pride of place. Many an elderly body gazing out over the shrouded moorlands, felt sure they saw a grey dim figure in a long cloak, blue bonnet, and walking stick striding boldly over the hills. A certain famous Whig pamphleteer, Daniel Defoe from London, noted for his honest writing, had great sympathy for the people of Scotland and what they had suffered under the last Stewart reigns, since he had been sent noth as a spy by the Government to find out the truth. Though he said that the exact number who died would not be estimated, one day at the Great Judgement all these would get their white robes. Daniel Defoe, being sent after the Revolution to Edinburgh to help in the cause of the Union of Scotland and England, wrote a poem about the Scots, commending their bravery, learning, and abilities, and deemed an incorporating union as the means to make Scotland a scene of prosperity equal to that in England. After many sore birth pangs, a richer Scotland did arise to play a major part in Britain's great advance throughout the world in the spread of freedom and justice and at the root of this growth, the spirit of the Covenanters was a chief seed.

THE END

In Memory of Our Scottish Covenanting Martyrs

In a dream of the night I was wafted away,
  To the muirland of mist where the martyrs lay,
Where Cameron's sword and his Bible are seen,
  Engraved on a stone where the heather is green.

It tells of a sword that 'gainst tyranny fought,
  When prelacy ruled and dangers were fraught,
And also his Bible which marked out the way,
  And pointed above to a land far away.

That Bible it brings to my mind a black time,
  When reading its pages was counted a crime,
And our fathers were hunted about like the deer,
  Because from its reading they would not forbear.

On that stone stands engraven in letters of gold,
  Many names of the martyrs that ne'er will grow old,
Whose blood cries for vengeance from under God's throne,
  The blood of these saints God will surely atone.

It stands there a lighthouse, far out in the deep,
  And marks out the graves where the righteous now sleep;
Their frail barge engulfed in mad prelacy's hate,
  Still pointing the way that our nation should take.

It brings back to mind many names I adore,
  Whose graves mark the altars of Scotland of yore,
Where the names of the martyrs in letters of fire,
  Illumine our minds and our spirits inspire.

It shews us true pilgrims like Abram of old,
  Who, peering the clouds, saw the City of Gold;
That city whose builder and maker is God,
  Its pathway well mapped out with fire and with blood.

O Scotland, dear Scotland, how can you forget,
  Those spots in the muirlands where martyrs once met;
Those doorways to Zion which often did ope,
  Their spirit to comfort and giving new hope.

COVENANTER

Printed in the United Kingdom by
Lightning Source UK Ltd., Milton Keynes
137176UK00002B/13-51/A